Outsourcing *for* Radical Change

Outsourcing
for
Radical
Change

A Bold Approach to Enterprise Transformation

Jane C. Linder
Research Director
Accenture Institute

⁴AMACOM
American Management Association
New York • Atlanta • Brussels • Chicago • Mexico City • San Francisco
Shanghai • Tokyo • Toronto • Washington, D.C.

This publication is designed to provide accurate and authoritative
information in regard to the subject matter covered. It is sold with the
understanding that the publisher is not engaged in rendering legal,
accounting, or other professional service. If legal advice or other
expert assistance is required, the services of a competent professional
person should be sought.

Library of Congress Cataloging-in-Publication Data

Linder, Jane C.
    Outsourcing for radical change : a bold approach to enterprise
transformation / Jane C. Linder.—1st ed.
        p.   cm.
    Includes bibliographical references and index.
    ISBN 0–8144–7218–4
    1. Contracting out.   I.   Title.
HD2365.L56 2004

    658.4'058—dc22

                                                        2003019920

Printing number

10   9   8   7   6   5   4   3   2

To my parents

Contents

Foreword

I have recently done some research and coauthored a book*
on managerial innovations in businesses and organizations. Using outsourcing to bring about strategic and radical change in organizations certainly qualifies as a managerial innovation. It has all the key attributes,
including the potential to improve organizational performance, the fact
that most organizations aren't familiar with it, and the preexistence of
some of the components of the idea.

Certainly the notion of turning to outsourcing providers for radical
change holds the potential for improved organizational performance. It
seems quite logical that specialists in certain business processes could
take over other companies' activities in those areas and make them substantially better. In fact, this type of outsourcing actually encompasses a
variety of other business-improvement approaches. Instead of a company's doing its own reengineering, customer relationship management,
or supply-chain optimization, it turns those initiatives over to other organizations that specialize in them.

Our research suggested that, in business and management ideas, there
is nothing totally new under the sun. Supposedly "new" ideas almost

---

*Thomas H. Davenport and Laurence Prusak, *What's the Big Idea: Creating and Capital-
izing on the Best Management Thinking* (Harvard Business School Press, 2003).

always consist of previously known components. However, innovative leaders can shape and recombine them to solve new problems.

Using outsourcing for radical organizational change is a new concept, but its underlying components are familiar. The idea of outsourcing is hardly new, and the idea of radical organizational change is certainly not novel. But taken together, they represent a management approach that is quite unprecedented. Plenty of organizations outsource, but they typically do so for marginal or nonstrategic processes that don't matter to their business success. And many organizations need radical change, but they rarely think of entrusting that objective to a third party.

Jane Linder's research for this book suggests that this approach is not only innovative but also effective. It has an advantage over more experimental management concepts. It actually works in the great majority of situations Linder has observed. My guess is that outsourcing radical change projects actually leads to a higher degree of success than when companies undertake radical change situations on their own.

Why is this approach more successful than many unfamiliar management approaches? Again, it is based on proven components. Experienced companies know how to use outsourcing effectively. Outsourcing providers know how to deliver sophisticated services effectively. While it may be a large conceptual leap, it's a small operational step to use outsourcing for enterprise transformation.

In our research on the implementation of business ideas, we found that "idea practitioners"—people who make it their responsibility to bring in ideas and make them a reality—are critical to the success of such initiatives. A key reason for the success of outsourcing for radical change is that the idea practitioners who champion the approach within an organization are the company's senior executives themselves. As idea leaders, they do more than simply create a healthy environment for new ideas. They personally drive outsourcing-based transformation from concept to results.

The other key idea practitioners in the picture are the senior executives' counterparts at the outsourcing providers. These individuals don't just recommend new ideas, as consultants typically would. They have the opportunity and the responsibility to implement what they think up. Therefore, the linkage between idea and action is straight and direct. Most of the outsourcing initiatives described in this book received a particularly high level of attention from provider executives because they knew that this form of project was something new for themselves and for their companies. There's nothing like this level of focus from senior people to overcome obstacles and ensure that needed changes get done.

This is an important book, not only because of the approach it describes but also because of the larger implications of that approach. Many business theorists have argued over the years that a company's identity is based heavily on the core competencies that it maintains. But if key competencies in a company's strategy are provided by other organizations, what does this mean for identity and culture? Linder's research begins to suggest that the ability to work creatively and collaboratively with external providers may be more important than any other single internal capability.

Jane Linder is well equipped to describe this phenomenon. With a background as both an academic and a practicing executive, she looks below the theoretical surface to how things get done in the real world. As soon as outsourcing for transformational change began to be adopted by companies, she started doing both executive interviews across many organizations, and detailed case studies of the most path-breaking outsourcing situations. The book is therefore both timely and based on solid evidence. Her role as an Accenture researcher gave her unique access to the company's important outsourcing engagements, but she also worked with nonclients and companies that had chosen other providers. It is highly unlikely that we'll see a better book on this topic anytime soon.

—Thomas H. Davenport

Preface

For as long as I can remember, I have wanted to write a book. This desire, like a fat, patient hen, has sat perched on my dream list—a short list of deep aspirations that keep watch over me. This item was in good company. I wanted to earn my doctorate. I did. I wanted to have wonderful children. They are amazing. I didn't want to hit my children. I didn't. Not once. I wanted to write a book. Now I have.

Many business books are not really written by the people whose names are on the front cover. That's not the case here. I worked with many wonderful colleagues during the process of researching this book, and I am indebted to them for their contributions, but I couldn't check it off my dream list unless I wrote it myself. So I did.

The story of how this book came to be is full of false starts and surprises. It actually starts with a house. I don't know how it got there, but this beautiful house appeared in my head one day. It was actually more than a house. It was a whole vignette. Picture yourself standing on the edge of a cliff overlooking the ocean. It's dark and stormy. Waves are crashing. Thunder and lightning roll over the rumbling ocean. Wagner is playing in the background. You turn around slowly. There you see a house perched on the hill behind you. It's all lit up, and its warm glow wraps its arms around you and brings you home. It brings you home to write.

So I decided to build the house. My husband-to-be graciously drove with me up and down the coast of New England looking for a piece of property that resembled the one in my head. We found it in Narragansett, Rhode Island, in the summer of 1999. I won't bore you with the details of planning and building the house, but in December 2001, we moved in. And it was just as I had pictured it. My writing room overlooks Narragansett Bay and Beaver Tail Light.

In addition to a place to write, I needed something to write about. At about the same time we spotted the land, I started a research project with Susan Cantrell on changing business models. You will recall that that time was the heart of dot-com mania, and talking about new business models was all the rage. Our project was not, however, about new business models. We reasoned that businesses would have to change the way they operated much more quickly than ever before as the Internet took hold, yet most of the companies we knew had a terrible track record at change. It didn't add up to us. How were they going to do it? We set out to find the answer.

We interviewed senior executives, evaluated more than a hundred business models, and accumulated evidence about how companies change their business models faster. For our efforts, we had published several articles and acquired a very solid understanding of business models and how they work. Unfortunately, by January 2001, with the Internet frenzy fizzling, no one seemed to be interested in business models any longer. Despite our surprising and provocative, if preliminary, answer to the question, we closed up the project.

Meanwhile, I had concluded that my organization was missing a critical capability. We did a fabulous job at deep, academic research projects, but we did not do a very good job of supporting our consulting colleagues' needs for focused, timely studies on current management issues. I decided to demonstrate that a small, dedicated team could produce high-quality, insightful management reports in 10 to 12 weeks instead of 10 to 12 months. Fast-cycle research was born.

Shortly afterward, the managing partner of Accenture's outsourcing practice, Marty Cole, came to me with a request. He had accepted an opportunity two months hence to give a speech to an august group of CEOs, and he was looking for some interesting new ideas to talk about. The new fast-cycle research capability was just what he needed. He asked if I could do a study on an emerging approach—using outsourcing for transformation. I agreed.

It was mid-May, and we were looking at a mid-July, hard-stop deadline. I pulled together a team of two summer interns, Matt Breitfelder and Mark Arnold, and an experienced research colleague, Al Jacobson of Hartwell Associates. In a mad dash to get our arms around this new idea, we tried to identify every example of transformational outsourcing that existed and to get in touch with executives who had been involved. We searched the Web, interviewed outsourcing experts and Accenture partners, and punctuated our days with white-board debates about what we were hearing and what it really meant. In the end, there were a few long nights, but we hit our deadline, and Marty Cole made a great speech.

Fast-cycle research had begun to prove its value, but there was much more to come. Thousands of copies of the management report were distributed to public- and private-sector executives as Accenture increased its overall commitment to outsourcing. Subsequently, through the hard work of Caroline Trotman, Ellen Marks, Mimi Wallk, Susan Nealon, Carol Lynne Jones, Linda Coppola, Martine Bertin-Peterson, Shari Wenker, and Chris Burrows, I got the opportunity to conduct eight additional fast-cycle research projects on outsourcing. Some of these also had a transformational theme, and others helped us fill in the details of the overall outsourcing landscape. As a result of this continuing rota of rapid-fire research, I personally interviewed hundreds of executives around the world about their experiences with outsourcing.

My research colleagues, Susan Cantrell, Joe Sawyer, Tim Wiley, and Christine Dawson, each made substantial contributions to one or more these projects, and Alice Hartley was an invaluable research associate for several of them. Suneel Gupta, Louis Carvallo, and Scott Crist helped as well. In addition to supporting us with secondary research, Gosia Stergios ran the behind-the-scenes processes to turn our words into works. On the public-sector projects, Tom Healy's unwavering sponsorship and thoughtful guidance gave us support for stepping out to the leading edge. Marty Cole played an equally valuable role on the private-sector side. Countless others helped by connecting us to their clients and by offering their own insights. Gary Stephen Pusey, Karyn Mottershead, John Rollins, and Alex Christou were especially helpful.

I am also indebted to the busy executives who took the time to tell us their outsourcing stories. Peter Bareau, Steve Owen, and Gill Lambley at NS&I and Marco Trecroce and Su Mills at Thomas Cook deserve medals for all they have done to help.

I owe special thanks to Alex Beal and to Tom Davenport. Alex was the one who suggested that I turn the growing body of research on transformational outsourcing into a book. Tom, as the executive director of the Institute, provided both the financial support and the organizational air cover for me to take the time to pull all the work together.

How did this dream ultimately come true? From February through June 2003, at every opportunity, I worked from my new home in Rhode Island. It was as I had hoped—a quiet, beautiful space with plenty of room for ideas. When the words got stuck, I took advantage of the calming power of the ocean to get them flowing again. It was a house for writing, and I wrote.

My wonderful husband not only put up with me during this time, he willingly served as sounding board and able counselor. He and my children never rolled their eyes when I needed to talk about outsourcing to get my thinking straight. I can't tell you how much it meant to me to have my own personal fan club during this time.

Writing the book also held a particularly juicy surprise. As I said earlier, Sue Cantrell and I closed up the business-models research with a satisfying and provocative answer to the question, How do companies change their business models faster when they are particularly inexpert at implementing deep organizational change? There is a far-reaching answer, but one that demands superior organizational capabilities that are frankly out of reach for most companies. By accident, writing this book turned up a second very good answer to the same question. And this answer is extremely accessible—it's something that anyone can use. My hope for this book is that executives will find this answer useful and effective in helping them make their organizations great.

PART I

The Case for Transformational Outsourcing

CHAPTER 1

National Savings and Investments Uses Outsourcing to Transform

This book is about transformational outsourcing. I hope to convince you that transformational outsourcing is a powerful tool that executives can use to achieve dramatic improvements in their organizations' performance. Most often when I introduce the topic, however, executives' eyes glaze over or they suddenly remember an urgent appointment. They don't see outsourcing as something they should care about. Yes, they know they can probably use it to reduce costs in some areas, but they would not consider it a strategic tool. So I tell them the story of National Savings and Investments. Then they get interested. Here's the story . . .

On September 30, 2002, Alan Cook took over as CEO of National Savings and Investments (NS&I), the home of arguably the most successful transformational outsourcing deal in the world. National Savings and Investments (NS&I), an executive agency of the Chancellor of the Exchequer, helps fund the UK national government by selling retail savings products. In 2002, it had more than £60 billion (almost $100 billion)* under management, making it one of the largest banking organizations in the nation. It provides about 20 percent of the government's funding, with

---

*British pounds converted to U.S. dollars at a rate of 1.664 dollars per pound.

the remainder coming from the Treasury's sale of gilt-edged securities. In a country with a population of 60 million, NS&I claims up to 30 million customers.

While it does not have a full line of banking products and services, NS&I competes head to head in some arenas with private financial-service companies like Barclay's and Abbey National Bank, as well as the UK building societies. It offers a range of savings products, from traditional individual passbook accounts and guaranteed income bonds to innovative products like guaranteed equity bonds and Premium Bonds. NS&I is the only savings institution in the UK that offers individuals the opportunity to win up to £1 million ($1.66 million) in prizes, tax free, without putting capital at risk.

Competition in the financial services industry goes beyond the established banking companies. Major UK food retailers like Tesco, J. Sainsbury, and Safeway threw down the gauntlet by setting up financial service centers in their supermarkets beginning in the mid-1990s. Not content simply to lease space to a banking partner, these companies branded their own products, built on-line banking capabilities for their customers, and offered a full line of appealingly priced products. In addition, a new entrant, Virgin Group, recently began soliciting entire banking relationships by offering a comprehensive account that consolidated loans, mortgages, cash, and savings in a single flexible account. For NS&I to succeed and continue to fulfill its mission, it has to compete aggressively on both product innovation and pricing.

Anatomy of an Outsourcing Initiative

In July 1996, National Savings, as it was called at the time,[1] was changed from a government department to an Executive Agency of the Chancellor of the Exchequer. This shift increased management autonomy, and more importantly, created an opening at the head of the organization for an executive CEO. Peter Bareau, an experienced banking leader from Lloyds, stepped into the post in July 1996.

What Bareau found as he surveyed the agency was somewhat daunting. The staff numbered 4,650 civil servants with an average tenure in the organization of some 20 years. Products and services were supported in three separate operational sites—Glasgow, Durham, and Blackpool—but each site managed only one segment of the product line. For example, if a member had invested in three or four products and wanted to transact with someone at NS&I, she or he would have to contact all the relevant physical locations; these were not connected in any way. If the product was an ordinary savings account, the facility at Glasgow was responsible; if it was a Premium Bond, the customer would have to deal with Blackpool (see Exhibit 1.1). Telephone support was minimal; most inquiries

Exhibit 1.1. Amounts invested in National Savings and Investments products at March 31, 2000.

Source: National Savings and Investments.

had to be conducted through written correspondence. Products could also be purchased through the nation's 19,000 postal offices, making NS&I products highly accessible to individuals in even the most remote regions. However, the postal service transferred customer orders to NS&I through a largely manual process. Twenty million of the agency's 55 million annual transactions were processed without substantive automation. The computer systems infrastructure had suffered from underinvestment and was no longer up-to-date, according to one executive. NS&I had invested scarce capital elsewhere, where demands were greatest. With an unwieldy legacy systems environment as its toolset, NS&I had introduced only three new products in the past eight years. Noted Bareau: "Our image was old. We weren't regarded as being dynamic."

Early on in his tenure, Bareau set about charting a course for the organization. His first initiative was to clarify the organization's mission. He established that one of the traditional aims—to make savings products available to the populace—was well managed by the private sector. The merits of its second aim—to provide a cost-effective source of funding for the national government—hinged on whether or not NS&I's all-in cost for raising funds was lower than that for gilt, the UK government's name for its Treasury bills.

During 1996–1997, with the help of outside consultants, Bareau and his executive team worked closely with the Treasury to develop a strategy. They looked at a full range of possible futures for the organization. This process established that NS&I created £100 million ($166 million) in value per year by being able to raise funds for an all-in cost that was lower than the cost of gilt. However, no one in the organization was under any illusions about whether this could continue without substantial investment in organization, systems, and infrastructure. If NS&I could not ably compete, it would not be able to replace an average of £10 billion ($16.6 billion) per year in redemptions with new sales. In this case, it would place a substantial drag on the government purse. Said Bareau: "If we didn't dramatically lower costs, improve products, build a customer database so we could market better, change our image, and add professional capabilities, our risk would grow and grow until we had no value left." On the positive side, Bareau now had a clear, visible metric with which to drive performance.

Again with the help of private-sector experts, Bareau and his team set a new strategy for the organization with an aspiration not just to survive but also to leapfrog private-sector competitors in the personal savings market. A senior member of his team pointed out the depth of the challenge: "We didn't have all the skills; we didn't have the technology; and we didn't have all the resources required to fulfill our mission. We were capital-constrained. It sounds perverse, but we even found it difficult to reduce staff numbers at the desired rate because we had limited financing available for redundancy payments. To succeed, we needed to transform the business very quickly in a way that was self-supporting. So we looked at the outsourcing model."

Bareau's small senior team, most of whom had significant private-sector experience, satisfied themselves that an outsourcing business model could work—that a private sector company could invest at the level they required and make a profitable business out of the opportunity. Through a unique process, they decided that the outsourcing would best be done in one comprehensive, radical deal rather than a series of smaller arrangements. Explains Steve Owen, the outsourcing project manager at the time (now partnerships and operations director): "We looked at our four key stakeholders: our staff, the Treasury, our customers, and ourselves as a strategic business. We identified what each stakeholder group would be looking for in detail, and assessed each option against these needs." That drove the decision toward a single provider to offer the single customer view, integrated systems, and investment commitment that NS&I needed for wholesale transformation (see Exhibit 1.2).

They went through the legally prescribed procurement process and posted a very broad tender offer in the OJEC, the *Official Journal of the European Communities*. From over 80 expressions of interest they received, the team qualified four groups—two companies and two consortia—as capable of moving to the next stage of the process. However, at that time, they still had not determined exactly where to draw the boundaries between what would be outsourced and what would not.

Rather than provide a detailed tender specification at that point, NS&I chose an innovative approach that still met the European procurement regulations and issued an Information Memorandum to the four groups. Recalls Owen: "We realized we had a lot to learn, so we didn't issue a formal tender at that stage. We described our business, our challenges and constraints, and invited them to come back to us with creative solutions. It was a deliberate attempt to draw in information and ideas." Between the summer of 1997 and the spring of 1998, NS&I talked with potential partners, evaluated proposals, and learned.

(*text continues on page 10*)

Exhibit 1.2. NS&I's objectives for the deal and its requirements of a private-sector partner to meet those objectives.

Objectives	NS&I required a private-sector partner to:
a) The transfer of responsibility and the risk for the delivery and enhancement of an integrated operational service.	■ Substantially increase operational efficiency through business process reengineering. ■ Meet detailed product and customer quality standards as measured by specified key performance indicators. ■ Accept progressive reductions in the fee if key performance indicators are not met. ■ Develop a link with the planned Post Office Counters Automation system. ■ Be responsible for transaction accounting. ■ Accept all risks associated with the year 2000. ■ Take on the risk of the impact of future legislative changes on the operational service. ■ Take operational responsibility for implementation of the first NS&I ISA product.
b) Cost reduction to the most competitive levels achievable throughout the contract.	■ Charge a declining fixed fee based on a "middle case" volume transaction scenario with a predetermined free band of volume variations around the "middle case." ■ Charge a different fee for each band of transactions above or below the "middle case" volume and free band. ■ Benchmark services and costs throughout the contract and offer downward-only price movements and/or improvements in quality service. ■ Share in higher than expected profits from NS&I work. ■ Share in profits and cost savings made from third-party business using NS&I assets. ■ Agree that severance costs above an agreed cap will be at the provider's risk.
c) A collaborative and flexible contractual relationship with a provider incentivized to support NS&I strategies.	■ Allow NS&I the right to audit all aspects of service delivery and key performance indicator calculations. ■ Maintain complete transparency of accounts relating to the performance of the NS&I contract and the third-party work conducted from the transferred undertaking. ■ Allow National Audit Office access. ■ Supervise, on a day-to-day basis, the processing services provided by Post Office Counters Ltd. ■ Ensure that the entity performing the NS&I contract remains an identifiable and separable undertaking at all times enabling NS&I to be able to regain control at any time. ■ Not charge for variations that are simply regular amendments. ■ Provide new products at no additional cost, with a marginal increase or decrease in cost if NS&I requires more or fewer of such products.

d) An equitable commercial relationship.

- Take a long-term view of investing in a partnership with NS&I.
- Agree that where new products or channels are fundamentally different, NS&I retains the right to tender more widely.
- Agree to a 12- or 15-year contract term with both parties able to terminate 5 years before contract end.
- Assume responsibility for staff, operational assets, and liabilities from NS&I.

e) The transfer and protection of staff.

- Maintain Investors in People accreditations.
- Retain a significant presence at all three sites for at least the first five years of the contract.
- Apply Transfer of Undertakings Protection of Employment rules to the transfer of staff.
- Provide redundancy and pension terms that are broadly equivalent to the Principal Civil Service Pension scheme.

Source: National Audit Office, May 25, 2000.

In April 1998, NS&I invited both General Data Services (GDS) and Newport Systems (not their real names) to negotiate further. The agency issued a formal tender specification that articulated clear requirements, a business model for the partnership, and even a draft contract. By this time, the NS&I executives had arrived at a fairly radical conclusion about core and noncore activities. In the core, they included owning their stakeholder relationship with the British government, and their product, marketing, and channel strategies. Everything else was considered noncore. "We had to get over the organization's mind-set," said Bareau, "that we couldn't possibly outsource operations that would impact the customer. People believed that to control those things, we had to own them."

To keep the competitive process lively and informative, NS&I actually negotiated a full contract with both suppliers. This forced discussions and analysis to an unusual level of detail and ensured that NS&I achieved the best possible terms and conditions. Bareau remarked, "We were very clear about what we wanted: investment, job creation for our people, a total transformation of the operational systems, a huge culture change, and risk transfer. In the end, everyone underestimated the cost, complexity, and risk of the transformation; but the alternative of having to do it ourselves kept us on track."

It was clear from the outset that modernizing NS&I would mean dislocating staff. Owen commented, "We had been getting smaller for a long time. In the 1960s, we had 15,000 staff. By early 1999, we were down to about 4,500. With an average length of service of over 20 years, many of our people had lived through the shrinkage. They didn't welcome it, but they did recognize the business reasons for it."

The executive team believed that, despite the disruption, a good outsourcing model would provide the best chance for workers to continue employment. According to the transfer of undertakings protection of employment (TUPE) regulations, an outsourcing provider would have to maintain workers' current terms and conditions at the transfer. Further, under UK law, if it wanted to make redundancies following the transfer, it would have to start a consultation process with employees prior to taking action. But NS&I sought a contract that would encourage the provider to win new outsourcing accounts that would utilize transferred workers. According to Owen: "If it worked the way we hoped, the provider would have a valuable asset—an operations center with robust infrastructure and trained staff—with which to gain new business. That's how we sold it to our people, the unions, and the local politicians in Glasgow, Durham, and Blackpool."

The NS&I team started communication with the staff from the beginning of the process. Owen explained, "We started with a very light touch, and as we learned more about the shape of the deal, we began to open up more robust discussions with the staff and the unions. We didn't say, 'This is good for you,' but we said, 'This is the best thing for the business, and we will do everything we can to protect you.' We were very open." They held "road shows" to address staff fears about pensions, pay, and new work expectations. Each session eased some concerns and opened up the next tier of issues. Because the business case for the outsourcing was very strong, the NS&I executive team believed that ultimately the staff would recognize the need for change. And they managed to avoid press coverage to ensure there was no misunderstanding in the public's mind. "We kept a low profile," said one executive. "This was not the privatization of NS&I. This was a simple business case."

The competing bidders both knew that creating new jobs for outsourced NS&I employees would be central to the winning strategy. A provider executive noted: "NS&I wanted to outsource the delivery of massive change, which they knew would require investment and expertise that they did not possess. In addition, they were unable to create new jobs to offset the reduced need for staff to service their own business. So they asked, 'What can the private sector do to create work for the people who will no longer be needed to support NS&I and its customers?'" GDS and Newport Systems took different routes to reassure the government, the unions, and the employees that employment prospects were improved by the outsourcing. Newport Systems framed the NS&I deal as a strategic acquisition: it would acquire 1 million square feet of space and thousands of people that would form the core of an administrative services center outsourcing model. This showcase deal would enable Newport to demonstrate its deep outsourcing capabilities, and it would provide a center through which it could service new outsourcing clients. GDS, on the other hand, claimed that it had the scale to absorb NS&I employees into its organization through normal business processes.

Newport Systems also recognized that its success would depend on winning the hearts and minds of the people. It insisted on having access to the NS&I staff during contract negotiations. It mounted a concerted communications campaign to explain what outsourcing would mean to the affected people and their families. These road shows were designed to demonstrate that "we weren't two-headed dragons," one executive remarked.

The NS&I team did have some concern about Newport's level of experience in both business process outsourcing and the banking industry. "GDS was much stronger in IT outsourcing," explained Bareau, "but what we were doing was at the radical end, and even GDS didn't have much experience in that." To mitigate the risk with Newport Systems, Bareau and his team established a relationship with Newport's headquarters management, which guaranteed the contract.

By the time both providers' contracts were negotiated, the NS&I team had invested a great deal of time to determine exactly what the organization needed. Again aiming for a balanced view, they based the final decision on their assessment of the needs of the four key stakeholder groups. They identified four primary objectives for each stakeholder group and developed a total of 64 evaluation criteria in all. For example, it was important to minimize the cost of raising funds, and customers wanted their phone calls answered by a human being within 20 seconds. Owen recalls, "It was not just a list of vague wishes; we had laid out an explicit transformation program based on the sort of business we wanted to be." No matter how the criteria were weighted, one clear answer emerged: Newport Systems. (Exhibits 1.3 and 1.4 compare GDS's and Newport's proposals.)

In December 1998, NS&I announced it would award a ten-year contract to Newport Systems, with an option to extend for five additional years (see Exhibit 1.5 for a comparison of the winning bid with in-house alternatives). The total value of the contract was £635 million ($1.56 billion). All of NS&I's operations, customer service, technology, and transaction processing, along with 4,153 largely unionized civil servants, would be outsourced to Newport, effective April 1999. NS&I would retain 120 full-time civil servants on the payroll to handle strategy, marketing, and product design and to manage the relationship with Newport.

Stepping into the Abyss

As the NS&I team embarked on their modernization, they faced several significant uncertainties. One executive explained: "There was no ques-

Exhibit 1.3. Comparison of Newport Systems and GDS bids.

This figure shows that Newport's bid for operational services was £21 million lower than that of GDS, and that its bid for accommodation was £36 million lower.

	Newport Systems			GDS		
	Operations £m	Accommodation £m	Total £m	Operations £m	Accommodation £m	Total £m
July	641	4	645	622	68	690
October	592	35	627	623	68	691
November	604	31	635	625	67	692

Notes:
1. All values are shown in net present terms at 1998/99 prices.
2. Newport's initial bid for the accommodation elements of the deal was an error and was corrected in October.
3. Both Newport and GDS were prepared to purchase or lease the accommodation. NS&I negotiated a leasehold option with Newport and a purchase option with GDS as these represented the best value for money solutions offered.

Source: National Audit Office, May 25, 2000.

Exhibit 1.4. Other significant differences between the final bids from Newport Systems and GDS.

Area	Newport Systems	GDS
Open-Book Accounting	Unfettered access.	A comprehensive list of reports available for NS&I's scrutiny audited by GDS auditors.
Benchmarking	Regular benchmarking on both service levels and its underlying cost base against best practice. Reductions in costs would go directly to the unitary charge.	Periodic future benchmarking of the service but related to average market service levels as opposed to best practice. Any reductions in cost would be shared through the profit-sharing mechanism.
Profit Sharing	50:50 share over base margin requirement calculated annually. An element of the deal reported separately for profit sharing. Any savings in contingency provision would be shared 30:70 with NS&I	50:50 share over base margin requirements calculated cumulatively over time and across cost areas. GDS would give NS&I a credit note to be offset against additional and/or changed GDS services. Savings in redundancy costs would feed through to the profit-sharing mechanism.
Telephone Call Center	Capacity: 2 million. Additional calls: 80p each.	Capacity: 2 million. Additional calls: £1.80 each.
New Products	Cap of £600,000 for each product even outside the number contained within the unitary charge. Rebate of £600,000 for each new product not introduced within the unitary change.	Not clear. Cost of additional new products not capped.
Fundamentally Different Products	Accepted NS&I's definition.	Proposed a more restrictive definition. Potentially NS&I would have difficulty classifying products as new as opposed to fundamentally different and thus have them included within the unitary charge. GDS also reserved the right to refer NS&I's decision on a new product to the dispute resolution procedure.
Accommodation	Newport has taken leases on the whole estate and will pay market rent of £4.1 million a year, recovered in the unitary charge, leaving NS&I with a salable asset. Newport will keep a presence at each of the three locations for at least five years.	GDS proposed to transfer purchased properties to another company and lease them. It also proposed to sell the Durham site within 2 years of contract commencement. GDS proposals required NS&I to underwrite a 10-year lease on required accommodation. Weak clawback provisions included, leaving NS&I little chance of sharing in windfall gains from property development.

Source: National Audit Office, May 25, 2000.

Exhibit 1.5. Comparison of NS&I's forecast cast budgets, the Public Sector Comparator, and Newport Systems's bid.

This figure shows that Newport's bid was superior to the Public Sector Comparator, and that both were within NS&I forecast cash budget. The Public Sector Comparator represents the best performance the government organization estimates it could achieve in-house.

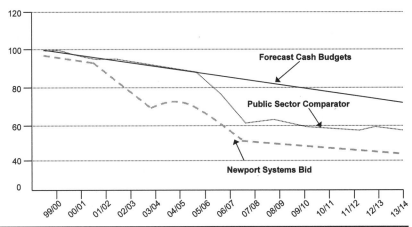

Source: National Audit Office.

tion that what we chose to do was very, very aggressive—the outsourcing route enabled us to bring a degree of certainty to the timescale for modernization."

To win the work, Newport Systems had to define the cost of running the operation posttransformation and to start charging at that rate on day one. One executive recalled: "There was a peak of borrowing at the outset to pay to operate under the old model. NS&I was to be charged about £100 million ($166 million) at the start with the intention that the two lines on the graph would converge in the future." In addition, Newport Systems was required to determine service levels for all NS&I activities and hit performance targets to avoid incurring penalty fees (see Exhibit 1.6). Up until that point, key performance indicators (KPIs) had not existed. According to a Newport executive, "Record keeping could have been improved—everyone knew what they were doing, but no one could spell it out crisply."

Newport Systems focused on executing an effective transition process to start the relationship off on the right foot. This included clear models for human relations support and counseling as people changed employers.

(text continues on page 18)

Exhibit 1.6. Key performance indicators.

Area of Coverage	Broad Description	Number of KPIs and Grading			Date of Introduction	Measurement	Frequency of Reporting
		Platinum	Gold	Silver			
Treasury Management	Banking of receipts and transfer from local banks to Bank of England. Transfer to and from National Loans Fund and National Debt Office	2	3	–	4 at April 1999 1 to be decided	Timeliness and accuracy of money movement	Daily
Product Delivery—Sales	Dispatch of customer documentation sales queries and updating of records	–	–	5	4 at April 1999 1 at October 1999	Timeliness of dispatch and response to queries and accuracy in compliance with customer's instructions	Daily or weekly monitoring with results reported monthly
Product Delivery—After Sales	Replies to queries, dispatch of statements of interest	–	–	7	4 at April 1999 2 at July 1999 1 at October 1999	Timeliness of dispatch Accuracy of replies to customers	Daily monitoring with results reported monthly. Quarterly for ISAs Annual
Product Delivery—Payments	Dispatch of payments and customer documents, queries	–	2	2	3 at April 1999 1 at October 1999	Timeliness of dispatch and accuracy in compliance with customer's instructions	Daily monitoring with results reported monthly
Product Delivery—Premium Bond Prizes	Informing major winners, dispatch of high value claim forms and of prize warrants, and automatic reinvestment of prizes	–	1	4	5 at April 1999	Timeliness of dispatch and accuracy	Monthly

Category	Description			Dates	Measure	Monitoring
Product Delivery—Customer Service	Customer inquiry calls	-	7	3 at April 1999 2 at July 1999 1 at October 1999 1 to be decided	Speed of answering and duration of calls Accuracy of fulfillment	Daily monitoring with results reported monthly
Customer Service—Research	Customer satisfaction with the service provided and customer complaints	-	5	5 at October 1999	Percentage of satisfaction	Continuous sampling with quarterly reporting of results. Daily monitoring with results reported monthly
Management Information	Delivery of standard and ad hoc management information reports specified by NS&I	- 2	4 11 29	4 at October 1999 23 at April 1999 4 at 1/7/99 13 at July 1999 2 to be decided	Timeliness and accuracy	Daily, weekly, and monthly

Note: NS&I did not introduce all of the key performance indicators at the commencement of the contract. Those not introduced immediately were in areas where NS&I had not previously measured performance or for new processes introduced under the contract, for example, the provision of management information by the private-sector partner to NS&I. Newport wanted to gain experience with these measures before they became subject to performance deductions.

Source: National Audit Office, May 25, 2000.

One Newport Systems executive stated proudly: "By sticking close to the unions, and being open and honest with them early on, we headed off the people issues before they became grounds for serious concern." The transfer on the day went very smoothly indeed. The next step was to reduce the cost of operations. The executive continued: "We made an offer for voluntary redundancy, and many people were happy to take the generous payoff. So the transition never caused the industrial relations fallout that would have been painful for Newport, NS&I, and its customers."

One of Bareau's first moves after his original strategy had been approved was to ask the current board members to resign and recompete for their positions. He also invited several members of the Treasury to enter the process. As a result, the composition of the board changed markedly. Bareau explained: "These people weren't unprofessional, they were just associated with the old way of doing things."

As Newport Systems stepped into the maelstrom of organizational transformation, it faced massive challenges. The scale was daunting. Said one seasoned executive: "It always looks easy when you have a blueprint, but it's much more complicated in real life." Newport planned to implement an entirely new IT platform, including hardware, networks, and software. It would transfer existing products to the new platform over one year. At the same time it would develop new products, implement new business processes, start up call centers and imaging centers, train employees, and keep the old systems running until all the migrations were proven effective. (Exhibit 1.7 shows Newport Systems's plan for the first year of activities.)

Newport considered the technology implementation fairly straightforward. For example, it phased in intelligent character recognition hardware that would allow payment documentation to be processed automatically. Newport had a core expertise globally in that kind of hardware. Other aspects of the transformation were more problematic. One executive explained, "The change process took more time than we envisaged, and we found that it not only took longer to make staff reductions but that the operation might ultimately require more staff than we originally planned to run it." Although some deadlines were missed, by the end of 2002, through a combination of redeployment and voluntary release, Newport had reduced the staff by 50 percent and introduced eight new or substan-

Exhibit 1.7. Newport Systems's gradual approach to the development and implementation of IT and human resource solutions.

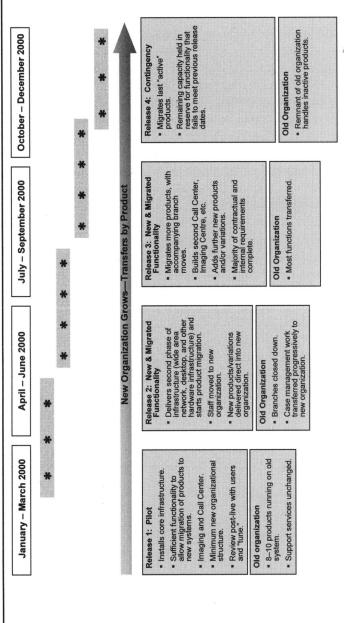

| January – March 2000 | April – June 2000 | July – September 2000 | October – December 2000 |

New Organization Grows—Transfers by Product →

Release 1: Pilot
- Installs core infrastructure.
- Sufficient functionality to allow migration of products to new systems.
- Imaging and Call Center.
- Minimum new organizational structure.
- Review post-live with users and "tune."

Old organization
- 8–10 products running on old system.
- Support services unchanged.

Release 2: New & Migrated Functionality
- Delivers second phase of infrastructure (wide area network, desktop, and other hardware infrastructure) and starts product migration.
- Staff moved to new organization.
- New products/variations delivered direct into new organization.

Old Organization
- Branches closed down.
- Case management work transferred progressively to new organization.

Release 3: New & Migrated Functionality
- Migrates more products, with accompanying branch moves.
- Builds second Call Center, Imaging Centre, etc.
- Adds further new products and/or variations.
- Majority of contractual and internal requirements complete.

Old Organization
- Most functions transferred.

Release 4: Contingency
- Migrates last "active" products.
- Remaining capacity held in reserve for functionality that fails to meet previous release dates.

Old Organization
- Remnant of old organization handles inactive products.

"Current" Organization Reduces—Transfers by Product →

*Migration of products to new systems in four tranches.

Source: National Audit Office, May 25, 2000.

tially improved products, at least one of which was the first of its type in the industry.

During this period, Newport Systems was undergoing a massive transformation of its own. It came to the partnership with obvious strength in technology, but a less solid footing in the banking industry and administrative service management. Steve Owen commented: "It's hard to transform a business process when you don't know the business you're in. We had to do more work than we expected to help them understand banking. They're also coming up the learning curve on business process outsourcing. But they bring a huge technology capability that we couldn't have tapped into ourselves. Together, we're a great team."

Newport had committed to redeploy 1,200 of the displaced NS&I workers to service new clients. In 2001, Newport was able to win a large contract from a UK bank for back-office processing services that required a staff of 700. An executive asserted: "Newport could never have won the deal without the experience it gained on the NS&I account." The UK bank had administrative functions like checking account address changes dispersed in numerous branches around the UK. As part of its grand strategy, the bank wanted to focus all its employees in High Street branches on customer-facing activities. It needed a whole new back office, so it sought a partner with people, space, and expertise. Newport Systems won the profitable deal against stiff competition.

It was also able to win an additional piece of work with the UK Passport Service within its existing UK government contract. The Passport Service wanted a seventh regional office, and Newport won with the proposal to build it in the NS&I facility in Durham.

Whole Business Thinking Makes the Relationship Work

From the outset of the contract, most of Bareau's team recognized that they had not shed management responsibility as conventional outsourcing wisdom promises; they had simply traded one type of management challenge for another. Bareau admitted that some things had not gone as well as planned. Initially, both partners acted as if a traditional relationship could deliver the results they expected. Bareau summarized: "We needed more joint working and joint strategizing, and less passing parcels back and forth. It got very antagonistic in places until we realized that what we were trying to do was ensure success for both of us. Increasingly we realized that everything we do must be holistic, including our business model. We can't say, 'We have ours and you have yours.'"

NS&I and Newport Systems executives began to exercise their joint governance process to actively manage the relationship (see Exhibit 1.8). This included an annual meeting between the Treasury Minister and the head of Newport, monthly board meetings that involved the CEOs of both Newport and NS&I, monthly business management meetings, and meetings of seven or eight task-oriented boards as needed. Owen explained, "These are all joint organizations focused on 'whole business thinking.' Every issue has a home."

Clear objectives and aligned goals were critical to success, but flexibility was as well. The contract established NS&I's ability to launch a certain number of new products each year for no additional fee to Newport Systems. But the NS&I team learned that they could set back the service-level achievements by defining complex products that were difficult to administer. "We are contractually cushioned from the consequences of our actions," Owen explained. "If we introduce a new product that's great for customers but an operational nightmare, [Newport Systems] pays the price. We learned to sit down together and work through the implications so we could make the right decision from a whole of business perspective."

In some ways, Owen asserted, NS&I's task was easier than functional outsourcing. "We were business oriented. We described the kind of business we wanted to be and the outputs we were after. You don't need reams of technical parameters and excruciatingly detailed definitions of business interfaces with this kind of deal. And we didn't have to be constrained by what was doable. We just sketched out what we wanted." Bareau attributed their overall success to the partners' commitment, saying, "This was a seminal contract for Newport. We got their absolute, top-level commitment. Without that, we might have found ourselves with much bigger problems. It carries you through the rocky places." Emphasizing the senior team's strong commitment, another executive said simply, "We had our names all over it."

Exhibit 1.8. Governance of the contract.

This figure shows that a formal governance structure has been defined for the contract.

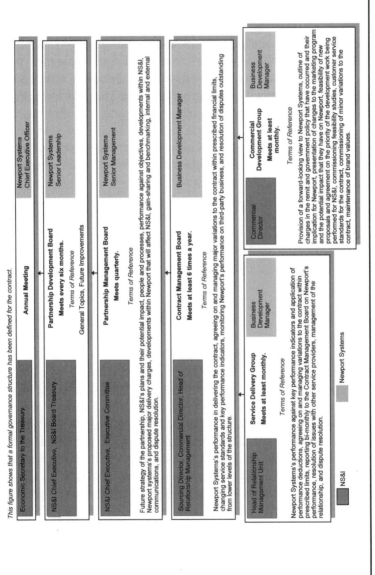

Source: National Savings and Investments.

Taking Stock

By all accounts, NS&I was actually accomplishing the bold agenda it had set forth (see Exhibit 1.9). In the National Audit Office's first examination of the deal—just six months after it was signed in January 1999—it found that although it was too early to conclude whether the outcomes envisaged in the partnership would be achieved, NS&I had secured a very good deal with Newport Systems. With a contract of this size and scope, however, the National Audit Office would be watching to determine whether the taxpayers really had received the benefits they were promised. The results of its second examination were delivered during May 2003.

The achievements that Bareau and his team had delivered in just four years after transferring its operational staff and assets to Newport Systems were:

- £176 million ($292.2 million) value added in 2001/2002, against a goal of £120 million ($199.7 million).
- Introduction of the first-ever equity-linked investment product, the guaranteed equity bond, which offers a return linked to the FTSE 100 index yet provides 100 percent security for capital.
- Establishment of a single telephone number for sales and 24/7 service with the ability for customers to buy seven different products with a debit card over the phone.
- 11.7 million call-center calls, a 57 percent increase over the previous year. Nearly 90 percent of these were answered first, and within 20 seconds, by a person, rather than a machine.
- Launch of a free lost-funds tracing service, which enabled 2,400 customers to be reunited with £3 million ($4.99 million).
- Transition of products to a common systems infrastructure.
- Adoption of a new name and modernized identity for the organization.
- Change from an "isolationist, civil service culture" to a market-led culture.
- Change from a complex civil service pay structure to a discretionary system with clear bonuses based on performance.

Exhibit 1.9. National Savings and Investments timeline.

1861	NS&I's original predecessor organization was established as the Post Office Savings Bank to encourage ordinary wage earners to provide for themselves.
1969	NS&I was separated from the postal service and established as a separate department accountable to the Treasury.
1996	NS&I was granted agency status, giving it more management autonomy.
	July. The Chancellor of the Exchequer appointed Peter Bareau as the CEO of NS&I.
	July. Bareau commissioned a strategic review of the organization.
1997	**January.** Consultants completed the strategic review.
	March. NS&I launched a search for a private-sector partner to undertake an extensive modernization program.
	July. NS&I issued an Information Memorandum to four bidders to solicit innovative solutions.
1998	**April.** NS&I issued an Invitation to Negotiate to two final bidders, GDS and Newport Systems.
	June through November. NS&I negotiated pro forma contracts with both final bidders.
	December. Newport was chosen as NS&I's outsourcing provider.
1999	**January.** NS&I and Newport signed a ten-year outsourcing contract with a 5-year extension clause.
	April. Newport formally took over NS&I operations along with 4,000 staff.
	April. Newport completed the technical work to enable NS&I to launch a new product, the Individual Savings Account.
	April through October. Two additional new products and five product variations were introduced.
2000	**March.** Number of operational personnel working on the NS&I Account now at 3,400.
2002	**June.** Value added for the 2001/2002 fiscal year reached £176 million.
	September. Peter Bareau stepped down after 6 years. Alan Cook from Prudential UK was named CEO.
2003	**January.** Operational personnel supporting NS&I now below 2,000.

Source: Personal conversations with NS&I executives, National Audit Office, May 2000.

- Reduction of staff from 4,153 to 2,050 to create a streamlined, low-cost operation.
- Establishment of a working group with the governments of Canada, the United States, and Ireland to benchmark the best practice cost and service levels for public-sector operations that sell retail debt.

By the end of 2002, the transformation of National Savings and Investments had entered a new phase. Targets for the coming year were focused on extending the wins, continuous improvement, and leveraging new capabilities. Cook recognized that the market's perception had not kept up with the pace of change at NS&I, and he was considering exactly how to unleash the organization's power.

What Do We Make of This?

This example is real, and it's working. The benefits have been documented by the National Audit Office of the UK government, so they are less subject to managerial puffery than most stories of this sort. This is not the only example of transformational outsourcing, but it is one of the best. It was executed well, but not perfectly. Nonetheless, by any measure we would choose, the results are unusually good.

Why is this so important? More than half of the business executives we talk to expect their companies to require radical change to succeed over the coming years.[2] The approaches most have used in the past to implement changes of this sort have been stunningly ineffective. As we will discuss throughout the remainder of the book, transformational outsourcing provides an alternative that actually works.

Notes

1. The agency was named National Savings in 1969. It adopted its current name, National Savings and Investments, in early 2002. For simplicity's sake, we will refer to it as NS&I throughout the document.

2. Unpublished Accenture survey, conducted in conjunction with the Economist Intelligence Unit in 2002.

CHAPTER 2

Outsourcing Isn't What It Used to Be

Transformational outsourcing is definitely not the most common form of outsourcing; it's an unusual and specific flavor. However, it's also an essential tool in every executive's bag of tricks. In some important situations, it's the only tool that works. These are bold assertions, but I'm confident that they're true. Let me take you through my logic.

What Is Outsourcing Anyway?

Until I asked executives this question, I thought outsourcing was well understood. In fact, the definition is quite fuzzy. Most leaders would agree that outsourcing involves purchasing services from an outside company. But that's where the agreement stops. Some argue that it isn't outsourcing unless a company's employees transfer to the service provider. Others would not hold that high standard, but would stipulate that the organization has to have once provided the service for itself. Still others would insist only that the organization could have provided the service for itself. After speaking to hundreds of executives, here's what I have found to be the real underlying concept:

Outsourcing means purchasing ongoing services from an outside company that a company currently provides, or most organizations normally provide, for themselves.

For example, if a company uses an outside company to do its manufacturing, most managers would say it "outsources manufacturing." This is true even if the company never made a single widget on its own. Why? Because companies generally manage their own manufacturing operations. By the same token, almost no company would say it outsources its investment banking, auditing, or garbage collection, because the vast majority of companies purchase these services.

This definition also establishes that projects, while they may be service purchases, are not usually considered outsourcing. When a company contracts with XYZ Systems to develop a computer application for them, XYZ's responsibilities end when the system is delivered. Outsourcing providers, in contrast, offer ongoing services. Their responsibilities end when the contract date arrives.

What's important about this definition is that the line between what is and what is not outsourcing moves over time based on accepted practice. For example, the mining companies in the United States and Canada at the end of the nineteenth century often operated company towns. Employees of these companies staffed stores, credit unions, and real estate development offices—certainly a much broader range of services than companies provide for their employees today. As late as 1966, the U.S. Naval Academy operated its own production facility to provide milk for the midshipmen. At the time when these services were handed off to a third party, the organizations would have said they "outsourced" them. Today, however, no one would refer to buying milk from a dairy as outsourcing.

In other words, if we take the long view, we can recognize that a deal that is considered radical—almost unthinkable—at one time is thoroughly commonplace at another. Do you recall the buzz that was created when Eastman Kodak decided to outsource its information technology in 1988? This $18 billion company shook the corporate world by announcing a $250 million, ten-year deal to outsource its corporate IT infrastructure: 17 data centers, all its networks and desktop systems, and some 650 of its 4,000 IT employees.[1] At the time, I was teaching at Harvard Business

School. To delight and amaze my students, I convened a debate between Kathy Hudson, Kodak's CIO at the time, and the chief operations officer of Fleet Bank. Now, the banker was no shrinking violet. It was on his watch that Fleet had expanded from a sleepy Rhode Island retail bank to one of the largest banks in the nation through years of acquiring and relentlessly integrating other institutions. Predictably, sparks flew. The Fleet executive condemned Hudson for giving up control of one of the key strategic levers in her business. She defended herself admirably by arguing that her ability to fix PCs and run data centers was never going to make one whit of difference to Kodak's future.

The point is not who was right. It is that, in 1988, contracting with an outside company to provide IT infrastructure services was considered radical outsourcing. Today, it's a low-margin business that some consider almost a commodity service. IT infrastructure services have moved some distance on the spectrum from radical outsourcing to purchased services. At the same time, some companies are now beginning to outsource services that many others would consider unthinkable. This sets the stage for us to talk about the real subject of this book: transformational outsourcing.

What Is Transformational Outsourcing?

As I said earlier, transformational outsourcing is a special variety of outsourcing. It involves outsourcing ongoing services that are critical to the performance of the business. So "what" is outsourced matters, and "how" the initiative is structured is also important. But what matters more is the purpose of the initiative—the "why" of outsourcing (see Exhibit 2.1). Transformational outsourcing is defined most clearly by the objective of the initiative. Transformational outsourcing is:

> Using outsourcing to achieve a rapid, sustainable, step-change improvement in enterprise-level performance.

Let's pull this apart and examine its parts in detail. First, we say "using outsourcing." Outsourcing, or for that matter any other management tool,

Exhibit 2.1. Transformational outsourcing defined by the "why" of the initiative.

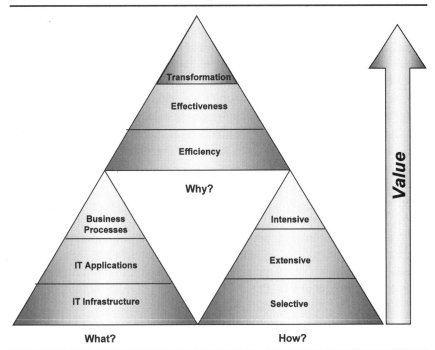

does not create an impact by itself. It changes a company's trajectory, it is hoped in the intended direction, when executives deliberately use it for their ends. In other words, tools don't make change happen; people make change happen.

Transformation implies a rapid, step-change improvement in performance. We would not call a program transformational if it took decades for the effects to become apparent. Nor would we put it in this category if it had only a small impact. *Transformation* means big change fast. Of course, all change is relative. We consider an initiative transformational when it achieves larger, faster, and more lasting impacts than we might reasonably expect. For example, Bill Parcells has a reputation for transforming football teams. He has taken three separate professional teams from sustained losses to playoff slots within two years of taking over as coach of each one. For a coach to have this kind of impact on a team's performance is extremely rare, hence transformational. Most would credit

Lou Gerstner for transforming IBM's notoriously self-absorbed and in-bred culture of the 1990s, even though even he would say it's still a work in progress.[2] What about that transformation was fast? Not much, but its speed still exceeded expectations because most of us would have called it impossible.

Making a big impact on enterprise-level performance means changing the things that really matter. Companies undertake no end of minor change initiatives every day. They improve their staffs through training; they adjust compensation to more closely align with corporate goals; they focus resources on higher-growth markets. These activities are all useful, but not transformational. Their impacts are imperceptible at the bottom line except over a very long time. A transformational initiative, in contrast, can noticeably double a company's stock price, shift its market share, or drive its profitability.

The target of transformational outsourcing has to be an entire operating unit. That's why we say enterprise-level performance, not organizational performance. If the impact cannot be felt at the bottom line, it's not truly transformational.

And finally, if the benefits were only temporary, we would not say that the enterprise has actually been transformed. Achieving a sustainable change in performance means that the organization has been set on an entirely new track. Nothing in business lasts forever, but a true transformation should provide benefits for an entire management generation—five to seven years.

Transformational outsourcing has gained some currency right now. As a result, many outsourcing vendors are touting their work as transformational. In most cases, it is not. And this media hype just confuses executives about exactly what the concept means and how it works. Just put the words *transformational outsourcing* in an Internet search engine, and you'll find that Compaq, Cognizant, Schlumberger, IBM global services, Alltel, Collaboratech, Cap Gemini Ernst & Young, and others all claim they can transform their clients' businesses through outsourcing by implementing new technologies. This isn't it. Transformational outsourcing often requires that new technologies are implemented, but the defining factor isn't the new technology. It's the purposeful use of outsourcing to achieve dramatic enterprise-level change.

A few examples might help to bring our definition to life. National Savings and Investments isn't the only example of transformational outsourcing, but it's a good place to start. The executive team of National Savings deliberately used outsourcing to achieve the changes the organization needed. The agenda certainly reflected big change fast: the CEO's aspiration was to go from near last in the industry to on a par with the leaders in three years. And the impact showed up clearly at the bottom line of the enterprise.

A company we'll call Archer Financial Group, a multinational financial services company, paints a similar picture in the private sector. In 1997, the company was facing demutualization and exposure to the scrutiny of public ownership. The board determined that the company had steadily slipped from a dominant market position to middle of the pack, and nimble new entrants were circling to take their share of the company's juicy customer base. It brought in a new CEO to lead a turnaround, with a mandate to pull it off within three years. After taking a thorough look at the organization and its resources, the CEO framed a broad vision about overall direction. He also recognized that the company lacked the culture, IT capabilities, and management bench-strength to execute the transformation.

He decided to position information technology as the engine of transformation for his business. Despite the fact that most of us would consider information technology a critical and high-priority activity in a financial services company, the CEO's push marked a big change for the role of IT in the organization. At the outset of the initiative, the IT infrastructure was weak, relationships with business leaders were passive, costs were high, and the function actually reinforced organizational silos instead of cutting across them.

Archer outsourced its entire IT operation to a global management consulting and technology services company. The CEO correctly understood that if he forced change in the company's systems, he would disrupt the complacent attitudes and power dynamics among his senior team. He used this wedge to cause the organization to completely rethink its market strategy, value propositions, product lines, and incentives and compensation. In short, he drove top to bottom change in the organization by using outsourcing.

With its outsourcing partner, Archer created a separate IT business unit to house a shared service center. They started with the basics: They drove duplicative applications out of the processing network and streamlined work flows. Then the CEO and the provider's leadership kicked off

technology-enabled change programs designed to cut down the dysfunctional organizational silos and change the company's focus from protecting turf to performance. They also implemented a report card that
measured contribution to strategic goals.

The results? In three years, operating margins increased from
$151million to $370 million, market share grew from 19.1 percent to 28.1
percent, assets under management increased 64 percent, and share price
doubled. As these two examples demonstrate, outsourcing offers a viable
approach for executing dramatic business transformations.

Transformational outsourcing is very different from conventional outsourcing.

Transformational and conventional outsourcing have very little in common (see Exhibit 2.2 for a comparison). To be totally frank, outsourcing
initiatives are extremely diverse. They don't fall neatly into one or two
buckets. But these two ways of using outsourcing are so different that it's
useful to describe them as archetypes.

Pick up any article or book about outsourcing and you will very

Exhibit 2.2. Different outsourcing relationships meet different objectives.

	Conventional Outsourcing	Transformational Outsourcing
What's at stake?	Risk of Disrupting Operations	Risk of Imperiling Strategic Agenda
	Little Value-Add on the Upside	Upside Opportunity to Drive Dramatic Business Improvement
How difficult is it to specify the performance required?	Easy: • Well-understood processes • Easily measured outputs • Clear link between outputs and benefits • Simple interface to nonoutsourced activities	Almost Impossible: • Effective behaviors and outputs only assessable by outcome, if then • Activities inextricably linked to non-outsourced work • Excellence requires industry-leading innovation
How much flexibility do you need?	Little: Annual Benchmarking Suffices	Extensive: Must anticipate and respond to dynamic competitive environment.
Power balance?	Could Replace the Vendor for a Better Deal; Unpleasant Transition	Could not replace the vendor.

quickly hit the idea of core and noncore competencies as the line of demarcation for outsourcing. The conventional wisdom goes something like this: To achieve excellent performance, any organization—let's call ours Flambo—must focus on doing a few things well. No organization can be good at everything, and Flambo is no exception. The first step in achieving excellence, therefore, is for Flambo's executive team to identify the organization's uniquely valuable collective learning and coordination skills that stand behind its core product and service lines—in other words, its so-called core competencies. [3] Everything else people in Flambo might do—the noncore activities—distract them from the highest and best use of their time.

To optimize focus and performance, Flambo should contract with other companies to take over these noncore functions and processes. As a result, their executives will be able to pay more attention to the important, core contributions. In addition, what is noncore to Flambo may well be core to an outsourcing provider; hence, they can be counted on to perform those activities efficiently and effectively. The advertised benefits from this conventional form of outsourcing include:

- Cost reductions of 25 to 30 percent
- Service improvements, like more responsive call centers and faster problem resolution in noncore functions
- Improved executive focus on core competencies, which theoretically leads to improved performance
- Access to superior—and continually improving—skills and expertise of the outsourcing provider

When managers are following the conventional wisdom, they use outsourcing to contract out functions and processes that require their scarce management attention, but don't offer any opportunity for competitive distinction. Their objective is not to change much of anything except their expense line and the way they use their own time. And the organizational-level impacts are expected to be positive, but minor. Even if the cafeteria becomes much more efficient through outsourcing, for example, no one would expect this improvement to have a noticeable effect on the bottom line. A search-engine company provides a good example of conventional outsourcing (see Exhibit 2.3). It outsources the process for responding to

Exhibit 2.3. Conventional and transformational outsourcing have little in common.

	Conventional Outsourcing	Transformational Outsourcing
Objective	Hand off noncore function to specialist provider to cut costs and focus managers on core issues.	Transform the operating model through partnering to achieve rapid, radical enterprise-level performance improvement.
Partner Role	Run support function.	Collaborate to transform business.
Approach	• Standardized services • Transaction-based, fee-for-service pricing • Narrow scale and scope of services	• Integrated services to radically change business • Outcome-based, risk-share financial structure • Accelerated delivery
Typical Benefits		
Inputs	• 20–50% cost savings • Access to best practices • Improved career opportunities • Improved management focus	• 50% cost savings • Access to critical skills • Improved career opportunities • Improved management focus
Outputs	• Same, consistent service level • Shared financial risk	• Higher, consistent service level • Improved flexibilty, speed • Shared strategic risk
Outcomes		• 50% market share increase • Revenue doubled • Basis of competition changed

e-mailed customer requests for support to India. "The reason for outsourcing is to save money," an executive summarizes. The process is well structured and well understood on both sides. The company provides templates, and the outsourcing provider's staff use them to respond to e-mails about navigation problems or requests to link to the company's site. The manager in charge of the relationship communicates with the provider largely through e-mail. This conventional view of outsourcing holds that:

1. Outsourcing is appropriate only for noncore activities.
2. The primary benefit of outsourcing is reduced cost.
3. When executives outsource a function or process, they can turn their attention to more strategic matters.

Is Conventional Outsourcing Effective?

A whole series of research studies on this question adds up to a single unqualified answer: perhaps. The Center for Naval Analyses did one of the only existing rigorous reviews anywhere that looked at the actual financial benefits achieved in 16 military outsourcing competitions accounting for $100 million in precompetition operating costs and more than 2,800 military and civilian positions between 1988 and 1996. It concluded that outsourcing improved costs by 24 percent on a simple before-and-after basis. If researchers also gave outsourcing providers credit for the fact that services had actually expanded, costs improved by 34 percent over what it would have cost the military to perform those functions by itself.[4]

Studies of private-sector outsourcing conclude that executives fully achieve their objectives at best about half the time. One study, for example, found that three-quarters of managers in companies surveyed believe that outsourcing outcomes have fallen short of expectations.[5] Another study found that 20 to 25 percent of all outsourcing relationships fail within two years and that 50 percent fail within five.[6] A 2003 Accenture survey of 325 U.S. executives found that only about 10 percent were completely satisfied with their outsourcing initiatives, although mean satisfaction for the respondents was above average—3.45 on a scale of 1 to 5.

Executives clearly want more benefit from their outsourcing initiatives than they are currently achieving. But without hard facts about what they set out to achieve, what they actually did achieve, and what changed along the way, it is virtually impossible to tell where the performance gap comes from. Do expectations run ahead of what is even possible to attain? Do they advance—despite accomplishments—like that juicy carrot that hangs just out of the cartoon rabbit's reach? All we know for sure is that executives want more out of outsourcing and that, as they become more experienced with the tool, they apply it to successively more sophisticated and complex opportunities in this quest. While transformational outsourcing still represents an extremely small fraction of the outsourcing population, executives are moving in that direction.

Transformational outsourcing holds a very different set of precepts from conventional outsourcing. It's entirely appropriate for any activity that is critical to performance or growth. Whether these are core or not is a separate question. Cost is and should always be a factor that managers consider in any initiative, but transformational outsourcing targets a broader value equation. Finally, transformational outsourcing starts and stays on the CEO's agenda because it is the tool he or she is using to achieve the company's strategic aspirations. What could be more important?

What Makes Us Think Transformational Outsourcing Can Work?

If the conventional wisdom provides us with clear rules of the road on outsourcing, but transformational outsourcing takes a very different path, what gives us confidence that transformational outsourcing will create the results we want? First, this way of using outsourcing is well suited to the problem of transformation. And second, in the hands of capable executives, like the CEOs of NS&I and Archer Financial Group, transformational outsourcing can be executed effectively. Let's look at each of these points separately.

The "Hammer" of Transformational Outsourcing Hits the Nail on the Head

We've all heard the criticism—especially of technologists and consultants—that when they have a particular hammer in their hand, every problem looks like a nail. Let's look at how the hammer of transformational outsourcing measures up to the other tools that executives can use to transform their organizations.

By its very nature, business transformation is risky and extraordinarily disruptive, no matter how it is approached. For instance, when Jim Collins went looking for companies that made substantial improvements in their performance trajectories to go from good to great, he found only 11 examples out of 1,435 companies for which he had data. Among the 16 turnaround companies that Frederick Zimmerman followed for 20 years, more than 40 percent failed.[7] Hannan and Freeman[8] argue that organizations stumble in the short term when their coherence is disrupted in order to adjust to compelling changes in their environment. Over the long term, they may be more successful, but the short-term disruption endangers their survival. Too much change, too radical a change, or change at the wrong time leads to chaos, loss of cultural glue, fatigue, and organizational breakdown.[9]

Some noted management scholars even say transformation is impossible, almost by definition. Remember that we defined transformation as "big change fast." John Kotter[10] notes that transformation efforts produce poor results because executives fail to sustain their commitment over the years that these take to implement. He also states that effective transformations must be anchored in the organization's culture. Well, culture represents an accumulation of behaviors practiced for so long that they become values. When transformation involves new behaviors, which it must by definition, it would certainly fly in the face of existing culture.

Forward-looking executives will avoid transformation when they can. Instead, they will opt for relentless incremental change, which has a much higher success rate.[11] In some cases, however, they have no other choice.

Transformation, again, by definition, depends on developing new or dramatically improved capabilities. If an organization had all the capabilities it needed to succeed, it wouldn't be failing. For example, when Gerstner turned IBM around, he demanded that business units cooperate to provide customer solutions instead of competing with each other.[12] This change involved shifting organizational structure, rewards and incentives, sales and marketing programs, and a host of other behaviors. Transformation relies on making and sustaining deep and well-thought-out behavioral changes of this sort.

Leaving aside speed for a moment, what tools can executives use to pull off a change of this magnitude? It turns out that organizations use one of four approaches:

1. Do it yourself through a concerted organizational change initiative. This was Gerstner's approach. It's also the way DuPont transformed itself from an explosives company to a chemical company after World War I.
2. Merge or acquire other organizations that have the needed capabilities. Seagrams transformed itself from a wine and spirits company to a media and entertainment company through a series of mergers, acquisitions, and divestitures. FleetBoston used acquisitions to turn itself from a minor player in the banking industry in the late 1980s—a Rhode Island community bank—to one of the ten largest retail and commercial banks in the United States by 2001.[13]

3. Form a joint venture with another organization that has the necessary complementary skills. The government of Brunei formed a 50/50 joint venture with Accenture to manage the country's treasury systems. This followed a debilitating scandal in the late 1990s during which a member of the ruling family was found to have diverted millions, if not billions, in public money to his private construction company.[14]

4. Outsource critical functions and processes to an organization with the ability to transform them.

What familiar options are not on this list? First, implementing a particular computer system doesn't appear. Despite vendors' claims to the contrary, this approach results in effective transformation only when coupled with concerted management initiatives. Technologies themselves, no matter how disruptive, do not create transformational change.[15] Second, strategic alliances do not appear to be an effective tool for transformation. We see this more by the complete absence of examples than by any specific research.

Outsourcing differs from other transformational tools in one extremely critical way: It offers reliable execution at speed. In every other case, the existing executive power dynamic puts up tall, virtually impenetrable barriers to the new capabilities that the organization sorely needs. Let's go through each alternative to outsourcing to examine why it doesn't work (see Exhibit 2.4).

Do It Yourself

The idea here is for the existing management to organically grow the missing capabilities. What that means is that executives steeped in other ways of succeeding must loosen their hold on the practices that got them to the top. Then they must embrace new and unfamiliar approaches. At the very least this makes them vulnerable and not especially competent for the time it takes to become expert in these approaches. In most cases, they will revert to what they know and what they know how to do when business hiccups, as it most surely will during a strategic transformation. For example, Xerox was unable to capture value from many of its breathtaking technological advances—the mouse and the Macintosh-type visual

Exhibit 2.4. Outsourcing works better for transformation than any other option.

	How long will your partner work with you?	Are new capabilities integrated?	Who's managing the critical new activities?	Who's calling the shots?
Outsourcing	For the term of the contract	Integrated	Experts from the skilled partner	You
Do It Yourself	N/A	Integrated	People who lack the right expertise and culture—You	You
Acquisition	"Permanent"	Integrated	The controlling partner	You
Joint Venture	"Permanent"	Segregated	Experts from the skilled partner	Shared with partner
Strategic Partnership	As long as it suits them	Coordinated	Experts from the skilled partner	Shared with partner

   Serious impediment to effective transformation.

interface, for example—because the company was being run by "copier people" who just couldn't see the value.[16, 17]

Acquisitions

Companies can acquire organizations with the capabilities they need. But the structure of an acquisition keeps the executives without these capabilities in charge. Just as in the "do it yourself" option, they must subordinate themselves to the acquired management team's priorities, expertise, and culture. This requires a power structure that would look utterly upside-down from the acquiring executives' perspective. Ask yourself how many times your organization has acquired a smaller company to get access to their expertise. When your company tries to integrate it into the core company—to absorb the new capabilities—the change backfires. Instead of transforming the core company, the initiative kills the acquired company.

Mergers frequently fare worse on this score. Those theoretical "synergies" that merger architects promise often turn into sustained organizational conflict. The commitment to different strategies, competencies, and behaviors that the two executive teams bring to the party engenders mutual distrust and disrespect. Instead of combining their abilities to transform the organization, they frequently battle over power and control so fervently that the company itself languishes. The Bank of New England's merger with Connecticut National Bank in the mid-1980s is a telling example. Initially, the two banks' executive teams believed that a well-regarded commercial bank and a successful retail bank would make excellent partners. When they stepped into a so-called merger of equals, these two organizations practiced political infighting so intently and so well that the company was unable to address the imperatives of the recession of 1990, and the bank failed. A review of all the bank combinations in New England over that decade revealed that, on average, merging banks actually lost substantial ground to competitors within two years after striking a deal.[18]

Joint Ventures

Carving out an organization that is dedicated to operating in a wholly new way does work. The joint venture has its own management and, often, the organizational latitude to develop the practices and culture it needs to succeed as a very different kind of company from either parent. That's all fine. What a joint venture doesn't do well is transform either original organization. For it to have this effect, it would have to be repatriated in a way that would infect its parent with its new behaviors. In short, the management team of the joint venture would have to take over in the parent company to instill their way of operating in it. At this point, it looks like a merger or acquisition, with all the problems we outlined above.

Outsourcing

Outsourcing is different from the other three options outlined above in one critical dimension: The power to implement new capabilities is placed clearly in the hands of the executives with the new skills. The outsourcing partner provides a management team that is experienced in the capability that the organization needs. And these individuals are empowered by the outsourcing process to implement the practices they bring with them. This is the only option of all the alternatives through which this is possible.

In the Hands of Capable Executives, Transformational Outsourcing Can Work

As we have seen from our examples, some companies have achieved transformation at speed through outsourcing. This is very much an emerging practice, but I have compiled 20 examples of transformational outsourcing. Seventeen of them have been in place long enough to show results. Of the 20 examples, 82 percent have actually achieved dramatic, organization-level results. And as we will discuss more fully later, all of them—100 percent—executed the transitional initiatives they intended. Where they failed to effectively transform, the leaders failed in strategy, not execution.

In a 2003 Accenture survey of U.S. senior executives, 54 percent of respondents agree or strongly agree that "outsourcing is one way the organization can implement dramatic changes effectively." We all know the reliability problems inherent in check-box survey data, but this kind of overwhelming response indicates that business leaders are beginning to recognize the potential in this approach.

Make no mistake: This is risky business. And, as with every emerging practice, the guidelines for making it effective are a bit unclear at this point. But it appears that outsourcing, unlike the other options that executives have at their disposal, can deliver transformational results reliably and at speed.

What Does It Take to Make Transformational Outsourcing Work?

That's the subject of the rest of this book. I will first review the most important aspect of transformational outsourcing: what leaders need to know. Then I'll take you through the process: how to decide what needs to be transformed; how to choose the right partner and shape the initiative; and how to manage the relationship over time to create the value you want.

Notes

1. See Kathy Hudson's presentation on the deal at http://ais99.sba.uwm .edu/outsourcing.ppt.

2. Lou Gerstner, *Who Says Elephants Can't Dance? Inside IBM's Historic Turnaround* (New York: HarperBusiness, 2002), p. 242.

3. C. K. Prahalad and G. Hamel, "The Core Competence of the Corporation," *Harvard Business Review*, May/June 1990, pp. 79–92.

4. Frances Clark et al., "Long-Run Costs and Performance Effects of Competitive Sourcing," Center for Naval Analyses, 4825 Mark Center Drive, Alexandria, VA 22311–1850, CRM D0002765.A2, February 2001, pp. 2–6.

5. E. R. Greenberg and C. Canzoneri, *Outsourcing: the AMA Survey* (New York: American Management Association, 1997), p. 4.

6. Marq R. Ozanne, *D&B Barometer of Global Outsourcing*, 2000, www.dnbcollections.com/Library/kbarom.htm.

7. Frederick M. Zimmerman, *The Turnaround Experience* (New York: McGraw-Hill, 1991), p. 72.

8. M. T. Hannan and J. Freeman, *Organizational Ecology* (Cambridge, MA: Harvard University Press, 1984), pp. 16–18. "Structural Inertia and Organizational Change," *American Sociological Review* 49, no. 2, pp. 149–164.

9. H. W. Volberda, "Towards the Flexible Form: How to Remain Vital in Hypercompetitive Environments," *Organization Science* 7, no. 4 (1996), pp. 359–374.

10. John Kotter, "Why Transformation Efforts Fail," *Harvard Business Review*, March-April 1995, pp. 59–67.

11. Jane Linder and Susan Cantrell, "Carved in Water: Changing Business Models Fluidly," Accenture Institute for Strategic Change Research Report, December 2000, pp. 8–10, www.accenture.com/isc.

12. Robert D. Austin and Richard L. Nolan, "IBM Corporation Turnaround," Harvard Business School case study #9–600–098, revised November 14, 2000, p. 6.

13. Banks ranked by total assets according to Online Banking Report, http://onlinebankingreport.com/resources/100.html.

14. Roger Mitton, "'Everyone Was Shocked' A Scandal Climaxes as the Sultan's Brother Is Sued," *Asiaweek.com* 26, no. 9 (March 10, 2000), p. 1, http://www.asiaweek.com/asiaweek/magazine/2000/0310/nat.brunei.jefri.html.

15. Jane Linder, "Outcomes Measurement in Hospitals: Can the System Transform the Organization?" *Hospital & Health Services Administration* 37, no. 2 (Summer 1992), pp. 143–166.

16. Douglas Smith and Robert Alexander, *Fumbling the Future: How Xerox Invented, Then Ignored the First Personal Computer* (New York: William Morrow, 1988), p. 122.

17. For a useful review of all the ways internal change initiatives are inherently self-defeating, see Andrew Molinsky, "Sanding Down the Edges: Paradoxical Impediments to Organizational Change," *Journal of Applied Behavioral Science* 35, no. 1 (March 1999), pp. 8–24.

18. Jane Linder and Dwight Crane, "Bank Mergers: Integration and Profitability," *Journal of Financial Services Research* 7, no. 1 (January 1993), pp. 35–55.

CHAPTER 3

Ten Imperatives for Leadership

To take advantage of the growing potential of transformational outsourcing, business leaders must change the way they think about and use outsourcing. First and foremost, senior executives must personally and visibly take charge of the initiative. CEOs may be unaccustomed to such an active role in outsourcing. However, they must stand at center stage at the outset of any transformational outsourcing initiative that works.

As a senior executive, you must be tired of hearing this particular drum beat. "Can't my people do this on their own?" you might wonder. The short answer is no. And this answer comes from executives who have been through the experience. For example, some years back, one of the world's top stock exchanges concluded it could not support the trading volumes it expected with a face-to-face bid and quote system. Following the "big bang" move from face-to-face trading to computerized quotes and phone calls, it had outsourced IT infrastructure and applications to streamline processes and improve reliability. Now the organization was ready to take on the challenge of transforming to fully computerized trading. Initially, the effort was championed by the CEO, but before he could move ahead, he was asked to resign over a different issue. His successor took up the charge. He lost his job fighting with the board to implement this radical change that would eliminate many of the exchange's market makers. A third CEO put his shoulder to the same cause. Ultimately, it was under his guidance that the outsourcing provider implemented systems and processes that completely changed the basis of trading on the exchange.

If senior leadership remains uninvolved, transformational outsourcing will fail. What must leaders do to ensure that this kind of transformational initiative is a resounding success? I offer ten imperatives for transformational outsourcing leaders. These aren't all the responsibilities that have to be executed superbly. These are the leaders' personal critical success factors.

Make the Hard Call

Transformational outsourcing isn't the right answer in every situation. Is it right for yours? Does your company need radical change in order to succeed in its industry? More than 50 percent of executives in a 2002 Economist Intelligence Unit survey of 225 executives around the world said their companies will need radical change to remain competitive in their industries. Is speed a critical factor for your company? How long do you have to implement the changes your strategic agenda requires? If you don't have the time and the resources to build internal capabilities, transformational outsourcing may be the best way to achieve rapid, radical change in critical processes.

If you can answer yes to the seven questions in Exhibit 3.1, you should consider undertaking transformational outsourcing. They add up to a single potent question: are you ready to make a long-term commitment to partner with another company to transform your own?

No CEO would take a decision to transform a company lightly. But embarking on a transformational outsourcing initiative is even more serious. Why? In the hands of capable executives, transformational outsourcing actually works. Unlike most substantial organizational change approaches, using this tool means you will implement the changes you envision and execute the strategy you have laid out. And they will take effect within a few years, not over a decade. Executives who are accustomed to slogging their way through organizational inertia with ineffec-

Exhibit 3.1. CEO self-test.

Seven quick questions to determine whether you should be considering business transformation outsourcing for your firm.

1.	Does your company need a radical change to be competitive in its industry?	Yes	No
2.	Is speed a critical factor in implementing this radical change?	Yes	No
3.	Are you willing to sponsor the initiative personally?	Yes	No
4.	Are you willing to accept a difficult transition?	Yes	No
5.	Do you lack the people and the skills necessary to accomplish it?	Yes	No
6.	Are you willing to work with a partner to accomplish it, even if it means ceding some control?	Yes	No
7.	Are you willing to share the benefits with your partner?	Yes	No

tive approaches will have to hold on to their hats. But they should also be very careful what they wish for.

Design a Good Business Model, Not a Good Deal

A good deal satisfies the parties the day it is signed. Ten minutes later, the world starts to change. Whether the deal will remain good for both parties is unclear; but the contract often keeps them locked into the arrangement despite the changes. Since transformational outsourcing focuses on making change, not contracting around it, its structure must be different. Partners in transformational outsourcing must design a business model that recognizes the dynamic process of creating value over time for both organizations. No one can predict all the changes that might take place, but a good model will establish structures and processes for taking advantage of change.

What does it take to design a business model? It's harder than it looks. We'll talk in more detail about this subject in Chapter 5, but let me go through the highlights here. First, you have to understand your stakeholders and what they value. These include investors, the management team, current and potential customers, and employees.

You must articulate exactly how each organization will generate value from the arrangement you envision. For example, in the National Savings and Investments example, Newport may or may not earn a profit from that particular relationship, but it created a showcase relationship that enabled it to win business from Barclay's bank and the UK passport agency that it might not otherwise have won. Some of the profits from these relationships can also be added to the National Savings and Investments tally (see the sidebar, "Newport Systems's Follow-On Opportunities," below).

Newport Systems's Follow-On Opportunities

The showcase NS&I initiative helped Newport Systems land these two outsourcing contracts.

- *Barclay's Bank.* Newport Systems manages all back office services on behalf of Barclays bank. The contract includes business process outsourcing, provision of new back office processing equipment migration, consolidation and reengineering of 140 branch-based customer service units and the already centralized Regular Payments Processing Centre. It also involved redeployment of 600 Newport–NS&I staff and transfer of 120 contractors/staff.

- *UK Passport Agency.* We have developed a new automated passport application system for the UK Passport Service, which has been rolled out to all seven of the organization's offices as part of a ten-year contract. On-site, our staff is responsible for the front-end processing of applications, the scanning of the documentation, and the cashiering of monies.

Source: The Web site of the company we are calling Newport Systems

Finally, you must identify the positive and negative dynamics in the process—the factors that will build and destroy value for both parties—to ensure the model actually works in practice. For example, when a large U.S. insurance company outsourced its IT infrastructure to a major outsourcing provider, executives assumed that the provider would be motivated to keep the technology up-to-date in order to continue to improve its own costs and profits. This turned out not to be the case. Why? This particular provider was having some earnings trouble at that point in time and valued short-term income so highly that even investments with a two-year payback looked unattractive.

Striking a good deal relies on negotiating skill and situational leverage; crafting a good business model takes "whole of business" thinking. That means the strategists must see indisputable value from the initiative when they look at it through their partner's eyes as well as through their own company's eyes.

For example, in 2000, the central government of Australia mandated that all of its IT infrastructure would be outsourced. It created clusters of government agencies that seemed to make sense—revenue agencies together, justice with police, and so on. Each cluster went through a tendering process to let its contract to a single provider or consortium of private companies. When the first clusters were going through this process, it was quite clear that others would follow. Many of the private companies that participated in these early tenders believed that winning one bid would almost guarantee substantial follow-on business from other clusters. In these negotiations, therefore, the public sector executives had enormous price leverage.

However, the benefits from this policy approach were very slow to materialize. By 2002, the government had abandoned its mandate and authorized agencies and departments to make their own independent decisions about what and when to outsource. In fact, the architect of the policy publicly admitted that the idea had been a mistake. The result? The prospect of follow-on outsourcing business for the existing outsourcing providers dropped substantially and immediately. And the government executives' leverage took a nosedive as well. Not all outsourcing companies would take this approach, but some of the involved providers are aggressively lobbying to renegotiate their contracts and dragging their feet in preparing documentation that would allow other companies to take over. In some cases they are allowing service levels to slip in a kind of passive-aggressive blackmail to make sure their government counterparts understand exactly how dependent they are on these suppliers. The government executives that struck these deals got very good prices. As they struggle to sort out how to disengage, they recognize that they did not design sustainable business models.

Own the Negotiation

In transformational outsourcing, you are not only crafting a contract, you are also establishing a relationship. Make no mistake; the contract is important. You and your partner will live by its terms and conditions for years. However, your process must have a higher aim. It must establish the principles and values that underpin a sustainable working model. Ideally, these are captured explicitly in the contract. In addition, the negotiating process sets the tone for the relationship between the partners. It establishes the way they will work together, they way they will resolve differences, and the way they will treat each other in stressful situations. The senior leaders of the organization are in the best position to keep a company grip on these priorities throughout the contracting process.

Most executives want expert assistance during this critical stage. Often they turn to lawyers, contracting experts, and outsourcing advisory companies. These companies can be quite helpful, especially when executives have little personal experience with outsourcing. Executives tell us that the relationship can run off the rails, however, if they allow the advisers to run the show. If an adviser's role ends when the contract is struck, their management horizon could stop there, too. Some count their contributions narrowly—scoring a win only if they squeeze an extra concession out of the provider. If they have to give in on intangible, immeasurable principles to win tangible, cost-related benefits, some will. Perversely, hard bargaining that pulls most of the value of a deal onto your side of the ledger may make your initiative worse, not better. Successful outsourcing arrangements provide sustainable value because they are good for both sides.

In some cases, executives simply delegate contracting to specialists or lower-level employees in their own organization with the same unfortunate result. For example, when a major casino entertainment company decided its corporate call center needed a performance boost to support the company's growth plans, it moved to outsourcing. Now, this is an organization that distinguishes itself by knowing its 13 million customers intimately. Many of its experienced customers call directly into the facility that they want to visit, but new customers call a general toll-free number and end up speaking to the corporate call center. This center was struggling to support 18 or 20 facilities, each of which had its own reservation system, and it was not providing the service that corporate executives expected. They made the decision to outsource.

Senior leadership delegated the process to operational managers. These folks went through the vendor selection process without getting a good grip on the leadership priorities for the initiative. As a result they chose a vendor based on cost. And for the next two years, the organization struggled to teach the provider's employees how to hold an unscripted, interactive conversation with a customer on the telephone. Eventually, the company's call center shadow department succeeded in getting the provider to achieve the kind of performance they needed. The accountable manager quipped, "Their people surely were cheaper than ours, but we spent a lot of time teaching them how to do our business. We sure weren't saying 'Boy, are we glad we outsourced this.'"

In conventional outsourcing, delegating the negotiations has unpleasant consequences; in transformational outsourcing, the results are disastrous. Instead of building a viable business partnership that is launched in the right direction, giving too much latitude to overzealous contracting experts can create a deal that undermines the very purpose of the initiative. Senior leadership must take the transformational outsourcing helm to navigate through these tricky waters.

Allocate Two Full Days a Week of Your Own Time for the Foreseeable Future

If this statement makes you gasp, you're not ready for transformational outsourcing. Many executives have been misled about the importance of their own personal involvement by one of the promised benefits of conventional outsourcing: the ability to focus management attention on more strategic matters. This promise is wrong twice over. First, even in conventional outsourcing deals, senior executives must stay intimately involved in the process to make sure that contracts and relationships reflect the real objectives of the organization and to ensure that workforce transitions are smooth. In transformational outsourcing, the outsourcing relationship is the strategic activity that matters most. It could not have a higher call on senior executives' time and attention.

The sourcing director at National Savings and Investments in the initial stages of the transformation was highly experienced in outsourcing when Peter Bareau recruited her. She had orchestrated 13 separate relationships for British Airways. On the question of conserving management time and attention, she snorted, "Some people think that if you have a problem, you can just outsource it, and it will go away. It never does. The leadership team at NS&I were clear from the beginning that we were just swapping one management challenge for another. We didn't underestimate the challenge. There was no guarantee of success. We were out to do something radical." Even with this preamble, some of the executives at NS&I would argue that they failed to understand how much of their time and attention the transformation would require.

Orchestrate a Dynamic Transition

Most experts will tell you to aim for a smooth transition—the more invisible it is, the better. That's not quite right. This is appropriate for conventional outsourcing, but it is a mistake in transformational outsourcing. You do want employees and current work flow to move transparently from your organization to that of your provider. On the other hand, unlike most outsourcing programs, your major aim in this initiative is to transform your organization. You'll want to leverage the transition your organization must go through to both symbolize and actualize new attitudes and behaviors. So on the one hand, some parts of the transition should be transparent and frictionless; other parts should help everyone understand that the organization has stepped into a new game for good.

The leader's role is to ensure that people affiliated with the organization recognize that the old ways have come to a stop. Of course, executives don't do this in a vacuum. The reason for stopping must be compelling and proximate so the employees have no doubt that the results are worth the effort. In some cases, the motivation is organizational survival. An NS&I executive explained, "What triggered us to transform? We were on the edge of the cliff, and everyone knew it." Companies can also transform themselves to leave a mediocre track record behind and head for a best-in-class position. J. Sainsbury, for example, had slipped into the middle of the pack among its UK retail competitors and initiated a transformational program to regain its leadership position in the industry.[1]

Before your organization can head off at full speed in a new direction, you must disrupt its comfortable web of routines. As a first step, work with your transformational outsourcing partner to engineer a full stop—not in employees' current tasks, but in their expectations and attitudes toward tomorrow. In other words, your organization must stop trying to continue doing what it is currently doing in order to begin doing what it should. The transfer of employees from one organization to another is a clear breaking point. Use this very real transition to communicate that you are changing the way the organization works.

Stopping is important, but it's only the start of change.[2] For an organization to be effective, it must also be turned and restarted. Turning means establishing new expectations, new goals, and new motivations. In transformational outsourcing, the leadership of both partners must help employees understand not just that things are going to be different, but how they are going to be different. Vague statements about financial goals won't do the job here. Leaders must communicate a plan that makes sense to the people who have to bring it to life. Many make public commitments to achieve bold strategic aims. Since this puts them personally on the hook to deliver what they've promised, it provides compelling evidence to skeptical employees that they have every intention to succeed.

We've talked about bold agendas and business models. We've talked about a dynamic transition. The years of capable execution that follow these planning and transitional activities are equally important. Five of our ten leadership imperatives address this part of the initiative.

Create Momentum

Stopping and turning set up the transformation; restarting the engines gets the organization moving again, but in a new direction. Just as in starting

up a new business, the leader's job is to get the flywheels spinning—
slowly at first, then faster. To do this, leaders must create organizational
momentum; this is a sense within the enterprise that the force behind
the initiative is growing and that progress is accelerating. Leaders create
momentum by orchestrating a continuing stream of meaningful wins.
When I say meaningful, I mean wins that count for something.

You'll want to kick off small, doable activities all over the organization to get things moving again. While training and setting organizational
structure are important, these are not enough. You'll want to focus on a
pipeline of visible outputs, if not outcomes. Some are in the marketplace.
Look at the timeline in Exhibit 1.9 in Chapter 1. NS&I's provider started
immediately to introduce new products that customers would buy. This
was a tangible accomplishment that marked a clear departure from the
organization's track record.

Skip Stitt, Deputy Mayor of Indianapolis under Stephen Goldsmith,[3]
emphasizes this leadership approach: "It is important to point out the
people who will have their streets paved for the first time in twenty-five
years because the process of managed competition generated savings that
the city could reinvest. It is critical to identify the neighborhoods where a
crime problem exists and then commit to hire additional police officers
for those neighborhoods using the managed competition savings. When
you are able to juxtapose the real winners and the people who believe—
sometimes wrongly—that they are losers as a result of the reforms, the
arguments get easier. We didn't just say, 'We want to privatize the wastewater treatment facility; what do you think?' Instead we said, 'We want
to put the wastewater treatment facility through a managed competition
process that protects both the environment and the public workers so that
we can avoid a 30 percent rate increase for our poorest citizens; what do
you think?' That's a totally different question. Not surprisingly, you get
totally different answers because of how you phrase the question."

This kind of achievement also lays the groundwork for a stream of
future wins. Launching a new product is an output of the new organization, but increasing revenues and profits by selling the product is an outcome. Starting with its first launch, NS&I could begin to build momentum
by tracking the sales from new products.

You'll want to rely on your partner for help in creating momentum.
As employees move into their new roles, their supervisors will introduce
them to new practices and expectations. Whether this means hiring new

workers, giving existing workers new tasks, establishing new ways of doing old tasks, or simply setting new goals and performance measures, workers in critical processes will be taking up their responsibilities with a fresh agenda. As they master new behaviors, they'll shake down the work processes and rebuild valuable organizational routines.

For example, John Fleming, the Deputy Minister of the Ontario Ministry of Community and Social Services, talks enthusiastically about the impact of working with the motivated and disciplined staff of a large outsourcing company. In this case, the provider's fee for a particular piece of work was based solely on the documented savings it could generate. Of course, these savings were critical for the Ministry as well. Fleming remarks enthusiastically:

> We learned a whole new definition of the word drive from [our provider]. We've learned about discipline, planning, risk assessment, and hard driving project management.
>
> For example, we had performance measures to tell us what we were getting out of the initiative, and we weren't getting there. Our partner drove us to ask, "Why is that?" and "What do we need to do to make it happen?" It was all about discipline, management, and finding incentives.

Fleming easily shares the credit with his provider because there was plenty to go around. Only six weeks after transitioning to the new process, his organization had generated CAN$35 million in savings, and was on track to bank CAN$200 million per year.

Be wary of picking off a few quick wins at the beginning of the transformational initiative without thinking through what comes next. You won't get momentum if demonstrable progress ramps up, but peters out quickly.

Manage the Relationship as if It Were Chinese Handcuffs

Remember Chinese handcuffs from your childhood? You stick a finger in each end of a woven tube. They go in easily, but when you try to pull them out, the tube lengthens and contracts. The harder you try to pull your fingers apart, the more stuck they become.

Transformational outsourcing relationships work like Chinese handcuffs. Once you sign the contract, you're in. No matter how clearly you set expectations, define roles, and specify outputs, there will be disputes—some of them quite acrimonious. Most people—and executives are no exception—respond to conflict by retreating to their corners. They adopt a we/they, adversarial approach and prepare to defend their terrain. Many pull out the contract in order to beat the other side over the head. It sounds a little immature, but the situation funnels responsible individuals down this unproductive path.

A natural reaction to outsourcing I call the "miracles syndrome" makes this tendency even worse. Whenever executives pay for a service—even when they openly acknowledge they could not manage that service themselves—they immediately develop unrealistic expectations about what the provider can accomplish. When miracles fail to materialize, executives' disappointment turns into recriminations, and the relationship slips into adversarial wrangling.

Leaders resist the temptation to pull back on the Chinese handcuffs. They move toward their partner, instead of away. And they coach their senior executive team to model the same kind of behavior. They open their books. They open their perspectives to appreciate the other side. They open their plans to creative joint solutions.

This kind of leadership works best when executives on both sides behave this way. But either partner can stake out and hold the high ground first. For example, a transportation services company outsourced information technology applications development and support. Executives would admit today that, during the process of negotiating the contract, those in charge gave up their objective of service improvement in order to achieve their cost reduction goals. Unfortunately, they did not communicate this shift in the value equation to the IT users in the company. When the provider took over and service responsiveness dropped—as planned—the users revolted. For an entire year, the CIO held daily meetings with the provider's operational leadership at which he beat them up for performing exactly as he had contracted with them to do. Needless to say, the relationship stumbled forward on rocky footing. One day, the CIO found himself facing an urgent and difficult requirement for which he was unprepared. Hearing of the need, the provider's account partner stepped in and offered to take care of it—for no fee. This act of rapprochement changed everything. Starting from this simple gift, the relationship grew into a trusting partnership.

Engineer a Commitment to Performance

An excellent relationship between a company and its outsourcing provider is necessary for success, but not sufficient. Outstanding accomplishments, of the sort that transformation requires, are created by a healthy tension between an intimate working relationship and a commitment to performance excellence. Leaders must stand up for both.

The conventional approaches to performance management in outsourcing don't go far enough. Service-level agreements, penalty payments, and even bonuses for overachievement do incentivize behavior, but they don't inspire commitment. The last thing you want are workers who are coin-operated. Psychological research shows that most people perform better when they internalize commitment, and that most people internalize commitment better when external incentives are minimal.[4] That is, people accept more responsibility for their behavior when they feel they have chosen their own course of action in the absence of strong outside pressures. They feel even more committed when they must actively work against outside pressures.

Instead of paying big bonuses to individuals, you will want to invite them to commit. Describe your joint organization as elite. Provide opportunities for them to volunteer to meet challenging targets. Recognize their contributions when they excel. Help them affiliate more with your joint effort than with their employer of record. Ask everyone to put his or her name and reputation on the line.

You should evoke the full force of the outsourcing partner's culture and incentive system to help you. The partner company can act as both a foil and an accelerator at the same time. For example, when the UK Inland Revenue outsourced its entire information technology operation to the world's largest outsourcing services company, the executives in charge asked for an open book arrangement. This was in direct opposition to the outsourcing provider's corporate policy. By convincing the local partners to work with them in this way, they created a divide between these individuals and their bosses back at headquarters at the same time as they made their own relationship with them more intimate. They made the local partners choose sides.

That's not all. They leveraged the provider's internal corporate competition for recognition and status. The upwardly mobile employees in every company are constantly tussling with each other for recognition as they work their way up the status ladder. The Inland Revenue recognized the association with a successful account was beneficial to career progression and took advantage of this common playground dynamic. If the outsourcing provider met the aggressive performance goals for the initiative and successfully delivered reliable, large-scale, and complex day-to-day services as well as a major software portfolio, the local partners would earn enough margin on the contract to make them heroes back home. If their performance was only mediocre, their margin percentage on this big contract would place them at the bottom of the pecking order.

Don't just invite commitment to outstanding performance; give your outsourcing provider the tools and support to deliver. Inject partners with a self-guiding instinct for acting on your behalf and instill personal accountability for high performance. The finance director at a UK-based grocery chain explains, "The head of our outsourced operation videoconferences in for my weekly meetings and shares sensitive business information, just like any other member of my senior team. Day to day, he understands the issues facing the business and the finance team, and can work with us to respond to them."[5]

You will also want to ensure that employees from both organizations feel connected socially and at parity professionally. For example, the BBC uses special events to bring in-house and outsourced employees together to break bread and compete in events, such as a quiz show about organizational knowledge. Last year, the outsourcer team won. The finance manager of a French chemicals company calls it "e clique," or personal chemistry. "We're not producing a finished product you can see and touch; it is intangible. That takes more trust. So we did not choose a company to work with, we chose a team—people we could connect with emotionally."

Face Forward

Transforming your organization means creating a new future for it. That means venturing into new market spaces, taking on new competitors, and operating at an entirely new pace. All of these self-inflicted changes come on top of the shifting business conditions inherent in any normal commercial environment. In conventional outsourcing, executives address the need for change with provisions in the contracts for continuous improvement, for periodic technology refresh, for contractual renegotiation, and if all else fails, for exit. Transformational outsourcing requires an entirely different approach. You and your partner need real strategic flexibility—the ability to change fluidly as threats and opportunities arise.

Leaders don't just make joint planning part of the expectations; they invite their outsourcing partners to join them in a scenario planning process before the contract is signed. That way, some of the hard thinking about how the partners will thrive in the future can be incorporated into the business model they craft.

Just as important, they make joint strategic planning a regular process—part of everyday management. Whether it's punctuated with quarterly meetings or annual off-sites will depend on the rate of change in the business. Regardless of its frequency, it should be a way for both partners to confirm or reshape the business model. Some companies even put break points in their transformational outsourcing contracts every three or four years. This kind of "breather" provides a structured time to take a fresh look at the future.

Taking a top-down look at the future is one half of the answer. You will also want to stimulate innovative ideas that come from individuals close to the operations or from other parts of your partner's organization. Thomas Cook,* the leisure travel company, schedules executives from its outsourcing partner to give a quarterly presentation on innovation to its board of directors. It bases a portion of its outsourcing partner's annual bonus on board members' perceptions of the quality of the ideas.

Recognize That You *Will* Underestimate the Task, and Plan Accordingly

Over the course of the past several years, I have talked personally with more than 200 executives experienced in outsourcing. I cannot recall a

---

*Throughout the book, for simplicity, I will refer to the Thomas Cook UK and Ireland subsidiary as "Thomas Cook." I will refer to its parent company as "Thomas Cook AG."

single one who claimed to have accurately estimated the time and effort the initiative would require. Not one. And some of these relationships fell squarely in the commodity category.

Let's face it. An ongoing business, with all its processes and people, is a complex organism. And each one is different. Your outsourcing provider may be more skilled at your particular flavor of industrial "organ transplant" than any other company, but I guarantee that you will both uncover issues you did not expect. The good news is that most unexpected issues just take hard work to resolve. You will want to plan accordingly. What do I mean by that? Create slack.

Microsoft, a company that experts consider one of the most capable in the world at managing large projects, puts one week of unscheduled time in every project plan. Over time, the company has learned that this week will be required. They don't know exactly how the time will be used at the outset, but they know they will need it.

In transformational outsourcing, you can expect to use more people during your transition than you have counted on. All the bonuses and penalties in the world won't make the work go faster. Put a 15 percent staffing contingency in your staffing plan. These are individuals at the worker level. Don't kid yourself that a few smart managers will be an effective substitute.

You can expect to make changes in what you want to do and what you need to do. In addition, your provider will hit unexpected snags. Put a 15 percent financial contingency in your plan to cover these unexpected costs. This should be over and above what your provider said they would charge you. Why not just hold the provider to its contracted price? Because the competitive process that gets you the best price may also incentivize your provider to cut corners. This kind of short-term thinking is your worst enemy if the big payoff is long-term enterprise transformation.

* * *

Transforming an enterprise may be one of the most daunting leadership challenges in the game. If you will be stepping onto that particular playing field, however, you will be gratified to know that you can use outsourcing to carry the day. And furthermore, if you personally engage and play with passion as I have outlined above, you are very likely to accomplish the transformation you envision. Since, unlike most management initiatives, you shall get your wish, frame it carefully. The next two chapters talk about the different ways you can use outsourcing to execute transformations and how to aim your approach to meet your strategic targets.

Notes

1. Susanna Voyle, "Why Sainsbury Put Its Money on a Wholesale System Change," *Financial Times*, June 13, 2003, page 12.

2. I use a simple but powerful paradigm for change: stop–turn–restart. Unlike the classical Kurt Lewin model—unfreeze-move-refreeze—this recognizes explicitly that organizations are bodies in motion.

3. Skip Stitt is now the senior vice president and managing director, Children and Family Services at ACS in Washington, D.C.

4. Robert B. Cialdini, *Influence: The Psychology of Persuasion* (New York: William Morrow, 1984), pp. 92–94.

5. Jane Linder and Joseph Sawyer, "Getting and Keeping Control in Business Process Outsourcing," Accenture Institute for High Performance research report, October 2003, p. 6.

PART II

Choosing Your Targets

CHAPTER 4

Transformational Outsourcing
Meets Strategy

Transformational outsourcing isn't right for every company. It represents a major strategic commitment. As we discussed in Chapter 2, most companies will get better results from relentless incremental change than from expensive, lurching transformations. However, in some situations, transformation is the only viable alternative. Let's start from the position that your organization has established its strategy and clearly understands its strategic imperatives, and transformation is on the agenda.

What Benefits Does Outsourcing Offer?

Executives use transformational outsourcing to achieve a clear strategic purpose. Outsourcing is not the only tool that executives wield to accomplish their goal; it is part of a concerted program to effect dramatic change. It is, however, a very important part of the agenda.

The single biggest reason for failure in outsourcing of any sort is that executives lose sight of their objectives. Some fail to clarify them in the first place. Others stop short of a complete picture by failing to consider

all the important stakeholders. Still others start off with a good understanding of what they want to accomplish, but lose their grip on it in the
press of contract negotiations, rocky transitions, or subsequent business
changes. Transformational outsourcing initiatives rarely fail, but when
they do, they fail for errors of strategy, not execution. In other words,
executives and their outsourcing providers implement what they intend to
implement, but this just does not produce competitive success. Leaders
will want to get their strategy in focus, then be perfectly clear about the
contributions they want from their outsourcing provider. Of course each
company's strategic imperatives will be highly unique and are outside the
scope of this book. I want to focus here on the distinctive benefits companies can derive by using outsourcing.

First, the outsourcing provider can bring top-drawer skills and capabilities to help your company execute its strategic agenda. Ideally, these
are capabilities your company needs in order to be successful at the new
strategy, but does not possess itself. For example, National Savings and
Investments did not have the technology expertise to develop the new
information system–based products and services it needed to remain competitive. Its outsourcing partner had a worldwide reputation for excellence
in IT.

Access to skills extends beyond the obvious mastery of the operational details of the area that is outsourced. The right partner can also
bring deeper and broader expertise in strategy and business processes.
The outsourcing provider adds its management team to yours, and it can
tap its knowledge of other companies and industries to bring good, new
ideas to your table. For example, the large multinational outsourcing provider of Universal Leven, the Netherlands insurance start-up, offers new
product innovation as well as policy processing services as part of its
value proposition. NS&I has staff responsible for new product development, but it works intimately with its partner to get a lead on technology
innovations that offer promising new opportunities.

Outsourcing can offer the benefit of *speed*. Through focus as well as
expertise, an outsourcing provider is frequently able to implement difficult changes in a fraction of the time it would take an in-house team. A
start-up gains speed to market through operations that are gassed up and
ready to fly. A Thomas Cook executive explained, "We could have raised
a team to implement SAP and reengineer our financial, HR administration, and IT processes. It would have taken our best people full time, and

I don't know who would have been running the business in their absence. And they still would have taken longer than the experienced team our provider put on the ground."

Outsourcing delivers an organizational *wake-up call*. Better than any other approach to dramatic change, outsourcing sends a message that shakes an organization out of its lethargy. Why? Because it represents one-way action. No matter what happens afterwards, the organization will never be the same. Leaders have taken a bold step. Employees are affected. Even those who are not directly affected hear an incontrovertible signal that their world has changed.

Outsourcing can *reduce costs*. Many, but not all, outsourcing initiatives involve some kind of cost reduction in the value equation. Frequently cost reductions in some areas are necessary to free up resources to invest in growth opportunities. And most cost-reduction objectives involve both streamlining the existing operation and putting in controls to reduce the internal demand for that operation. For example, when a transportation services company outsourced its IT function, its provider implemented a disciplined process for making new IT requests. The business managers who had previously just picked up the phone to get their friendly IT representative to change a report format or run a special information request now had to write a justification memo and submit it for approval through the manager of change control. Needless to say, the utilization of IT resources for trivial changes dropped radically, and the company was better able to direct its IT efforts toward high-payoff activities.

Companies that create their own high-performing service units before they outsource are likely to get smaller improvements from transitioning to an external provider at that point. But low-wage-rate areas like India, central Europe, China, and the Philippines offer substantial cost-reduction potential over operations in areas like western Europe, the United States, Japan, and Singapore.

Many executives fear a loss of control from outsourcing, but in the event, they find that *operational visibility* actually improves. By making responsibilities and information flows more clear—both of which are required as a matter of course during the process of handing an operation over to an outsourcing provider—the organization will develop solid, detailed information about how its operation works. It can then use this information to make better decisions about how to improve both costs and revenues. We will hear more about the Thomas Cook story in Chapter 6, but its finance director's comment about this type of benefit is particularly apropos:

> Cosourcing makes visible the costs and implications of decisions. [When you have this information] it may lead you to make different decisions about what you offer to customers. For example, now that I can see all the costs associated with doing a particular type of business, I may decide I no longer want to offer it. I anticipated getting this kind of benefit from our cosourcing initiative, but I did not know how powerful it would be. Previously, people had no way to understand the implications of their actions, and now they do.

For growth-oriented companies, outsourcing offers access to *instant capacity* as the business expands. We're not talking about utility computing here, although computing infrastructure is far from irrelevant. What growing companies really need is access to processes that work. Whether this involves supply chain capability, phone-ready call center staff, or an administrative center that knows how to integrate a new acquisition, an outsourcing partner can offer just-in-time sips of process capacity that would normally come in fire-hose quantities.

Outsourcing gives a company *financial flexibility*. Transformation is expensive; it means new computer systems, moving expenses, redundancy payments, training, investments in new products, services, and markets, and a whole host of other kinds of cash obligations. In fact, the companies most in need of transformation are often the least able to afford its upfront costs. You and your partner can work out a funding dynamic that takes advantage of the financial strengths of both companies. Through innovative financial solutions, which are entirely legal and unimpeachable, an outsourcing provider can help smooth out these costs. For example, providers often buy a company's existing assets—computers, facilities, equipment, and the like that are associated with the operation it will take over. The company gets a cash infusion as well as lower recurring costs—for immediate positive impact on both its balance sheet and its income statement. Of course, this immediate benefit is paid off over time as the provider keeps a larger and larger share of the operational cost improvement it generates. It the transformation is successful, though, growing profits more than cover these costs.

Even when the outsourcing provider does not pay up front for physical assets, it can use its own capital to fund new technologies, facilities, staff, training, and a wide variety of investments that generate a stream of benefits. The company pays for services rendered, either with fixed fees or "by the drink" payments that are geared to service volumes. In the early years of a relationship, the provider pays the difference between total investment and the service fees. In later years, with the benefit of planned improvements in operations, the service fees more than cover costs and give the provider a reasonable margin.

For example, many organizations have more difficulty securing capital funding than annual budgets. Family Christian Stores could never have afforded the investment it made in new information systems. By working with its outsourcing provider, it was able to pay for these over time with profits from growing sales. Public-sector organizations frequently rely on outsourcing partners to provide capital investment in technology, which the government then pays for "by the drink" with its annual budgets. In one Accenture study, converting capital into expense was the most frequently mentioned objective for business process outsourcing. Fifty-eight percent of the organizations in the study counted it as either their primary or secondary goal.[1]

Finally, partners can bring *third-party funding* into an outsourcing initiative. This makes sense when the outsourcing provider has such a solid track record that it reduces the perceived risk for the initiative. As a result, the cost of borrowing can be lower than it would be for the company on its own. The company must ultimately pay off the debt, but it can do this with the savings it generates from the transformational initiative. Accenture's work with a major grocery chain illustrates this approach. The initiative involved Accenture's taking over the chain's entire IT operation, including infrastructure and applications, with an intention to reduce the cost of maintaining so-called legacy systems and invest in new IT capabilities that would drive its business transformation. As Exhibit 4.1 illustrates, Accenture purchased the IT assets, giving the company a cash infusion on day one. Accenture also set about reducing its information technology cost base. This freed up resources that could be put to more strategic uses. Accenture also guaranteed that the chain's ongoing IT cost would be lower than its historical spending, and that that rate of spending would grow more slowly than before. Accenture was paid for its efforts by a third-party financing company, so Accenture did not have

Exhibit 4.1. Creative financing opens a whole range of new options.

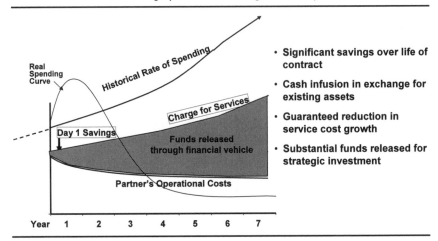

Source: John Rollins, Accenture.

to invest its own scarce capital. The grocery chain will repay the loan over time with its improved profits.

Bankers are not known for their risk-taking. In the case of the grocery chain's initiative, the reputations of the two partner companies helped convince the financing company of the merits of the deal. In the Family Christian Stores example, it was the provider's reputation alone that attracted a financial partner to the deal, making it affordable for the small company.

Outsourcing providers can bring all these benefits to the table. As we have seen above, executives need different things from outsourcing to achieve different purposes. The successful executive teams explicitly set down what purpose they are trying to achieve and what specific benefits they are after. They rank these in priority order, and they keep this ranking in mind as they set out to craft an outsourcing initiative to transform their enterprise. When things change, as they inevitably will, they review their objectives as the starting point for correcting their course.

Sizing Up the Strategic Challenge

Because this book is about a management tool, we end up looking at strategic questions from the inside out. That is, we ask, "Where can executives use this tool to accomplish what they want?" You will want to do the analysis from the other direction, asking, "What are my company's strategic imperatives, and how can I address them?" You will want to compare various approaches and use the one that makes the most sense in your situation. As Charlie Feld, chairman and CEO of the Feld Group, says, "Run the other way if you hear executives say 'I believe in outsourcing,' or 'I don't believe in outsourcing,' for that matter. Choosing the right management approach should be thoughtful and appropriate as opposed to a matter of religion."

With these caveats in mind, let's review four ways in which organizations use outsourcing to transform. We will look at how each taps different benefits and takes a different strategic course (see Exhibits 4.2 and 4.3).

1. Out-of-nowhere companies start up rapidly.
2. Crouching tigers clear the path to growth.
3. Fallen angels catalyze broad cultural change.
4. Born-again companies achieve radical renewal.

Exhibit 4.2. Organizations use outsourcing in four ways.

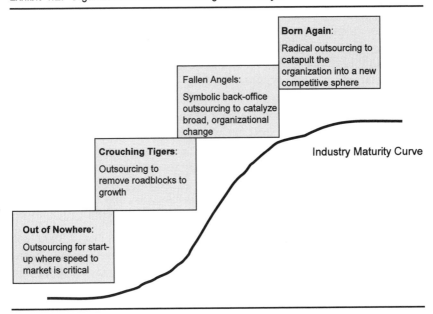

Exhibit 4.3. The four types of transformational outsourcing differ on key characteristics.

	Rapid Start-Up	Pathway to Growth	Catalyze Change	Radical Renewal
Description	Outsource to put a new business in operation at scale rapidly.	Outsource to fix a key process that stands in the way of growth.	Outsource to signal broad change and focus on adding value.	Outsource to radically improve core operating capabilities.
Primary Objectives	1. Speed 2. Expertise 3. Volume-based costs	1. Expertise 2. Speed	1. Cost 2. Standardization	1. Speed 2. Expertise 3. Capital
Cost of Outsourced Services	Higher than internal costs	Equal to internal costs	Lower than internal costs	Lower than internal costs
Target Number of Providers	Fewer is better to conserve scarce management time.	Fewer is better to create a coherent capability.	Fewer for coordination and scale, more for breadth of expertise.	Fewer is better for coordinated strategic delivery.
Key Relationship Features	Cost smoothing, by-the-drink pricing	Cost smoothing, tight organizational integration	Cost reduction and continuous improvement incentives	Risk and benefit sharing; deep strategic alignment
Exit	Bring service back in house to reduce cost	Bring service back in house to master critical capability	Benchmark and recompete to sustain low cost position	No exit; permanent partnership
Example	TiVo customer support	Family Christian stores	Thomas Cook	National Savings and Investments

Out-of-Nowhere Companies Start Up Rapidly

Starting up a company is the ultimate transformation. It means creating a substantial going concern where nothing existed beforehand. Theoretically, every start-up, from a pizza shop to a dry cleaner, could be considered a transformation of sorts. I want to be a little more selective. For our purposes, I want to limit our discussion to start-ups that make big change fast. These are organizations that need to launch and scale rapidly in order to succeed. They have big appetites. They want to get an innovative new model to market first, set an industry standard or take on entrenched industry leaders. If they move slowly, they fear they will be overtaken by larger companies with more market power.[2]

For example, TiVo, a start-up television service provider, used outsourcing to get access to business capabilities that were gassed up and ready to fly. Its goal? To take a new market by storm. In 1999, start-up TiVo launched a wholly new type of television solution. It provided an easy-to-use system it called a personal video recorder. Without the muss and fuss of digital storage media or arcane VCR programming codes, a fan could record up to 80 hours of TV and replay it at his or her convenience. The system could even track down favorite shows despite schedule or even network changes.

At the outset, TiVo realized that its success would depend on creating a market where none existed. With strong partners in Sony, Hughes, and Philips Electronics, and a technology lead, TiVo set out to both establish and dominate the market before competitors could get traction. TiVo's leadership believed that speed would be essential, so they turned to outsourcing. The company outsourced distribution, manufacturing, the process of setting up retailers, public relations, advertising, and customer support.

The way it outsourced customer support is particularly telling. TiVo's unique product had unusual needs. Since it was an entirely new concept, TiVo knew it had to invest in helping each customer understand, install, and use the new product in a way that specifically suited them. Ordinary call-center scripts and routine approaches wouldn't do the job. TiVo needed distinctive customer support in force from the start.

TiVo turned to ClientLogic for flexibility and a cooperative commitment to help TiVo improve the process over time. TiVo's provider worked closely to jointly establish processes and develop innovative training materials and incentives to enable the agents to "think like a TiVo" customer. In addition, TiVo gave agents the product to use in their own homes. As a result, TiVo's outsourced staff have mastered the open-ended dialogues and investigative problem solving they need to provide real customer solutions. Using TiVo's CRM application, they're able to feed a rich description of customer problems back to TiVo's product development and marketing organizations. Over time, they have cut the initial cost of support per subscriber by 94 percent.

The jury is still out about whether TiVo's bid to take over the personal video recording market will work. The company is not profitable, and competitors like Microsoft are salivating at the opportunity to join the feast. Whether or not TiVo will benefit from its first-mover lead is a question for its strategists. But it could never have executed its chosen strategy without relying on outsourcing.

Out-of-nowhere start-ups use outsourcing to put well-oiled operations in place quickly and to pay for them by the drink. In this way, a small but growing organization gets the mature capabilities it needs to take on bigger, stronger competitors without spending scarce seed capital and scarcer management time building an organization from scratch. If the company takes off, it also has access to the outsourcing provider's bench strength to support its growth. These advantages, however, come at a price. Most start-ups would find it cheaper to grow organically. But it does take longer. So the start-up would only opt to outsource if speed to market were pivotal to its strategy. When its growth trajectory slowed, it would consider bringing outsourced operations in-house to cut costs.

In Polaroid's early days, for example, it relied on contract manufacturers like Timex—yes, the watch people—to manufacture many of its high-end cameras for all the reasons outlined above. When the company's spectacular growth slowed in the mid-1970s, it brought manufacturing in-house. (It actually contracted hardware manufacturing out again in the late 1990s as it struggled to trim its high cost structure.)

Crouching Tigers Clear Pathways to Growth

Organizations use outsourcing to make dramatic improvements in under-performing functions and processes that are roadblocks to growth. These companies have big strategic aspirations that are being stymied by a deficiency in some key capability. It could be manufacturing or information systems, the ability to integrate acquisitions, or the capability to develop new products. Whatever the arena, executives recognize it as a critical roadblock, and they remove it through outsourcing.

For example, in 1992, Family Christian Stores, then named Family Bookstores, was an under-the-radar subsidiary within publishing giant News Corporation. (Family Bookstores was owned by Zondervan, which was owned by HarperCollins, which was part of News Corporation.) Les Dietzman, a retailing veteran with experience at WalMart and Dayton Hudson, joined the organization to pursue a "higher mission." When he arrived he saw an unexpectedly compelling opportunity for transformation. He believed that the small Christian retailer could grow substantially under his leadership. By 1994, he had developed an overall vision for company growth, and he led a management buyout to get the authority to make it happen. At the time, Family Bookstores had 120 stores and $130 million in sales.

Dietzman believed that information technology was standing in his way. In his mind, it was the foundation for everything he had to do: site selection, store management, supply chain, pricing, and management reporting. But Family Bookstores's systems had been run by its parent company, and these were designed to meet the needs of a publishing company, not a retailer. To replace his publishing systems with a top-drawer, retail-oriented information technology capability that would support the company's growth would take an investment of $7 million—resources FCS did not have. So Dietzman turned to outsourcing.

He worked with Accenture to structure an innovative deal to get FCS the systems, the expertise, and the operational capability it needed at a price it could afford. Accenture hired FCS's existing information technology staff and recruited some new employees to take over IT. The unit replaced every piece of hardware and software in the company over an 18-month period. It then operated, scaled up, and improved IT support as the company expanded. Its leader sat on Les Dietzman's executive staff and functioned as the company's CIO.

Accenture helped FCS pay for the IT transformation by bringing a financial partner into the deal—GE Capital. GE Capital paid Accenture for the upfront project work, the software, and the IT infrastructure. In turn, FCS paid off the $7 million investment with interest over the seven years of the agreement. In addition, as FCS reached its sales targets, its outsourcing fees to Accenture increased accordingly. That way, the company used its own growth to pay for the IT capability it needed to support the growth. In the words of one executive, it was a "Cadillac deal for a reasonable price."

How did Family Christian Stores fare? Today, it is the nation's largest Christian retailer. It has grown from 120 to 330 stores, and its sales have tripled.

Crouching tigers want fast implementation just as out-of-nowhere start-ups do, but they want expertise even more. The missing ingredient for these companies can be anything from marketing or product development to supply chain management or information technology, and they need it fixed in order to grow. These companies do not necessarily want to reduce overall costs in their roadblocked function. But they do want to siphon spending out of tactical activities and direct it toward programs that will contribute to the strategy. They usually need access to new capital as well—either directly from the outsourcing provider or from a third-party financial partner that likes outsourcing's risk profile.

Because the new capability must be tightly integrated into the tiger's operation, these companies often prefer cosourcing rather than strict outsourcing. In other words, the provider takes over responsibility for the roadblocked function or process, but the retained employees remain on the tiger's payroll. This puts the tiger in a better position to upgrade its internal capabilities and ultimately bring the operation back under its own control.

We often think of crouching tigers as small companies that rely on larger and more mature outsourcing providers for the skills they lack. It can work the other way around as well. In the pharmaceutical industry, many of the large companies that are facing empty product-development pipelines are turning to small biotech companies for drug discovery. For the most part, these large companies manage the relationships contractually, but leaders are moving toward a cosourcing approach.[3]

Fallen Angels Catalyze Change

Traditional outsourcing often involves moving back-office functions and processes to a third-party company to improve costs, focus, productivity, service quality, and flexibility. Some organizations outsource the same operations in a way that makes it transformational. These companies are failing to thrive. They're comfortably settled into the wrong performance trajectory, and they need strong action to change their tack.

Executives use this kind of outsourcing to communicate—and to catalyze—a broad organizational change. As with any other type of transformational outsourcing, it is not the only initiative executives have under way. It can, however, symbolize the depth, speed, and extent of change that executives intend.

Executives at British Petroleum, for example, describe their transition from a stodgy, bureaucratic oil company to a nimble competitor.[4] In 1987, the Thatcher government sold its majority stake in BP to the public, completing the company's privatization. According to one executive at the time, "The company had a history of being managed in a bureaucratic, cumbersome way." Between 1990 and 1992, more than 22,000 jobs were eliminated, layers of management were removed, the corporate headquarters staff was slashed, and BP experienced its first financial loss in 80 years.

At the time John Browne led BP's upstream business—oil exploration (BPX). According to one colleague, "He needed to shake up the organization to communicate that things were going to be radically different." To redirect his organization, he cut staff and refocused capital expenditures in order to "spend less to find more." In addition, he undid BPX's traditional hierarchical management approach and created separate business units, each with its own accountable executive. Instead of having control over only 40 percent of their spending, Browne's autonomous "asset managers" each had personal authority over 90 percent of their costs, and they had the freedom to do what it took to make money.

Overhead support, like finance and accounting personnel, was part of the revolution, but in a very different way. Browne believed that finance and accounting was not an area in which BPX could create a competitive advantage. He did not just paint a cost-cutting target on it, though. He teed it up for radical change to make a point to the rest of the organization. In a bellwether deal, BPX consolidated all the accounting outposts that dotted its far-flung empire and outsourced the entire process. His immediate goal was cost reduction, and he believed that economies of scale would deliver these results. However, his aspiration did not stop at the company borders. Browne reasoned that if he could get his competitors to use the shared service center too, his costs would improve even more.

Ultimately six oil companies and several other services companies joined the North Sea finance and accounting center in Aberdeen, Scotland. By 1997, BPX had cut its finance and accounting costs in half, while its volume of work doubled, for a breathtaking improvement in productivity. BP has gone on to outsource a wide range of activities that it considers distractions, just as it shrewdly sells properties that no longer produce profitably. Changing these "noncore" and "no-longer-core" activities is only part of the transformational agenda, but it is an important part. These moves send a clear signal to the rest of the organization about where and how the company does distinguish itself. Just as surely as firing an executive who fails to meet her numbers, these actions help remaining employees who understand what happens to operations that don't create value.

Going beyond the obvious benefits of wake-up calls and cost improvements, fallen angels often look for deeper impacts as well. When they make management information clean and visible; for example, they can improve the quality of decisions. How? The senior team stops arguing about what the results are because that is no longer in question. For the first time, they may be able to see which of their products or services are actually profitable. They can turn their attention to what they should do about it. They can also tap off-balance-sheet financial slack to fuel innovation. And, unlike out-of-nowhere start-ups and crouching tigers, fallen angels are likely to keep outsourcing relationships in place over the long term.

Born-Again Companies Achieve Radical Renewal

Companies and public enterprises that need a radical renovation of critical processes and functions don't have many options. Outsourcing is one way to replace the engine in the airplane while it is in the air. We're not talking about catalyzing change. We're not talking about clearing away a roadblock to growth. We're talking about changing the guts of the organization so that it becomes dramatically more effective.

These companies will not survive unless they find market traction quickly. National Savings and Investments executives used outsourcing to radically reshape their organization. Out of 4,500 employees, only 120 were retained in the original organization. The rest transferred to the outsourcing partner. Before the initiative, NS&I management questioned whether the organization should even survive. Four years later, it boasted a sleek, low-cost operation that was one of the most competitive in the financial services industry.

NS&I is probably the best example of radical transformation through outsourcing, but it isn't the only example. In 1986, one of the largest financial institutions in the UK—we'll call it Consolidated National—entered the Spanish market. It established two small branches with a narrow product line and very limited service: It made mortgage loans.

At the end of 1992, the CEO of the Spanish bank engaged a consulting company to conduct a strategic review to determine why the bank consistently lost money and to define a more effective direction going forward. The consultants' report drew a line in the sand. It gave the CEO two choices: leave the market or play the same game as the other banks in Spain. That would mean selling a full range of products to a clearly defined target market with a capable staff in a large number of convenient branches.

The CEO decided to stay. However, his situation was anything but enviable. He lacked the information systems, the data center, the branch infrastructure, and the staff to run the bank the consultants recommended. And parent company management had lost patience with his financial performance; they were looking for profitable operations. The CEO didn't have money, and he didn't have time. He turned to outsourcing.

By the beginning of 1994, the CEO had chosen an outsourcing provider and had signed a six-year contract. Over the next 18 months, the provider implemented a full-line bank's information systems platform, opened 23 new branches, hired staff, and defined and developed new products. It also brought seasoned partners to the table to help the CEO define and implement bank strategy. One executive from the outsourcing provider described the relationship this way: "We had a very informal relationship. Our company paid no service penalty in six years. In many of its points, the contract did not match what we were really doing, so we managed the work like we were partners. We worked side by side to continuously improve the bank's performance."

Consolidated paid for the help in an innovative way. The provider charged a minimal monthly fee until the systems and processes were put in place and the bank reached a threshold volume of assets under management. After that point, the provider received a percentage of the assets as its payment. The more the bank grew, the more both partners earned. In 1997, the bank approached break-even results, and in 1998 it was profitable.

For companies seeking radical renewal, outsourcing is a lifeline. These companies need all the benefits that transformational outsourcing can provide. An NS&I executive said it best: "We didn't have all the skills; we didn't have the technology; and we didn't have all the resources to fulfill our mission."

*   *   *

How Far Should You Go?

We have talked about how the four uses of transformational outsourcing differ strategically, but there's one more important decision that executives must wrestle with no matter which purpose they embrace. They must decide how far they intend transformational outsourcing to take them.

This is really a question of horizon, and it matters because it influences how executives shape and manage their outsourcing relationships. Executives have two choices. They can use transformational outsourcing simply to reposition their company, or they can use it also to accelerate their performance improvement. I have yet to encounter an executive who is using this approach to "ennimble" an enterprise—to give it the capability for strategic agility, so we'll hold that part of the discussion for Chapter 12, "Transformational Outsourcing Horizons" (see Exhibit 4.4).

Reposition

The most narrowly focused leaders—sometimes the most desperate ones—use outsourcing to achieve their most urgent purpose: to reposition the organization. In other words, they want to move their company to a better competitive situation. They'll deal with what happens next when they get there.

Start-ups and turnarounds often fall often into this category. Their needs are pressing, and the stakes are survival. In that kind of situation,

Exhibit 4.4. Goals for transformation through outsourcing.

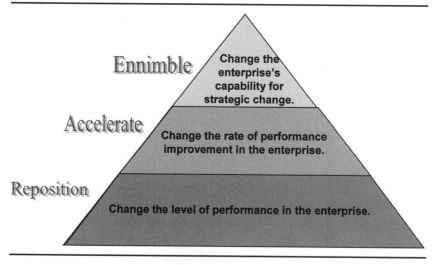

it's hard to think beyond the current tectonic pressures. Some other transformational outsourcing initiatives can fall into this category simply because executives have not attended to longer-term planning. In still other situations, executives intend to outsource to gain a new position, but to bring the function or activity back in-house once it is established. In this case, they want to take the responsibility for changing the performance trajectory on their own shoulders.

The executives who want to reposition their organizations focus primarily on putting robust working processes in place as quickly as possible. They are racing against time, and they measure their success primarily by whether or not they have met the deadlines they have set for themselves. For example, Consolidated National's CEO charged his outsourcing provider with implementing a full-service banking capability in nine months.

Another example, a nonprofit organization we'll call Mana, also illustrates the point.* Mana is owned by a consortium of the 50 largest industrial-products companies in the world. It was launched in the late 1990s to help all the companies deal with the growing pressure for safe and effective disposal of hazardous materials. By 1998, this company had to be ready to accept declarations from member companies detailing the number of units of each type of hazardous material that was disposed of. It also had to be ready to present invoices back to the companies so they could remit their handling fees promptly and in the right amount. (These fees were designed to finance the cost of removing and recycling the packaging waste.) Mana's president recognized that his company would be ineffective if it could not guarantee accuracy. In addition, he was responsible to the member companies for spending the money to administer the shared system wisely.

In order to start up quickly and meet the pressing deadline with quality work, Mana management believed they could not afford the risk of trying to hire and train a new workforce. So they outsourced finance and administration, customer contact, and information technology functions, under the leadership of a small core staff of employees. They did meet their deadline and achieve the accuracy their member companies expected.

Since speed to operation is the most pressing goal to executives who

*Some details of this example have been changed to protect the identity of the firm.

are repositioning their organizations, these organizations often absorb costs that come with a pedal-to-the-metal schedule. Mana, for example, estimates that its outsourcing fees cost 50 to 60 percent more than it would spend for an internally staffed operation.

Companies that aim for repositioning can state their objectives clearly and incentivize their provider for meeting them. They need not worry about governance processes to drive continuous improvement, benchmarking service levels to ensure their company remains competitive, or complex incentive schemes to motivate innovation. These companies can also make the strategic trade-off between single or multiple providers more easily. Coordinating a multiprovider environment requires more management attention, but the natural competition keeps an edge on the relationship as providers angle for increased business. This takes a toll on commitment and trust, but motivates operational improvements. If repositioning is the goal, these improvements are generally not as important as the ability to work closely with the provider.

Accelerate

Some companies choose to frame transformation as a longer-term initiative. Ultimately, they seek both to reposition the organization and to accelerate its performance trajectory. In other words, they don't just want to use outsourcing to get to a better spot, they want to use it to equip the organization to improve faster than the competition once they get there.

Companies that are using outsourcing to catalyze change or remove a competitive roadblock frequently fall in this category, although start-ups and turnarounds can as well. Leaders that intend to accelerate their trajectories want to drive improvement in key functions and processes, but they don't intend to stop there. They outsource to an especially capable partner to establish a top-quartile trajectory that includes continuing investment, innovation, and industry leadership. For example, in 1991, British Petroleum outsourced its North Sea finance and accounting operations to Accenture. BPX, the upstream exploration unit, transferred more than 300 workers to a shared services center in Aberdeen, Scotland. At the time, BP's agenda was to transform its enterprise by creating a best-in-industry cost structure, by focusing firm management on value-adding activities, and by establishing a driving, aggressive culture. This outsourcing initiative, by itself, helped BPX reduce its finance and administrative costs. But management did not stop there. The leaders of the initiative worked with their outsourcing provider to leverage the asset—to bring additional clients into the center to improve economies of scale beyond what BPX could achieve on its own. BP leadership reasoned that no matter how well the company performed finance and accounting activities, these would not make a difference for its competitive position. The best it could do was to minimize the cost of a high-quality operation. All in all, six additional North Sea oil and gas companies transferred their finance processes to the center including Talisman Energy (U.K.), Conoco (U.K.), and Total-FinaElf Exploration (U.K.). BPX executives brag that they have reduced administrative costs every year for a decade—ultimately halving costs while transaction volumes doubled.

Going for acceleration requires that executives stay tuned to the external business environment in order to guide the step-change and subsequent improvements effectively over the longer term. And they must shape their outsourcing relationship in a flexible way to enable it to react to business changes. If they neglect these steps, they can emerge from a serious and expensive change effort with a company that is no more likely to be successful than when they started. For example, one of the world's largest telecommunications service companies asked a network equipment company to take over operations of its legacy voice network and to build it a new digital network in order to execute its strategic shift toward voice over IP and digital data services for the commercial market. Throughout the process, the two companies held annual "reality checks" involving senior executives in both. The purpose of these analyses was to determine whether the strategic direction continued to look appealing. If, in these sessions, the leadership reached the opposite conclusion, they had the flexibility in their relationship to stop and change course.

An acceleration agenda also involves devoting management attention to long-term plans, continuous operational improvement, and innovation as leaders shape the outsourcing initiative. We will talk more about how to incorporate these elements into the relationship in the following chapters. Suffice it to say that the contract duration, metrics, incentives, planning, governance, change control processes, and relationship-management aspects of the outsourcing initiative must all be constructed with the improving trajectory in mind.

*   *   *

In this chapter, we have addressed two major strategic questions that face transformational leaders:

- What is the major purpose of our transformational outsourcing?
- How far do we want it to take us?

With these grounding purposes set forth, we can now turn our attention to filling in the blanks with a clear set of objectives for this strategic initiative: transformational outsourcing. Executives who intend to use outsourcing for transformation (and even those who don't) should write down exactly what they hope to accomplish and how they will know they are successful. They can then use this clear statement of purpose for the duration of their outsourcing relationship to continually remind themselves and their partners what they set out to do.

How do executives craft an arrangement that fulfills their strategic purposes? Read on.

Notes

1. Jane Linder, Susan Cantrell, and Scott Crist, "Business Process Outsourcing Big Bang: Creating Value in an Expanding Universe," Accenture Institute for Strategic Change research report, July 2002.

2. Ibid.

3. Jane Linder, Sam Perkins, Srinivasan Rangan, Philip Dover, "The Drug Industry's Alliance Archipelago," Accenture Institute for Strategic Change research report, November 2003.

4. For more on the changes at BPX, see Joel Podolny and John Roberts, "British Petroleum (A1): Organizing for Performance at BPX," case study from the Graduate School of Business, Stanford University, #S-1B-16A2, 1998, revised April 2, 2002, and "British Petroleum (A2): Organizing for Performance at BPX, Graduate School of Business, Stanford University, #1B16A1, July 4, 1999.

CHAPTER 5

Crafting a Business Model
That Works

We have reviewed four major ways to use outsourcing for transformation, some choices of horizon, and a host of potential benefits. Now we want to help you determine how to craft an outsourcing initiative that fulfills the strategic agenda you have set for yourself.

In the past, executives have used an adversarial negotiating process to create the terms and conditions of a relationship. The assumption behind this process is that each company will ensure its own well-being. This process doesn't provide a sound enough foundation for a transformational outsourcing relationship. No executive should enter such an important outsourcing deal unless he or she is convinced it can be sustained for the duration of the commitment. That means explicitly designing a business model—actually a joint business model—that benefits both partners.

Many executives use the term "business model," but they frequently have difficulty defining it.[1] Let's agree that a business model is an organization's core logic for creating value (see sidebar below, "What Is a Business Model Anyway?"). It is:

A set of value propositions and operational processes for delivering on them, designed as a system that relies on and builds tangible and intangible assets in order to create value.

___

What Is a Business Model Anyway?

A business model is an organization's core logic for creating value. It is a set of value propositions and operational processes for delivering on them, designed as a system, that relies on and builds tangible and intangible assets, capabilities, and relationships in order to create value. In a for-profit company, creating value usually means making money.

Since organizations compete for customers and resources, a business model must highlight what's distinctive about the company: how it wins customers, woos investors, and earns profits. Effective business models are rich and detailed, and the components reinforce each other; change any one component, and you've got a different model.

___

Leaders create viable joint business models in three steps:

- Stakeholder analysis
- Business model design
- Scenario planning

Stakeholder Analysis

The first step in designing a working business model is to identify the critical stakeholders. These are the constituencies on both sides of the initiative that have a stake in its outcome. National Savings and Investments counted customers, employees, the Treasury, and management as the four key stakeholder groups. For Newport Systems, stakeholders in-cluded headquarters management, business unit management, investors, and employees. When NS&I decided to work with a single provider rather than multiple vendors, and when it chose a provider, executives looked at each decision from the point of view of each stakeholder group to arrive at the best overall choice (see Exhibit 5.1).

However, they went even further. They also considered Newport Sys-tems's key stakeholders in order to make sure the arrangement their part-ner had proposed would be sustainable. NS&I recognized that Newport had set itself very aggressive targets and that missing these would under-mine its profits. Peter Bareau and his team reasoned that, with this out-come, they would risk losing the support of headquarters management and investors. To head off this problem, the NS&I team deliberately estab-lished a direct relationship with Newport's corporate leadership to person-ally secure their support.

When Don Brown of the UK Inland Revenue got involved in the agency's outsourced information technology systems and processes, he addressed this issue by stating up front that the provider deserved a rea-sonable profit. Although we would not consider this outsourcing initiative transformational, it illustrates the point. Open-book accounting helped the provider guard against incurring debilitating losses as well as ensuring his own fair share of windfall profits. This kind of forethought makes for a more sustainable relationship.

Business Model Design

Transformational outsourcing means making radical changes in an organi-zation's existing business model. In most situations, it also means estab-lishing a very tight connection to the business model of another company—the outsourcing provider. Most executives ignore this perspec-tive. They think about outsourcing as a deal. Of course, the deal is only the beginning. What they really want is an ongoing operation that creates value—in fact, more value for both partners than they had before. To achieve this objective, executives have to go beyond deals and create busi-ness models that work.

What makes a good business model? First, it's important to under-

Exhibit 5.1. Examples of NS&I stakeholder objectives.

Stakeholder	Objective
Customers	• Appealing new products • Competitive prices • Convenient service • Low investment risk
Employees/Unions	• Job security • Career growth and opportunities
UK Treasury (owners)	• Low cost of borrowing • Low financial risk • Low performance risk • Low millennium compliance risk • Low fraud risk • Demonstrated best approach to execution
Management	• Financial success • Financial and operating slack • Effective, low-cost operations • Low performance risk

stand that business models are like insects: Their diversity is stunning, and a slight variation in key components can make all the difference between a Darwinian winner and an also-ran. And no single business model stands out as being financially superior. However, the better models do share certain characteristics.

First, they offer unique value. Most often, this involves a combination of product and service attributes that offer more appeal, either a lower price for the same benefit or more benefit for the same price. Lowes Home Improvement Warehouse, for example, combines the low price and selection of a superstore with the knowledgeable advice you'd find in a full-price specialty hardware store. Historically, DuPont has commanded premium prices because of customers' trust in its brand.

Good business models exhibit a virtuous and self-propelling dynamic. They create value, not only through sound logic, but *also with* "round" logic. In other words, the components of the model reinforce each other (see sidebar below, "Business Model Logic Is 'Round' as Well as Sound"). In our NS&I example, the more Newport improves the call center, the more likely it is to win business from other clients, which creates jobs and increases volumes, which enable it to improve its value to NS&I as well.

Better business models are also hard to imitate. Whether through patents and proprietary assets, a lock on scarce resources, or superb execution, models that can't be easily imitated provide barriers to entry that protect their profit streams. This makes them durable—that is, profitable over time. Internet companies like eBay and Yahoo that win big audiences early, for example, can benefit from increasing returns to scale. The bigger they get, the more each new customer contributes to profits. Why? Because customers value the presence of other visitors—the larger the audience, the higher the value.

Finally, better business models are grounded in reality. They are based on assumptions of customer behavior that actually hold true. They have cost structures that can be supported by the revenue streams, day in and day out. These criteria sound obvious, but many companies—new and old—don't have a clear picture of where they make money and why customers prefer their offerings. One of my previous studies on this topic found a shocking statistic: 62 percent of executives interviewed could not easily articulate their company's business model.[2] And many companies are stunned to find out how many of their customers actually cost them money!

Business Model Logic Is "Round" as Well as Sound

To illustrate "round" business model logic, we will walk through a simple business model—an Internet-based, business-to-business office products supplier. Let's call it Office supplies.com.

- Officesupplies.com sells office products at dealer cost over the Internet.
- The great prices attract small and midsize companies accustomed to paying 25 to 40 percent markups.
- Good service—including wide selection, next day delivery, and phone center support—keeps customers coming back.
- Good service and good prices build volume.
- High volume enables Officesupplies.com to negotiate purchase discounts with wholesale suppliers.
- These discounts, along with a lean cost structure, give Officesupplies.com its profit, and the ability to lower prices further.
- Profits attract capital for growth.
- Growth helps the company attract top talent, which enables it to continue to improve its Web site and to sustain excellent customer service.

Since most executives are unfamiliar with the process of designing business models, let's start with the basics. Then we'll talk about why this kind of analysis is especially important for transformational outsourcing and how to apply it.

Designing a business model is a disciplined way of thinking through how your company will make money. Since organizations compete for customers and resources, a business model highlights the distinctive activities and approaches that enable the company to succeed in comparison to others in its industry—to attract and satisfy customers, employees, and investors and to deliver products and services profitably.

A business modeling approach has one essential advantage over many other strategic frameworks: It is dynamic. Rather than painting a static picture of an organization's functions, business modeling provides a more realistic operating view of how the key elements of the moneymaking (or value creation, for the public sector) process work together and reinforce each other (see Exhibit 5.2). To begin to design a business model, you will need to answer the following three related questions:

- *What stakeholders will we target and what value proposition(s) will we offer them?* Starting with customers, we need to ask ourselves what, exactly, do we intend to provide for them, and what, exactly, will they give us in return? This value proposition should include both the tangible and intangible parts of the exchange. For example, if our company installs lawn sprinklers that we stand behind, our reputation for quality is part of the value proposition. Further, by identifying the customers we intend to serve, we can state specifically why we believe this segment will prefer our products and services over the others they might choose. We will want to continue this analysis with other important stakeholders such as investors, employees, and the executive team.

- *How will we deliver what we promise profitably?* How should we operate? What are the critical capabilities we need to meet our promises to stakeholders and make a profit in the process? Will we need to hire workers? Will we sell directly to customers or through channels? Will we do our own manufacturing? Will we need the cooperation of local government officials? You'll want to focus on the most important and distinctive elements of the delivery proposition for this analysis. For example, outsourcing software programming to India may be critical to the delivery proposition for a packaged software company that intends to compete on quality and price. It may be almost irrelevant to a professional services company that leverages deep personal relationships to win long-term contracts.

- *How will we finance our enterprise?* What kind of cash flows and cost structure will we have? How will we support that through investment or profits? What will we have to pay for capital and where will we get it? How can we make the most of our financial assets? For example, busi-

Exhibit 5.2. Business model overview.

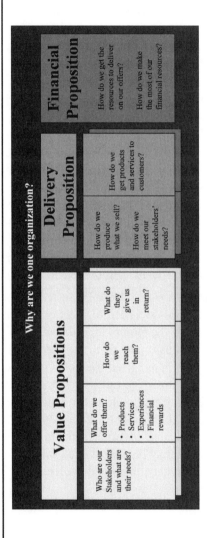
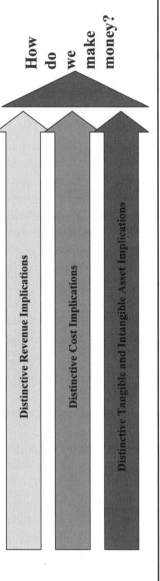

nesses that get cash up front from their customers—before they have to pay for the costs of goods and services—have a business model advantage over companies that get paid after products have been delivered.

I call these "related" questions because they are not independent. In fact, they are highly intertwined. As a simple example, a company that intends to offer the highest quality automobile in the industry for a premium price—its value proposition—must have access to designers, engineers, and manufacturing capabilities to build such a unique product: its delivery proposition.

Each of the three business-model design questions hides a myriad of detailed considerations. And some of these are critical to the model. For example, one model's value proposition might ask customers to pay for their automobiles in full when they receive them. Another model might allow them to pay over time. The latter could include charges on the unpaid balance, which could, of course, improve the model's overall profitability. For example, furniture retailer Heilig Meyers used to concentrate its stores in rural areas where patrons had less access to easy credit. The store's product margins were vanishingly small, but, for a time, it made healthy profits on financing charges. When credit card companies pushed into its customer segment with aggressive direct-mail campaigns, its sales remained high, but its profits tanked. It filed for bankruptcy in 2000.

By answering the three key questions, you will develop an understanding of how the organization creates value today. Your business-model dynamic has first-order effects that keep the basic business going. And to completely understand your model, you will want to articulate how it continues to create value (see Exhibit 5.3). The key here is to identify the tangible and intangible assets that are built as by-products of ongoing company operations.

Now we're talking about second-order effects that enable the organization to adapt, grow, and thrive (see sidebar, "Officesupplies.com Keeps Delivering Value," below). Operating businesses both rely on and create tangible and intangible assets. These include facilities and patents, as well as brand equity, know-how, relationships, and knowledge. For example, a business may rely on existing customer relationships for this month's sales. The new products and services also build the relationship. These are the critical capabilities your organization draws on to operate, and

Exhibit 5.3. Articulating a business model.

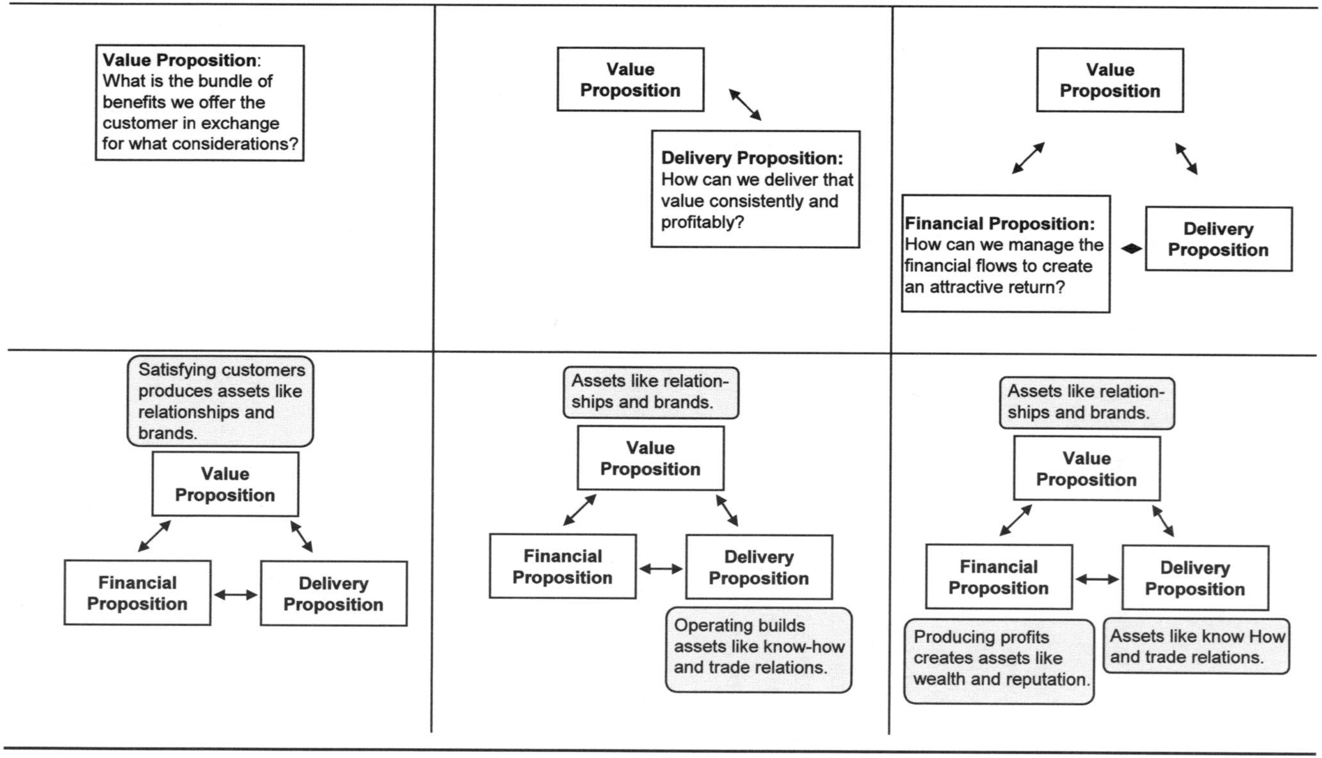
Value Proposition: What is the bundle of benefits we offer the customer in exchange for what considerations?
Value Proposition
Delivery Proposition: How can we deliver that value consistently and profitably?
Value Proposition
Financial Proposition: How can we manage the financial flows to create an attractive return?
Delivery Proposition
Satisfying customers produces assets like relationships and brands.
Value Proposition
Financial Proposition
Delivery Proposition
Assets like relation-ships and brands.
Value Proposition
Financial Proposition
Delivery Proposition
Operating builds assets like know-how and trade relations.
Assets like relation-ships and brands.
Value Proposition
Financial Proposition
Delivery Proposition
Producing profits creates assets like wealth and reputation.
Assets like know How and trade relations.

they are the capabilities you build through the normal course of doing business.

Officesupplies.com Keeps Delivering Value

Officesupplies.com's dynamic goes further than just keeping its basic business rolling. In addition to first-order effects, the company has a second-order dynamic. This tells us how the company leverages its important assets, capabilities, relationships, and knowledge to grow and thrive.

- Officesupplies.com's business model gives it an important asset: a base of satisfied small and midsize business customers.
- Officesupplies.com leverages this asset by expanding its offerings to these customers to include other convenience goods and services at excellent prices, such as office furniture, payroll services, insurance, and temporary help.
- The broader product/service line increases Officesupplies .com value for convenience- and cost-oriented customers.
- This improves customer retention and increases sales.
- Increased sales enable Officesupplies.com to continue to expand its product line, customer service, and marketing reach.
- This expansion fuels further sales growth and increases profitability.

Businesses extend and leverage these tangible and intangible assets to grow and increase their value. For example, a business could introduce new products under a successful brand. It could take manufacturing know-how in one product sector and use it to enter a new sector. This second-order dynamic makes a business model viable over time. It gives it the ability to adapt incrementally as business conditions change.

To outline your organization's business model(s), follow these steps. Remember, you have already identified your key stakeholder groups and their needs:

1. Identify the important sources of value you provide to each key group. Lay out the key factors underlying your ability to attract and retain these stakeholders: why do they prefer to deal with your company compared to others?

2. Identify what each stakeholder group gives you in exchange for the value you provide.

3. Lay out the key factors that enable you to deliver your value propositions profitably and consistently. These make up your delivery proposition and your financing proposition.

4. Lay out the tangible and intangible assets that you build as a result of operating this business, and that can you can use to propel it forward.

5. Test the logic. Do the value propositions attract enough resources to enable the organization to deliver profitably? Do the operations build enough lasting assets to attract investment and fuel profitable growth?

Use the information to construct a diagram that shows "round" logic. If your organization has several divisions, ask yourself: Why is this one company? If you can identify the reason, make sure that factor is prominent in the operating business model. If you can't, show the divisions as separate models.

Applying Business Model Design to Transformational Outsourcing

Transformation through outsourcing means making a substantial change in your organization's business model. National Savings and Investments adopted a new business model when it outsourced its operations to Newport Systems. On the cost side, it capped, then reduced its operating costs; it passed some of its fraud risk to its partner; it eliminated the need for capital investment in technology. At the top line, it contractually obligated its partner to implement dramatic improvements in customer service and convenience; it required its partner to develop a stream of new products at no additional operating cost; and it gained a share of the revenue its partner could earn serving other clients with its customer service center.

These changes, implemented through outsourcing, altered the business model. Before outsourcing, executives at NS&I would have said, "We create value by offering risk-free investments. Customers are willing to endure our inconvenient service because they value risk-free investments so highly. The Treasury is willing to live with our modest returns to them because we require limited capital investment and running costs." After the business model shift, executives would say, "We create value by offering innovative, risk-free investments coupled with superior customer service. Customers prefer them because they are among the most competitive products in the financial services industry. The Treasury continues to support our program because we deliver funds to it at a substantially lower cost than its other sources. We attract the best management talent because of our record of innovation and superb execution. Finally, we self-finance the investments we need to keep our operation competitive."

The NS&I team went through a business-modeling thought process before they decided to use outsourcing for transformation. They reasoned that a processing center staffed by loyal and experienced employees could create more value in the hands of a private-sector company than it could buried inside a government operation. They also understood that some of the costs and risks associated with implementing and operating new financial services technologies would be lower for experts than for themselves. If part of their operation would have higher value and lower risk-adjusted costs, they concluded that an outsourcing provider could make money, NS&I could get the benefits it was seeking, and a joint business model could work.

Scenario Planning

Since transformational outsourcing initiatives are likely to last for seven to ten years, planning for the future is an essential part of creating a sustainable relationship. The business landscape will certainly shift during that time. Scenario planning is a powerful planning approach that enables an organization to prepare for these changes.

Scenario planning is not new. Royal Dutch Shell pioneered the method more than 25 years ago.[3] It entails crafting three to five provocative but plausible scenarios that describe a company's business environment five to eight years in the future. This is far enough in the future to free planners from the drag of current realities, but not so far that it seems irrelevant. Executives consider the implications of each scenario by "back casting"—standing in the future and looking backwards. This turns out to be much easier than standing in the present and trying to predict the future.

Scenario planning recognizes that trying to define a single view of the future is unrealistic. In scenario planning, the object is not to forecast one future, but to identify a range of plausible futures. Good business plans prepare an organization to do its best no matter what shape the future takes.

Scenario planners start by identifying the key uncertainties in the relevant business sectors. These can be political, regulatory, social, technological, and economic questions. Planners then create narratives of the future in which these uncertain factors are resolved differently. For example, one of the key uncertainties in consumer finance is how quickly and in what direction aggregation will develop. Over the past decade, customers have demanded and received consolidated statements—they get one overview statement from each company with which they do business. Now they want to see a complete picture of all their finances—a consolidated statement across all the companies they deal with. How will this happen? One scenario might envision intermediaries like Yodlee, tax preparer H&R Block, or independent financial planners inserting themselves between most consumers and their financial institutions. Another scenario could posit that Microsoft includes this capability in its 2006 release of Windows. The aggregation question is only one uncertainty that a narrative would address. It would also take a position on regulatory changes, new patterns of consumer demand, technology developments, and other important factors.

Through a systematic process, an organization's strategy team plants its feet in one future at a time and looks backwards. They ask themselves pointed questions like, "What did our organization have to do to get here?" With the benefit of 20/20 hindsight, they prepare a road map that describes their company's actions that led it to succeed in this particular scenario. They combine the success pathways that come out of all the scenarios into a comprehensive road map to the future, paying particular attention to forks in the road and critical events that trigger their company to favor one strategic option over another.

By itself, scenario planning is a valuable approach to long-term planning. For transformational outsourcing, it is essential. Executives can use the results of a scenario planning process tactically. They can identify minimum and maximum transaction volumes and business risks, for example, under a more comprehensive range of assumptions about the future.

More important, however, executives can use scenario planning strategically. By inviting the outsourcing provider to participate in this kind of long-range planning process, they can create a rich context for designing a sound joint business model, and a migration plan that sustains value. Most of the private-sector organizations that transform through outsourcing work with a consulting company initially to set the strategy, review the alternative approaches, and frame the initiative. This provides a great start, but it does not go far enough. When they have selected a partner, and at least once a year for the duration of the contract, they should put their strategists and industry experts together to look at where they are going.

Are We on the Right Track?

A company and its outsourcing provider are about to enter into a risky, long-term commitment. Mont Phelps, CEO of Netivity Solutions, a networking services company, uses a story about Formula-1 racing to explain what long-range planning is all about. He describes a swarm of cars streaking around hairpin curves. If drivers watch only the cars right in front of them, their rapid short-term adjustments will slow them down and make them constantly feel a little off balance. And they'll never be able to look ahead to set their direction and find opportunities to pass. Executives will want to engage with their partner in joint long-term planning to validate their business model, explore opportunities for innovation, clarify directions for growth, and prospectively stress test their outsourcing relationship.

Validate the Company's Ability to Address the Stakeholder Needs

You're making a significant change in your organization's business model; it is imperative to make sure the new model provides the benefits stakeholders want and produces the value you expect. If it does not, your transformation is likely to result in failure. For each stakeholder group, the team should be able to answer the question, "Why will our stakeholders continue to (or begin to) prefer our organization, given this new model?"

Employees are a particularly problematic stakeholder in transformation. In the cryptic words of one executive experienced with transformational outsourcing, "You're never going to convince turkeys that Christmas is a good idea." We'll talk more about the details behind workforce transition approaches in Chapter 8, but it is essential to consider this stakeholder group as you design your organization's new business model. If your organization needs transformation to thrive in its business environment, you will probably be dislocating employees no matter how you implement the change. Some outsourcing options may, however, provide more advantages for employees than others. Articulating the benefits for employees that result from the transformation is just as important as anticipating the issues you will have to resolve.

Explore Innovative Approaches That Maximize Value

Having partners in the picture opens new opportunities. They bring skills and assets that can be factored into innovative new models that benefit you both. For example, an organization called the National Information Consortium operates the Web portals for 17 states in the United States under a model that works for both sides of its public/private partnerships. NIC builds and operates a Web portal for each state. The portal offers insurance companies access to government motor vehicle records for a modest fee. These fees compensate NIC for its work in developing, hosting, and maintaining the portal site. So the state government and its constituents have the benefits of a portal essentially for free.

The government of Hong Kong goes even further. Its government Web site presents both government transactions and related commercial offers in a one-stop-shopping mode. For example, couples applying for their marriage licenses can also arrange for flowers and a photographer for their wedding at the same time. The private companies pay advertising fees, which completely cover the cost of the Web site.[4]

These examples are just meant to illustrate the potential variety of ways organizations can work together to create value for both. As you begin exploring the potential of outsourcing for transformation, you will want to invite a range of partners to discuss their ideas with you. Most companies find that the proposals they receive from different vendors vary quite widely. You can incorporate the best ideas from these diverse offers to create a composite model that maximizes the value for your organization. Of course, to get these benefits, you will have to convince at least one outsourcing provider to work with you in the way you describe. For example, the state of Connecticut solicited proposals for providers to take over its information-technology function and to consolidate operations into a shared services center. Because of its difficult fiscal situation at the time, the state wanted the vendor to begin charging immediately at a rate that anticipated the savings that would be gained through the consolidation. Concerned for its own profitability, its chosen vendor was unwilling to agree. The two parties abandoned the deal.[5]

Thomas Cook shows an interesting contrast (see Chapter 6 for more details). Thomas Cook solicited proposals to outsource its finance and accounting, human resources administration, IT, and project management to a company that would consolidate all these processes into a single shared-services center. The CEO's intention was to catalyze significant organizational change, integrating the fragments of the company that had been pieced together by acquisition. He sought to create a vertically integrated enterprise that acted as one company. In the process, he also intended to realize rapid improvement in reported earnings. So he was shopping for an outsourcing provider that could provide superb operational capabilities, but also one that had a good grasp of financial engineering. Of the four vendors that submitted proposals, only one was willing to use its own financial strength to provide the quick profits that Thomas Cook needed to make its transformation work.

Here's how the financial proposition worked. Thomas Cook provided packaged holidays for which customers paid up front. The UK and Ireland subsidiary was short on profits, but its pay-first-travel-later business model gave it ready access to cheap capital. The successful outsourcing partner had the opposite financial position. It had strong profits, but was capital constrained. The two companies used their complementary financial profiles to create benefits for both. The outsourcing provider took over Thomas Cook's operations at a guaranteed cost that instantly improved Thomas Cook's reported earnings. Thomas Cook used its own cheap capital to pay for systems development and IT–related expenditures that could be capitalized. These would "trickle" into the income statement slowly, so the impact would be gradual.

Financial engineering of this sort is often associated with outsourcing. It is especially useful during transformational outsourcing because this is often a time when a company's need for investment exceeds its resources. In this kind of situation, executives can team up with financially solid outsourcing partners to give their companies the financial slack they need to reestablish their ability to operate profitably.

Clarify How Their Company Might Grow and Change Over Time

A business model works in a competitive context. As important factors in the landscape change, it must be adjusted so that it continues to deliver value. Forward-thinking executives not only understand their current business model but they also have considered how it might change given different future scenarios. They have laid plans to shift their model appropriately.

In the early 1990s, when British Petroleum first outsourced its finance and accounting processes for its North Sea operations, its agenda was to catalyze deep organizational change. The enterprise's majority owner had been the British government until 1987, and it still held the vestiges of a government bureaucracy. The newly appointed CEO of BP Exploration (BPX), John Browne, shattered whatever was left of the organization's complacency by driving out waste, eliminating organizational layers, and outsourcing every function and process across the enterprise that was considered noncore. One executive described his objective at the time as: "to make his organization lean and mean."

At the time BPX had accounting organizations dotted all over the company. It worked with an outsourcing provider to pull these into a single finance and accounting center in Aberdeen, Scotland. Over the first four years of the relationship, this consolidation achieved significant cost savings. But that was only the beginning. The architects of the outsourcing model also wanted to take advantage of the fact that oil industry competitors were accustomed to collaborating. They envisioned capturing the benefits of further economies of scale by serving multiple companies in the North Sea with the same service center. Ultimately, six other oil companies and two service companies also contracted with the center to provide their accounting services. As a result, BPX's finance and accounting costs declined 50 percent by 1997 at the same time as the amount of work done by the center doubled.

Now, as the economics of producing oil in the North Sea become less and less attractive, BPX is scaling back its operations in the area and, simultaneously, the resources it devotes to finance and accounting. According to the BPX executive who originally crafted the relationship, "We can turn on a dime." BPX asked the outsourcing provider to downsize the operation to keep pace with BP's reallocation of resources to other, more profitable oil fields.[6]

Evaluate the Model from the Outsourcing Partner's Point of View

Many executives have difficulty articulating even their own company's business model. To test the strength of any long-term partnership, they should consider the model from their partner's point of view. NS&I executives should put on Newport Systems hats, for example, and assess the value delivered to their stakeholders. Will this outsourcing arrangement meet the corporate parent's standards for return on investment over time? Will customers buy more from Newport Systems because they value this new capability more highly than what competitors can provide? By going through this analysis, both partners can identify foreseeable risks and evaluate the long-term viability of their joint model.

For example, NS&I's Peter Bareau surmised that Newport Systems's UK practice would experience some ups and downs in earnings as it worked to execute the aggressive transformational agenda. He concluded he should form a relationship with executives of the parent company to ensure that the UK practice would get the support it needed from above when these issues arose. Peter Bareau and his team reached this conclusion by thinking through Newport's stakeholders and business model as well as their own.

In retrospect, this kind of analysis seems like an obvious need. At the start of an outsourcing initiative, the need may not be so apparent. A few years back, for example, the central government of Australia decided to outsource its IT infrastructure using a unique, "cluster" approach. It created logical groups of government agencies that would be presumed to have similar IT needs—grouping social service agencies in one cluster and law enforcement agencies in another. Each cluster was mandated to outsource its IT infrastructure—mid-range hardware, desktops, help desk, and networks to a vendor that could reduce costs below the existing baseline. Some clusters issued requests for proposals while others were still organizing their information. The large, experienced vendors that bid on the earlier opportunities clearly factored two considerations into their "loss leader" prices. First, they intended to increase their revenue by charging for out-of-scope work. Second, by having an inside track, they would be more likely to win additional contracts with other clusters. Additionally, some less experienced vendors simply underestimated the costs they would experience.

With about half the cluster outsourcing deals completed, the Australian Parliament paused the mandate and commissioned an independent report on the situation. The Humphrey report[7] pointed out that the cluster approach had failed to generate the anticipated savings. Progress on the second agenda—economic development—did not outweigh the perceived reductions in IT support and service quality. As a result, the cluster outsourcing mandate was withdrawn. Agencies were still encouraged to outsource either singly or in groups, but the decision authority about exactly what, when, and how to outsource was left with agency executives.

There are two business-model implications in this story worth noting. When the government changed its outsourcing approach, the clusters that had outsourced early in the process still had ongoing contracts to manage. By withdrawing the mandate, the government instantly shifted the revenue calculus for those sophisticated vendors that hoped to get more business by being on the inside track. Almost immediately, these vendors began "whining and complaining," in the words of one government executive, that the deals were unprofitable and must be renegotiated. In some cases where executives had implemented careful change management to control extra charges for out-of-scope work, the vendors were particularly dissatisfied. One government executive charged that his cluster's vendor responded passive-aggressively with service delays and poor quality in an attempt to force the government to the bargaining table.

The situation in another cluster was equally debilitating. Its unsophisticated vendor underpriced the contract. As a result, it never provided enough equipment or staff to offer the level of service to which it had agreed. Its "anarchistic" processes did not enable it to diagnose service issues and implement appropriate responses. The result was a consistently poor record of service. The government executive who crafted this deal stated, "Constructing deals comes down to common sense in the end. If it doesn't seem right, then it's probably not right. If the price looks low, don't believe it. And if you do sign up for it, you can be sure you will have trouble later unless the outsourcer can convince you that they can provide the service and make a profit. A cheap deal is not a good deal unless it is sustainable. You get what you pay for."

I don't want to lay the blame for these nightmarish experiences at the feet of the government executives. Their outsourcing providers as well as their central government policy makers certainly had a share in the responsibility. However, the architects of this approach may have avoided some of the pain if they had taken the time to project the providers' business model as well as their own. They might have been able to anticipate the impact of withdrawing the opportunity for future business as well as the result of accepting a bid at an unsustainable cost.

Create Strategic Flexibility

By combining stakeholder analysis, scenario planning, and business-model design, organizations can give themselves strategic options through outsourcing. These can range from simple break points in the contract to well-defined growth opportunities that they intend to create with their partners.

For example, Thomas Cook characterized its transformation as "Fixing the old and creating the new." It recognized that its first order of business was to reset its cost structure in order to make operations profitable. As its outsourcing and other initiatives achieved these early milestones, the company would turn more of its attention to growth. To instantiate this agenda in its outsourcing relationship, Thomas Cook took several steps. It created a break point in the contract with its outsourcing provider after three years. At this point, the two organizations could part ways, renegotiate, or simply extend the contract. The company also promised to provide a million-pound ($1.66 million) bonus if its partner could reduce costs below an agreed baseline by that time. These two provisions ensured that the provider worked first on establishing a cost-reducing model that at least broke even by year three. It also made sure the Thomas Cook management stayed closely involved because they might soon get the operation right back.

The year-three break point also provided both parties a tangible hook for talking about successive phases of the model. Although the relationship is only in its second year, and both partners are clearly focused on getting systems in place, people transitioned effectively, operations settled down, and costs reduced, they are also starting to discuss future opportunities. These include moving the center to a low-wage-rate country to further improve costs or growing revenue by offering services to other companies. These changes would involve changes to the partnership's joint business model, and the contractual break point puts this kind of discussion on the table.

For transformational outsourcing to work, executives must manage it expertly—not just as they design the relationship but also as they continue to shape it over time. Most do not use the process I have outlined above to craft a business model and plan with their partner, but they should. To summarize, executives should:

- Prepare a stakeholder analysis to clarify the important stakeholder groups and their needs. This analysis provides the basis for framing the value propositions that are an essential component of business model design.
- Design alternative business models based on proposals from outsourcing providers, examples from other companies, and internal innovation.
- Project partners' models to ensure that they are commercially viable and sustainable.
- Use scenario planning to project business and regulatory changes. This should be a normal part of a company's strategic planning. For transfor-

mational outsourcing, you will want to join with one or two top-candidate partner companies, before finalizing your relationship, to think through the changes that are likely to affect both organizations.

• Evaluate alternative models and use your view of the future to stress-test their ability to deliver value to both parties over the long term.

Notes

1. I did much of my work on business models with Susan Cantrell. See "So What Is a Business Model Anyway?" Accenture Institute for Strategic Change research note, March 2000; "Changing Business Models: Surveying the Landscape," Accenture Institute for Strategic Change research report, May 2000; "Carved in Water: Changing Business Models Fluidly," Accenture Institute for Strategic Change research report, December 2000.

2. Jane Linder and Susan Cantrell, "Working Models," Accenture Institute for Strategic Change Research Note, January 2000.

3. See Peter Schwartz, *The Art of the Long View* (New York: Currency/Doubleday), 1991.

4. Jane Linder and Thomas J. Healy, "Outsourcing in Government: Pathways to Value," Accenture Government Executive Series Report, May 2003.

5. Jane Linder and Thomas J. Healy, "U.S. State and Local Outsourcing: Value in Leadership," Accenture Government Executive Series Report, July 2003.

6. Geoff Gibbs, "BP Axes 800 North Sea Contract Jobs," *The Guardian*, June 1, 2002, http://www.guardian.co.uk/recession/story/0,7369,725898, 00.html.

7. Richard Humphrey AO, "Review of the Whole of Government Information Technology Outsourcing Initiative," published by the government of Australia, December 2000, ISBN 0–642–74056–9.

PART III

Making Transformational Outsourcing Work

CHAPTER 6

Thomas Cook: Catalyzing Change

In April 2003, Stefan Pichler, CEO of Thomas Cook AG,* looked over the interim financial report from the UK and Ireland business with satisfaction. Despite savage shocks to the travel industry over the past two years, the organization he had bought was now turning in the kind of profit he had projected. He had supported the bold steps the Thomas Cook UK and Ireland leadership team advocated to transform the operation from a sleepy, fragmented operation to a successful player in the competitive UK travel industry. His international company had not only adopted the Thomas Cook name but also was watching its subsidiary's transformation program with increasing interest.

Manny Fontenla-Novoa, Thomas Cook's new CEO, was extremely gratified with the organization's accomplishments to date. It had taken out £140 million ($233 million) in costs over the past 20 months. He knew, however, that slimming down the cost structure was only the beginning of the journey. He considered how to achieve a second step-change in the organization's performance: a radical improvement in top-line growth.

---

*For simplicity's sake, I will refer to the parent company as "Thomas Cook AG," and the UK and Ireland subsidiary as "Thomas Cook" throughout the book.

Background

In early 2003, Thomas Cook, headquartered in Peterborough, UK, employed over 13,000 people and operated through a network of 650 travel shops. Wholly owned by Thomas Cook AG (formerly C&N Touristic AG), Thomas Cook was part of one of the world's largest travel groups (see Exhibit 6.1).

As well as having 650 Travel Shops and over 700 Bureaux de Change, the organization operated a tour-operations business that included brands such as Signature, Cultura, JMC, Sunset, Neilson, Club 18–30, Style Holidays, Sunworld Ireland, and an airline with a fleet of 24 aircraft— Thomas Cook Airlines. Thomas Cook also had one of the largest direct travel businesses in the country, taking bookings over the phone and tele-

Exhibit 6.1. Selected financial statistics.

Thomas Cook (€ Million)

	1998/1999	1999/2000	2000/2001	2001/2002
Consolidated Sales			2100.8	2702.4
Profit Contribution			87.2	46.3

Thomas Cook AG (€ Million)

	1998/1999*	1999/2000*	2000/2001	2001/2002
Consolidated Sales	4632.4	4980.5	7814.7	8062.6
Operating Income	105	117.3	86	(50)
Net Income	61.9	55.7	25.4	(122.8)
Goodwill as % of Shareholder Equity			131	150

*Originally reported in DM, converted to euros at 1.9558 DM per euro.

Source: Thomas Cook AG annual reports.

text. In addition, it boasted one of the leading Internet travel businesses and a television channel.

For decades, Thomas Cook Group had been used by a series of clever parent organizations in a variety of ways, from a source of cheap capital to a strategic foothold in the travel industry. From 1948 through the mid-1990s, as it was traded from team to team, it continued to buy up smaller UK companies in retail travel, package tour operations, and charter airlines (see Exhibit 6.2). In 1999, it was owned by Carlson Leisure Group (22 percent); Westdeutsche Landesbank (27.9 percent), Germany's third largest bank; and Preussag AG (50.1 percent), a German industrial and steel company that was in the process of converting itself into a travel operator.

By early 1999, Thomas Cook had been managed for 20 years by financiers. In addition to offering travel in the UK, Ireland, Canada, India, and Egypt, it also included a financial company that issued travelers checks and exchanged foreign currencies worldwide. The 162-year-old company's brand was widely known and well regarded, but its leadership had never seen the merits of integrating all the acquisitions they had made over the years. Alan Stewart, the chairman of the financial services side of the company at the time and chief financial officer of the group, recalled: "I pushed our shareholder company to take the decision to split the business into two halves. So we put a legal structure in place that allowed us to operate as two separate companies. When we pulled the travel business out from under financial services, we realized it was losing money."

The "battle for the beaches" reached fever pitch in 2000, when C&N Touristic AG, one of Germany's largest travel groups, made a bid for Thomson Travel, the UK's holiday travel market leader since 1974. Preussag stepped into the bidding, ultimately paying £1.8 billion ($2.995 billion) for Thomson. However, to get EU approval for the acquisition, Preussag agreed to sell its stake in Thomas Cook. In a complex deal, the financial services half of Thomas Cook was sold to Travelex for £440 million (732 million) and the travel half to C&N Touristic for £550 million ($915 million). According to Stefan Pichler, C&N's chief executive, "Preussag have paid DM 189 million [$432.5 million] per percentage point of UK market share [for Thomson]. We will pay DM 121 million [$276.9 million]. Preussag bought Thomson on a multiple of 17.5 times earnings. We will pay 12.5 times earnings."[1] The deal was final on

Exhibit 6.2. Thomas Cook (TC) key events, 2000–2002.

5/2000	- TC closes 38 high street shops because of overpenetration.
12/2000	- C&N Touristic AG buys Thomas Cook.
4/2001	- C&N Touristic purchase of Thomas Cook receives regulatory approval.
	- Alan Stewart named CEO.
5/2001	- Stewart informs C&N that Thomas Cook profits for the year will be poor.
6/2001	- C&N Touristic adopts the name of Thomas Cook AG.
	- TC initiates business transformation program.
8/2001	- TC unveils 5-year strategy, voluntary career breaks, shorter hours, and co-sourcing.
9/2001	- Terrorists attack World Trade Center.
	- TC announces significant organizational changes, relocation, massive cost cuts, redundancy programs, and Accenture as the co-sourcing vendor.
	- TC changes distribution mix to focus on selling its own products through its retail outlets.
	- TC records a £50 million loss.
11/2001	- TC launches Thomas Cook TV station.
	- Thomas Cook AG board approves co-sourcing arrangement with Accenture.
2/2002	- TC renegotiates tour operator and supplier contracts to improve costs.
3/2002	- Shared services center goes live.
	- TC transfers 500 people to Accenture.
	- TC outsources IT legacy maintenance to Syntel.
	- TC launches new tour operations brands to cover high, mid-range, and low end
5/2002	- TC launches new strategy with a focus on value innovation, customer centricity, operational excellence, and cultural change.
7/2002	- TC vacates London headquarters office.
	- TC launches Blue Sky, a brand for selling holidays direct to consumers
	- Thomas Cook AG rebrands the corporation.
10/2002	- TC reports a £30 million profit.
11/2002	- Accenture completes implementation of SAP financials in the shared services center.
	- TC transitions remaining distribution and tour operations financial staff to Accenture.
	- TC establishes service-level agreements for finance and IT.
	- TC reverses pay cuts and pays 10% bonus to all employees who participated.

Source: Personal conversations with Thomas Cook executives.

April 1, 2001. Within a few months, C&N Touristic had adopted a new corporate name, Thomas Cook AG.

Eating Their Own Dog Food

In his position as chairman of the financial services business, Alan Stewart had led the effort to sell both halves of Thomas Cook. The travel company's new owner immediately asked Alan to take over as the CEO of the UK and Ireland travel business with Ian Ailles, who became the group finance director. Stewart recalled: "We sold the business with projections of modest profit in the first year after the sale, with steep growth afterwards, resulting from the integration of the parts." Ailles continued: "Prior to April 1, Alan and I were intent on maximizing value for our previous parent. We were very much the sellers; we had pushed the price. Now we had to take on the responsibility of the buyer to make the company profitable. We knew it wasn't the gleaming machine we had sold. But we didn't really know how broken it was."

Thomas Cook had been built by acquisition, so the assorted pieces were not operating as an integrated business. For example, about 70 percent of the tours sold through Thomas Cook's 650 retail outlets were provided by other tour operators. The distribution division's managing director argued that his organization made a higher margin when it sold other companies' holidays and, as a result, the Thomas Cook tour operations division was losing money. In addition, the charter airline was struggling with on-time performance, which exacerbated its low yield factors. Further, the company was located in 23 physical office facilities spread all over the UK and Ireland (not counting the retail shops), including an expensive headquarters building in London's West End district. Its other supporting infrastructure, from its IT systems and information flows to its HR administration and financial organization, reflected a patchwork of disparate and disconnected processes. Ailles summarized: "The business was needlessly complex."

Undertaking Business Transformation

By May 2001, Stewart and his new leadership team realized the company's profit was going to be significantly worse than what he had projected when he sold the company. In July, he convened his team and the company's senior managers for a one-day "state of the company" meeting to get his people ready for what was to come. More than 300 managers arrived at headquarters expecting to hear the usual—that everything was fine. Instead, Stewart and his team promised to be truthful about the condition of the business. They announced that Thomas Cook was on track to lose £50 million ($83.2 million) that year. If it did, they said, it would not survive. They promised radical action.

Stewart believed that Thomas Cook's performance problems started with management. To get ready to take on the transformation, he made several changes to his executive team, including replacing the managing director of tour operations and its airline, bringing in a new HR director, promoting the communications director and legal director to members of the executive board, and establishing a new post, group business transformation director.

To create a plan for transformation, the leadership team began an intensive series of sessions during July and August, fondly called the "bunker" meetings because they took place in a dreary basement office near the London headquarters. Their goals were to reduce the company's cost base by £140 million ($233 million); to pull together its autonomous operations into a vertically integrated model; and to establish a clear brand strategy to drive sales growth.

Under the banner "Fixing the Old and Creating the New," the senior management team crafted a new five-year strategy for Thomas Cook, as well as a new organization and a plan for consolidating the company and streamlining the cost structure. They laid out an aggressive agenda that included establishing a new branding strategy, rolling out a new corporate identity, and making capacity reductions in tour operating, eliminating unprofitable flying routes, centralizing cost centers, and using strategic sourcing (see Exhibit 6.3).

They planned to announce the transformation program on September 16, 2001, but the terrorist bombing of New York City's World Trade Center on September 11, 2001, intervened. Stewart recounted: "It was a tragedy, but it didn't change anything we had to do. It only made our radical actions more imperative. It also helped us with the message. The whole industry was in turmoil, and our people recognized that we had to take dramatic steps."

Building One Company

In order to weld Thomas Cook UK's disparate operations into a streamlined, vertically integrated organization that acted like one company, the

Exhibit 6.3. Transformation agenda.

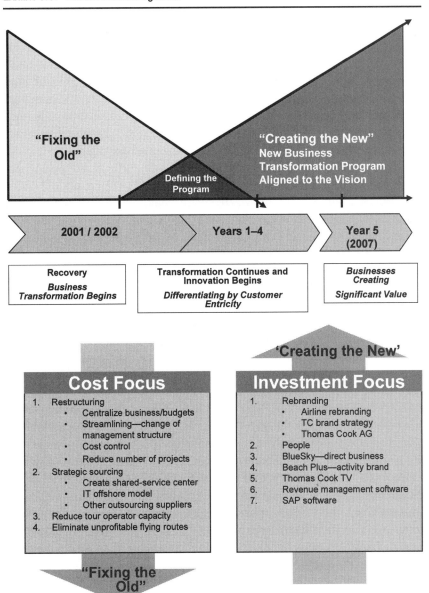

Source: Thomas Cook.

leadership team brought its three business units together under a single, global brand identity and drove aggressive operating changes in each.

The distribution business led by Andrew Windsor also dramatically shifted its business mix. It increased the proportion of Thomas Cook in-house vacations it sold from 30 to 60 percent of its sales. It also rationalized its channels, rebranding its larger "high street" shops, consolidating call centers, and adding both a new travel TV channel and a direct-to-consumer sales channel. To strengthen its sales focus, it eliminated administrative duties from the shops and created new incentive pay structures to reward associates for selling its own travel packages.

The airline business, renamed Thomas Cook Airlines, eliminated unprofitable routes and freed up six planes to be used in Thomas Cook AG's new Belgian flying program. Management collaborated with the parent's other flight operations to get economies on fuel, ground crews, airplane leases, and even foreign-currency hedging. In addition, they found entrepreneurial ways to use excess capacity to boost revenues. Finally, they substantially improved operational reliability and on-time performance, which reduced contingency costs and improved customer satisfaction.

In a market where overcapacity had always been an issue, Manny Fontenla-Novoa, then the managing director of tour operations, took the bold decision to reduce the number of vacation packages it would sell by 18 percent. Fontenla-Novoa said: "Reducing capacity also gave us an opportunity to take a good hard look at our product portfolio and eliminate many properties that didn't meet appropriate customer satisfaction levels." He also decided to move all of the tour operations functions based in South London to the Peterborough location. Fontenla-Novoa continued: "We had a very loyal and experienced team in London, but we knew if we wanted to act as a more vertically integrated business it would make more sense to have these people in Peterborough, together with the distribution business. It is a testament to their loyalty to the company that many of them chose to make the move." Management used an EVA framework to change the unit's focus from revenue to margin and yield. They consolidated customer contact and service teams, established three solid brands to segment the mass market, and invested in niche brands to increase market penetration. The intense customer focus paid off in increasing customer satisfaction and a return to profitability.

Unlike many large organizational change programs, the management team did not make communications an afterthought. "We wanted no leakage until the program was ready to go," explained Stewart, "but it was essential to have our communications director involved in the discussion from the outset." The director of public relations and communications planned a comprehensive campaign to build trust and loyalty through honest and open communications with employees throughout the transformation. She consolidated all the internal publications into a single, bimonthly newsletter that was distributed to all employees. She worked with Stewart to produce regular CEO updates—in print, in video, and face-to-face—so employees would feel informed amid the fast-paced change effort. She insisted that management share both the good news and the bad news with employees before they heard it from the press. She believed that the communications campaign not only improved loyalty among workers but also increased the feedback that management received about how plans were working.

Consolidation and Cosourcing

While the management team worked on improving business-unit operations, they knew that pulling the company together at the center and driving down administrative costs were also urgent. Stewart put all the major cost elements of the business under one individual—Marco Trecroce. His title was group business transformation director, and his first task was consolidation. "I told Alan that if he wanted to transform the business quickly, he would need me to own line responsibility for a number of cost areas and let the rest of the business focus on revenue growth and margin improvement while I worked on the costs. That should be my job," summarized Trecroce.

Trecroce identified and tracked 24 separate initiatives, including outsourcing ticket processing to Lufthansa, contracting with a company in India for IT legacy system maintenance, and outsourcing desktop management and mail distribution in the UK to a third company. One of the most significant activities was creating a shared services center for IT, finance, HR administration, and project management. Trecroce worked with consultants from Accenture, a major multinational consulting, technology, and outsourcing company, for several months to develop a solid business case for the initiative.

Cost reduction was important to Trecroce, but the shared services center had an even higher purpose. It would enable Thomas Cook to create a single administrative locus with a single set of information systems under the management of experts. This would deliver the culture change that Trecroce wanted and would enable Thomas Cook's own management to concentrate on selling vacations. Ian Ailles, the company's finance officer at the time, explained: "The finance consolidation was driven by geography. We had a finance team in Peterborough supporting the distribution business and one in London supporting the tour operator. We were closing that location. At the time we had four general ledger platforms and different charts of accounts. This was the ideal opportunity to get synergy and drive savings, and SAP was a key part of the answer." Trecoce added: "To begin to work like one company, we had to concentrate on the back office first."

After crafting the business case for the shared-services center, the senior team considered, then rejected, the option of implementing it internally. "You use a partner to give you the momentum of change," Ailles pointed out. "When you're doing it yourself, no matter how hard you try, no matter how many new people you hire, you will get slowed down by the treacle of the organization. Marco and I are the chemists. We needed to use a partner as the catalyst."

After an initial review of the capabilities of four outsourcing providers, Trecroce shortlisted two large multinational companies and issued a formal request for proposal. He opened up intensive discussions with these organizations citing four clear and equally important criteria for vendor selection:

- Speed to implementation
- Skills and expertise, in streamlining back-office systems and processes and beyond
- Ability to smooth the profit impact of the transformation
- Contract flexibility

With Accenture's fingerprints on the business case, however, the other shortlisted company had difficulty believing that the decision was not predetermined. "We were serious," Stewart said. "We would have chosen them. But in the end, they could not understand the financial flexibility and the reinvestment approach that we needed. Accenture did."

Thomas Cook chose Accenture as its partner in a "cosourcing arrangement" to build and operate the shared services center. They opted for cosourcing to emphasize that Thomas Cook would retain control over strategy, policy, investment, and procurement; and Accenture would focus on operational management. Stewart continued: "Cosourcing gives us the ability to generate savings over and above what we had expected, then choose whether to invest those savings through Accenture—like a bank account we can draw on—or to bank them ourselves through our P&L. This would be investment money that would not be in our budgets, but which we could control. It's a good way of running a business—it gives us some operating slack."

In negotiating the contract details, Thomas Cook and Accenture first agreed on a level of work as the baseline. Both parties recognized that significant year-one investments would be required to achieve the anticipated savings. These investments were projected to pay off with step-change decreases in costs in years two and three. Thomas Cook pressed hard for Accenture to take on the risk of achieving the benefits. Trecroce argued:

> At first, their concept of risk was pocket money. But if you only hand over the responsibility for running the back office to them, what is their incentive to get better? They have a high return on investment model, and they want more return, not less. So they want you to pay a high margin to them for providing a service, and that margin will not reduce in the future. So we had to develop a deal that transferred the responsibility for delivering benefits by making sure they have to take some of the financial pain if they don't produce the benefits.

The contract incorporated a £1 million ($1.66 million) bonus if Accenture was able to reduce operating costs below the baseline by the end of year three.

Alex Christou, the partner responsible for Accenture's European travel services practice and the Thomas Cook relationship, described the contract negotiation process as standing in the "middle of the hourglass." He had to construct a business case that would both appeal to the client and work for Accenture. He recalled: "Given Accenture's focus on EVA,[2] we had to find a way to reduce the huge capital needs of the deal without destroying its attractiveness to the client." To leverage the financial strength of both partners, Christou proposed an arrangement that would make the much-needed profit improvement to Thomas Cook immediate and sustained. In exchange, Thomas Cook would provide investment capital for the transformation program. It would also continue to own the IT and physical assets that would support its parent company's agenda to build purchasing power (see Exhibit 6.4). Christou explained:

> Accenture takes on all the legacy costs, and we are only able to re-cover the contract amount, as set out in the business case. That gives Accenture a first-year loss of, say, 30 percent of revenues. We have to draft Accenture experts into the center—that costs us anywhere between 10 and 30 percent of revenues. Then we have a cost for implementing the shared service center and SAP of 50 percent of year-one revenues. Before you know it, you're up to 90 percent in the red in the first year of the deal.

Exhibit 6.4. Outsourcing financial model.

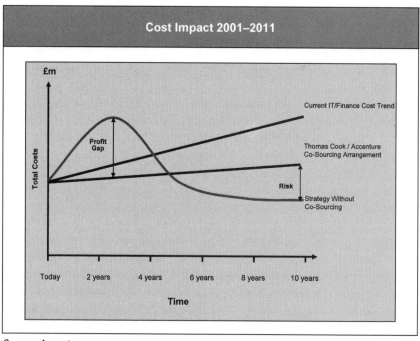

Source: Accenture.

In exploring options for the deal, it became apparent that Thomas Cook had ready access to capital just after the peak sales push for the summer vacation season. Christou continued: "Their access to capital was superior, so we suggested that they fund aspects of the transformation program." Thomas Cook was able to capitalize many of these costs to soften the short-term impact on the P&L. The net effect was an immediate and sustainable profit improvement for Thomas Cook and an acceptable capital performance for Accenture. "This was one of several examples," Christou recalled, "where open discussions helped us jointly shape the most commercially attractive deal for both parties." It also illustrated the new degrees of freedom offered by a partnering model in contrast to a traditional consulting fee-for-service arrangement.

In October 2001, Thomas Cook eliminated 570 positions, implemented a pay freeze, and announced a £50 million loss for the fiscal year. It also announced the cosourcing agreement with Accenture. The next step was to get approval from the board of Thomas Cook AG.

Thomas Cook's German parent questioned the merits of outsourcing. They were extremely concerned about a potential loss of control and with making a long-term commitment in a business environment that was rapidly changing. Stewart and Trecroce addressed the latter issue by including an official break point in the ten-year contract after three years. At that point, Thomas Cook could exit the deal: bring the operation back in-house, transfer it to another vendor, or consolidate it with the parent company's other European operations. With this provision and Alan Stewart's personal guarantee, the board ultimately agreed to co-source with Accenture in December 2001.

Managing the Transition

The shared services center was sited at the new Thomas Cook headquarters in Peterborough, 76.5 miles north of London. The plan for implementing it was aggressive (see Exhibit 6.5). In March 2002, five months after signing the contract, finance and payroll staff from distribution, as well as all IT staff from tour operations and distribution and some from airlines, were slated to transfer to Accenture. By November, SAP financial systems were to be implemented along with a new chart of accounts, and the finance staff from tour operations would be moved to the center. At the same time, the HR team was charged with harmonizing employment

Exhibit 6.5. Transformation program release plan.

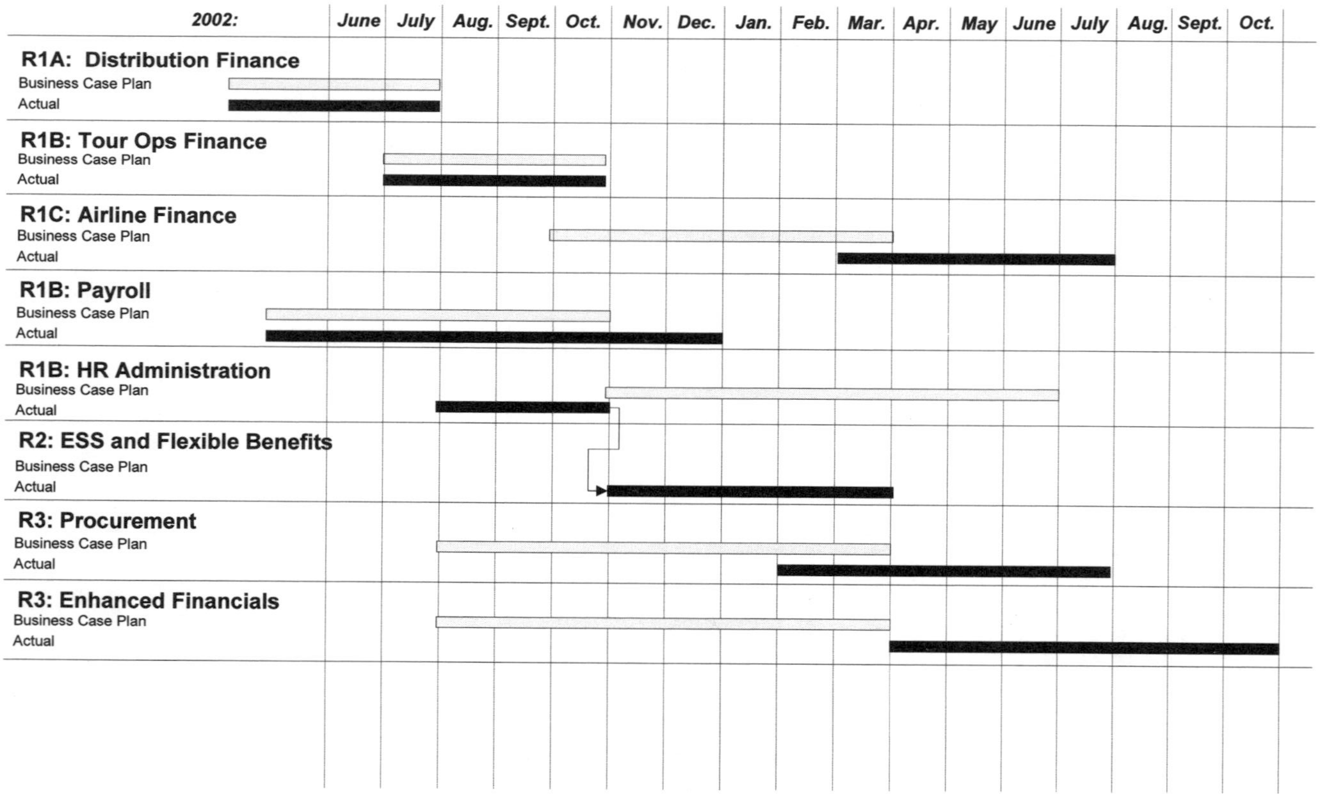

Source: Thomas Cook.

terms and conditions across the entire organization. The director of HR explained: "We had 86 different contracts and hundreds of different processes. The data was scattered everywhere. Even finding out where we were was tough."

Thomas Cook's senior team opted to hold off transferring HR administration until early 2003 to keep people-related processes intact during the other moves. The director recalled: "We were TUPEing[3] people across, we were dealing with the unions, and we were supporting the business through redundancies. We did not want HR going through a transition at the same time."

Time was of the essence, but implementation phasing was critical. Some steps could not be done simultaneously. For example, the center's organizational model and cross-functional systems had to be put in place before the tour operations finance people and processes could be transitioned to the new corporate standard. In addition, the tour-operations staff had to apply for their jobs in the center, which required a preestablished organizational structure with clear job descriptions.

Of course, some employees chose to leave the company rather than commute or move to Peterborough. In order to guarantee a smooth transition, the Accenture team had to master the details of Thomas Cook's financial processes so that the work could be transferred to Peterborough even if the employees were not. The uncertainty around exactly who would join the staff and who would not heightened the importance of broad and effective knowledge transfer. In some cases, employees' redundancy payments were explicitly contingent on transferring their knowledge effectively. Ultimately, 2,300 employees left Thomas Cook, 400 joined Accenture, and Accenture hired additional workers to bring the center up to speed.

Since Thomas Cook was experiencing pay freezes during this period, it asked Accenture to adopt the same policies for a time. One executive remarked: "We couldn't have people on the Accenture side getting jam while our retained staff got [only] butter. We agreed that we would coordinate our pay strategy, and when we lifted our freezes, Accenture would as well." Despite the fact that the center staff worked alongside their Thomas Cook colleagues in Peterborough and under similar terms and conditions, separation was emotionally difficult. Both Thomas Cook and Accenture took explicit steps to smooth the way.

Accenture convened the affected employees to introduce them to the company. The general manager of the center took the time to meet each individual personally during the transition. Thomas Cook mounted an extensive internal communications program to keep all the workers informed and to solicit their cooperation. Frequent, straight-talking updates from Alan Stewart were distributed to all employees during 2001 and 2002, including those in the shared services center. And the senior leadership team kept their ears to the ground to gauge the sentiment.

Communicating effectively required a delicate balance. On one hand, the leadership team believed they could be successful only if they shared both the good and the bad news openly with the workers. At the same time, they did not want the media reporting that Thomas Cook was in trouble because of the potential negative impact on consumers' perceptions. Yet the unions were actively using the pay cut issue to gain media attention and even got MPs involved. The HR director said: "We managed to gain the support of most of the workforce because people saw the huge transformation agenda and the savings measures we put in place; it wasn't just about cutting their pay. Over 79 percent of the employees participated in the voluntary pay reduction.[4] The decision was taken by the business not to include those employees earning slightly above the minimum wage. Some of those individuals even came to us and asked why they couldn't participate." The company implemented cuts on a sliding scale from 15 percent down to 2 percent, with the most senior executives taking the largest percentage to show their leadership and commitment.

Trecroce shaped the unique measurement approach he developed to calculate Accenture's bonus specifically to encourage the emphasis he wanted. The annual measurement schema had five interrelated elements: service levels, quality and standards, incremental improvement, cultural fit, and innovation (see Exhibit 6.6).

But Accenture's first biannual performance review was based solely on cultural fit. Service-level agreements were not established until November 2001, and financial penalties for any nonperformance were left out of the equation for the six-month transition period. Trecroce explained: "A smooth transition means no one drops the ball, and the work keeps getting processed. In reality it doesn't work that way. You have to be patient. Accenture is inheriting people who need to be retrained. There's a new organization, a new way of working, different rules. For example, they're not processing their usual accounts payable; it's accounts payable across the entire business. It is very challenging. If Ac-

Exhibit 6.6. Measurement approach.

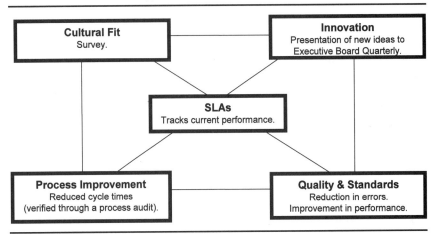

Source: Thomas Cook.

centure can get the people transferred over and make them feel wanted and get their heads around what the business needs, they're doing a good job. For the transition period, their bonus was based on how their internal customers rated them. Now that the center is established, we'll add the quantitative metrics in."

Thomas Cook and Accenture had a clear and consistent focus on partnership from the outset of the cosourcing arrangement, but they hit a few bumps in the relationship anyway. "At the beginning," one executive explained, "there was a lot of 'them and us.' From our point of view, we had done our TUPE; now it was Accenture's job to make things totally different. When it wasn't totally different from day one, we thought we needed to call them over and bang the table. We expected miracles. At the same time Accenture was learning. While they had project skills, that wasn't the problem. It was the day-to-day running of the co-sourced center, which was not their core skill." Over time, both sides learned the process of working together to make the joint operation successful. The executive continued: "We both had to learn not to act as different companies, but as a new company being formed together."

The Accenture team met unexpected difficulties coordinating effectively with the other outsourcing vendors working with Thomas Cook. During the complex and intense initiative to consolidate operations, replace financial systems, and implement HR self-service, Accenture had to work intimately with Syntel, the Indian company responsible for legacy systems maintenance; PinkRoccade, the desktop management company; and Fujitsu, the Web-hosting company. Despite the coordination costs, Trecroce insisted on a multivendor environment. "You always need to maintain an edge in your supply relationships," he maintained.

Making Progress

Trecroce summarized the transformation to date as an "£80 million [$133.1 million] turnaround in 20 months, reflecting the organization's progress from a £50 million [$83.2 million] loss in fiscal 2001 to a £30 million [$49.9 million] profit reported in October of 2002." Thomas Cook had exited 16 of 23 corporate locations, reduced unprofitable capacity, cut the number of vendors from 17,500 to 5,000, reduced the number of IT projects from 119 to 23, eliminated 2,300 positions that lowered payroll expenses by £43.5 million ($72.4 million), and cut discretionary spending by more than £87 million ($144.8 million). Strategic sourcing, including implementing the shared-services center and making property consolidations, netted another £19 million ($31.6 million) (see Exhibits 6.7 and 6.8). Thomas Cook had also returned salaries to their 2001 levels, repaid employees' lost pay, and added a 10 percent bonus on top for everyone who participated in the program. The senior management team congratulated the organization for delivering the level of profit they had originally promised Thomas Cook's German parent.

As important as the cost savings were, the dual benefits of consolidation and information transparency promised even more value. Ailles recounted: "Moving functions to a third party helped us consolidate. That got us process efficiency, which is important. But it also makes visible the costs and implications of decisions. This is a huge win. When you run the machine yourself, you paper over the cracks. But when you give it to a third party, it becomes quite visible when things are broken. This may lead you to make different decisions. For example, you may decide to stop offering a particular type of product because it costs so much to process that it is actually unprofitable. Before we co-sourced, business managers often didn't understand the cost implications of their actions. I

(text continues on page 130)

Exhibit 6.7. Transformation accomplishments and future plans.

Fixing the Old	Creating the New
The Airline Story	
▪ Aggressive focus, reduced costs £30m. - 4 airport bases and associated routes closed down. - Capacity reduction of over 15%. Freed 5 aircraft to establish TC Airlines Belgium. ▪ Contingency costs reduced from £7m (2000) to £2.6m (2002) by improving operational reliability and customer focus. ▪ Savings delivered through synergies between JMC Airlines and TC Airlines pan-European group. E.g.: Fuel purchase controlled centrally (£1.5m savings); renegotiation of aircraft leases. ▪ EVA has delivered a greater focus on Airline as a low-cost producer by removing the focus on profit for Airline only. ▪ Improved on time performance from all UK bases (August 2001 vs. August 2002). LGW 69.2% vs.74.6%; MAN 62% vs. 78%.	▪ Exploited opportunities to create centers of excellence and purchasing expertise across all TC Airlines. E.g. Fuel, foreign currency hedging, aircraft purchasing, ground handling agreements, engineering, uniforms—rebranding exercise. ▪ Integrated two new A330-200 series into Airline and won a section of Hajj contract against intense competition. ▪ Proactively chased Ad hoc and Subcharter work delivering opportunities for some £2.3m additional profit. ▪ Focus on full utilization of existing contracts generating an additional £2m from excess baggage, cargo, and pre-flight sales.
The Distribution Story	
1. More Effective Channel Management - Location strategy for branch network based on convenience and footfall. - Segmentation of branch network into 4–5 shop types based on primary customer segments. - Creation of competency and output-based pay scheme for sales staff. - Eliminate nonsales activities in branches, e.g. ticketing. - Focus on improved product knowledge through training and incentives. - Launch of TC TV. **2. Increased Vertical Integration** - Increased communication between Distribution and Tour Operations through colocation in Peterborough. - Sales of in-house products increased from under 30% to over 60% through increased in-house product knowledge and incentives. **3. Other Activities** - Rebranding of branch network. - Launch of Thomas Cook Credit Card (in association with MBNA)—200,000 customers to date.	**New Branch Property Strategy** - New focus on convenience and mall-location (away from small declining towns towards big mall–locations). - Closed 24 shops and opened two new format stores. **Segmenting the Shop Network** - Development of 4–5 shop types for different customer segments. **New Competency and Output-Based Pay Scheme for Branches and Contact Centers** - Sales consultants to be incentivized by level of product knowledge as well as sales volumes. **Change of the travel consultants workload** - Removed administrative tasks from branches and contact centers. - Centralized ticketing operation. - Made 60 administrators redundant. **Improving staff's product knowledge** - Introduction of new training courses. - Incentives to sell and to learn (e.g. new pay scheme). - Incentives to travel through staff discounts on holidays. **Thomas Cook TV** - Launched December 2001. - Expanded to NTL in September 2002. - Sales triggered reached £2.2m in August 2002.

(continues)

Exhibit 6.7. (Continued).

Fixing the Old	Creating the New
The Tour Operations Story	
▪ Appointment of a new management team in November 2001. ▪ Increased profit focus helped to recover from a £29m loss in FY 2000/2001 to a predicted profit of £0.5m profit in FY 2001/2002. ▪ Relocation and consolidation of Tour Operations team to Peterborough/Bradford and Brighton. ▪ Full capacity and product review using an EVA framework. ▪ Trading and operational management shifted focus to margin and yield—ensuring problem stock and routes were the focus of tactical promotions.	▪ Embedding revenue management principles and processes. ▪ Developing reciprocal strategic alliances with third parties. ▪ More detailed targeting of consumer offers on problem stock/routes/dates. ▪ Capacity management to meet seasonal and regional demand. ▪ Decision-making process created on vertical integration basis in combination with EVA principles. ▪ Launch of 3 brands (Thomas Cook, JMC, Sunset) based on customer-centric methodology focusing on customer delivery. ▪ Customer contact and service centralized under Tour Operations.
The Finance Story	
Organization and Culture Changes ▪ Total change of senior management within Finance (top 10%). ▪ Cost control focus. ▪ Move to predictive integrated management information. ▪ Elimination of non-value-added reporting. **Greater Market Focus** ▪ Benchmarked the processes to market. ▪ Early adoption of new accounting policies. ▪ EVA development and implementation. ▪ Support for business strategy development.	▪ Colocation of finance personnel from each Business Unit (in Peterborough). ▪ Co-sourcing of Finance to Accenture and set-up of UK Shared-Service Center. ▪ Outsourcing of internal audit. ▪ Implementation of SAP for Finance, Accounting & Payroll. ▪ Reduction in number of reporting levels within Finance. ▪ Head count reduction within Finance of 35%. ▪ Improved cash management.
The HR Story	

Culture Change
▪ HR acting as a commercial strategist and business partner.
  - Replaced two out of three divisional HR directors to bring new skills to the business.
▪ Supported transformation from a devolved to a vertically integrated company.
  - Move to Peterborough.
  - Consolidation of locations.
Cost Reduction
▪ Managed the process of streamlining the business.
  - 18% of workforce left the organization.
  - 40% of management left the organization.
▪ Reduced cost base within HR by 20%.
	HR Administration Functions to Be Transferred to Shared-Service Center
	  - Cuts down administration burden of department and allows focus on more strategic initiatives.
	  - Transition to begin February-April 2003.
	Succession Planning/Management Development.
	  - Examined management development needs and potential successors for top 50 management positions.
	  - Discovered need to develop leadership skills.
	  - HR will start implementing management development activities once restructuring is complete.
	Implementation of SAP—HR Module.
	  - Management and employee self-service (for Center, Distribution and Tour Operations from February 2003).
	  - Supplies companywide management information for the first time and thus allows for better management.
	Introduction of flexible 'flex' benefits to give employees ownership of and flexibility over their own benefits
	  - Focus on individual choice.
	  - Improves retention and recruiting.
	  - Tour Operations and Distribution by April 2002 (8,000 employees).

Source: Thomas Cook.

Exhibit 6.8. Transformation benefits to date.

- **Consolidation**—13 out of 22 offices and five airline bases were closed and the staff were relocated.
  - ➤ **Reduced costs by £5.4m.**

- **Centralization**—business functions centralized along with operating budgets.
  - ➤ **Reduced number of projects from 119 to 23.**

- **Streamlining**—Streamlined senior management, took voluntary and compulsory redundancies, and introduced pay cuts.
  - ➤ **Reduced payroll expenses by £43.5m.**

- **Cost Control**—Discretionary spend was reduced for marketing; procurement was centralized and contracts were renegotiated.
  - ➤ **Earnings related**   £52.9m
  - ➤ **Marketing**   £18.1m
  - ➤ **IT Costs**   £7.5m
  - ➤ **Procurement**   £3.5m
  - ➤ **Other**   £5.3m
  - ➤ Total   £87.3m

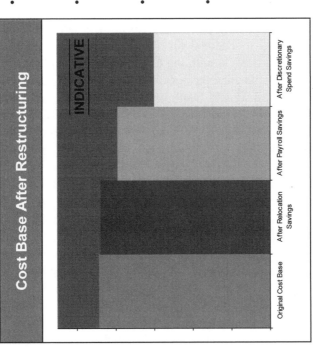

Cost Base After Restructuring

INDICATIVE

Original Cost Base | After Relocation Savings | After Payroll Savings | After Discretionary Spend Savings

Source: Thomas Cook.

knew this capability would be valuable, but I had no idea how powerful it could be."

Trecroce emphasized the importance of meeting the deadlines set for the shared-services initiative. "From the time we transferred the people, until ten months later, we hit our dates. As a result our credibility both inside Thomas Cook and with our parent has shot up." The CEO of Thomas Cook AG was so impressed with the UK and Ireland transformation that he outlined a similar agenda for the rest of the company, including outsourcing.

Creating the New

In pulling off the financial turnaround, the senior executives at Thomas Cook recognized that they had gotten only partway through their transformational agenda. They had set the stage. Some said they had accomplished the easy part. What remained was to chart a strategic course that would catapult the organization from third place in its industry to the top (see Exhibit 6.9). Fontenla-Novoa described the organization's vision and spirit: "We intend to become the leading vertically integrated leisure travel company in the UK with the lowest cost base and the highest customer satisfaction. We have gained confidence as an organization over the past 18 months, and we will continue to experience further change as the organization progresses toward meeting its strategic goals."

The organization launched several new initiatives to stimulate innovation. The team brought in an expert on value innovation from INSEAD, a leading European business school. She helped them brainstorm new opportunities to move into specialty businesses and to find new market spaces in an attempt to shift away from a me-too strategy.

Additionally, in the contract with Accenture, Trecroce had included an innovation requirement. Part of Accenture's bonus depended on making a quarterly presentation to the executive team on breakthrough ideas. Trecroce and Christou were in discussions about the potential to turn the shared-services center into a revenue-generating operation. They were also toying with the idea of using Accenture's patented Web-based simulation software to improve the sales effectiveness of its 10,000 retail and call-center staff. The senior team believed this could dramatically im-

Exhibit 6.9. Thomas Cook 2003 strategy.

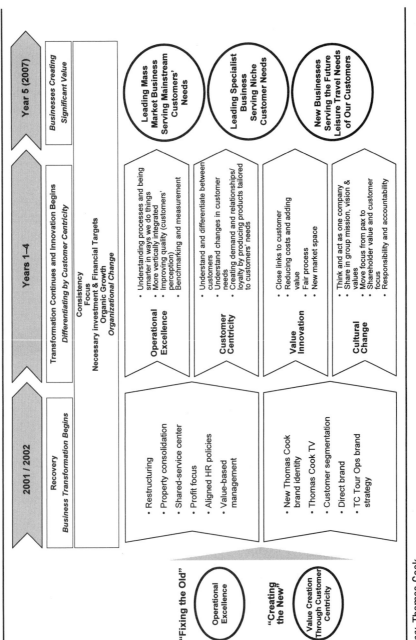

Source: Thomas Cook.

prove the company's customer focus. Accenture had already helped Thomas Cook expand its corporate portal to improve its ability to communicate its one-company mission, vision, and values throughout the company. Finally, Trecroce had recently attended an Accenture review of new technologies and was mulling over the possibilities of using radio frequency identification (RFID) tags to improve luggage handling. While Trecroce was pleased with the activity, he wanted to see more initiative from Accenture on innovation. "Perhaps I should have given them more leeway," he mused. "They have blinkers on around the business case, so they may not be able to see the forest."

Thomas Cook faced other challenges in addition to achieving the business case. Fontenla-Novoa ticked off the organization's priorities going forward:

> We need to deliver the results we set out to achieve in our business plan. That means we have to be aggressive with our cost base and aggressive with our suppliers. We have to talk to our customers and make sure we are delivering everything they expect from us and more. We need to continue to meet our financial performance targets. We need to continue to invest in our people. And finally, we need to further develop our road map for the future. We said we want to achieve 30 percent of our profits from the specialist businesses in the future. How are we actually going to do that?

Although Thomas Cook was in the early days of establishing joint planning processes with Accenture, Trecroce reflected on the role of the cosourcing arrangement in creating the organization's future: "I am quite confident that the relationship with Accenture will stay in place for ten years. But it will reinvent itself several times in increments of three or four years."

*   *   *

The reason I wanted to share this story was to communicate the complexity and management challenges that executives take on when they decide to use an outsourcing initiative to support transformation. Let me just point out a few highlights that I think we can take away from the Thomas Cook example:

- *Control.* In a business-critical situation, the management team believed they got more control, not less from outsourcing. What they really got was less direct say over worker tasks and more managerial control over decisions and cost structure.

- *Transition.* The first 18 to 24 months of the cosourcing required high-intensity management. This was not a handoff; it was a hands-on experience.
- *Process Understanding.* The transition process and the effort to design metrics drove Thomas Cook management's understanding of the way the company worked to a level of detail that the senior leadership had never had before. This understanding positioned them to make sound decisions about strategic execution.
- *Financial Flexibility.* By working with Accenture, the UK business unit found financial flexibility that an operating unit does not usually have. It has off-budget funds, which give it more latitude for innovation and experimentation.
- *Future View.* Thomas Cook leaders held fast to their long-term and whole-of-business perspective. It's easy to lose this in the press of a financial turnaround. They did not.

Notes

1. Dominic O'Connell, "Proposed Takeover Would Put German Firms Ahead in European Holiday Industry," *Sunday Business*, December 24, 2000.

2. Economic Value Added, a concept that measures company performance by the returns it is able to generate that exceed its weighted average cost of capital for the capital employed.

3. TUPE stands for Transfer of Undertaking (Protection of Employment). It is the UK law that ensures individuals retain their employment terms and conditions when their organization transfers them to another company.

4. By law, any pay reduction must be voluntary. Thomas Cook proposed the percentage reductions it would ask employees to accept at each salary level, then suggested that individuals contact HR if they felt they could not.

CHAPTER 7

End-to-End Performance Management

According to a recent survey, 24 percent of executives intend to use outsourcing to achieve significant changes in their organization, but they also hold a healthy skepticism about whether it will work.[1] Excellent strategy and business-model design must be matched with superb execution for a company to achieve its objectives. Chapter 6 offered a case study of how one company did just that. In this chapter, I talk about three important components of great end-to-end execution: metrics and incentives, strategic governance, and communications processes for sustaining a high-commitment relationship.

High-Stakes Outsourcing Introduces Performance Management Problems

An old business adage states that good managers match accountability with control. To get good performance, at least according to this old saw, managers just identify clear goals, establish consequences for good and bad performance, then follow up systematically. With conventional outsourcing, this works just fine. It does not represent the whole management picture, but it covers a good part of the terrain. An experienced company can easily establish a performance baseline, clearly articulate the cost savings and service levels they want, and anticipate the journey in between. Since the vendor oversees a discrete activity, accountability and control are neatly matched.

But transformational outsourcing relationships aren't so simple. As executives target complex, mission-critical process change through outsourcing, they face a host of new execution challenges (see Exhibit 7.1). First, they don't have mastery over the outsourced process at the start. Some companies have only a tenuous grasp on the functions and processes they intend to outsource, as these sprawl across departments, units, and geographies. Simply establishing a baseline can take months.

Business-process dependencies complicate matters. In more invasive outsourcing relationships, the vendor's domain isn't a discrete and independent component of the organization. The outsourced operation links to other business processes in rich and interdependent ways. For example, a large UK equipment manufacturer outsourced both its IT function and some business-process improvements in two separate contracts. When the

Exhibit 7.1. Transformational outsourcing requires a more sophisticated relationship.

	Conventional	Transformational
Approach	**Contractual:** Motivate outsourcer to hit specific, measurable output targets.	**Committed:** Do what it takes to achieve dramatic improvements in enterprise-level outcomes.
Purpose	To get what you ask for	To get what you need
Example Incentives	• Cash bonus for hitting target • Penalty payment for underperforming	• Share of new business venture • Showcase operation that builds provider's reputation
Example Metrics	• System availability • Cost reduction target	• Revenue • Earnings per share
Key Governance Mechanisms	• Contract • Regular operating review for evaluation	• Jointly developed strategic agenda • CEO-level collaboration • Regular board review
Benefit	Achieve competitive parity in activities that have little upside value.	Achieve enterprise-level outcomes.

business-process improvement team recommended changes to the engineering work flow, it affected the IT outsourcer's CAD operation as well as the company's product developers. As one provider succeeded at its mission, it caused the performance of the other one to slip.

The need for flexibility also interferes with simple performance-management approaches. Holding a provider accountable for meeting operational-level service agreements, for example, might get a company the transactional performance it asks for. But the right performance goals will help focus the outsourcing provider on doing what the company needs. This means that partners must have a way to change the targets when that is what the business calls for.

After defining a viable joint business model, executives must develop end-to-end performance management that supports capable execution. This framework of metrics, incentives, governance, and communication must help them keep their strategic purpose in the center of the crosshairs. It must incorporate the ability to shift gears when necessary. And it must tap the wellsprings of commitment that any organization needs to drive real, lasting change.

In this chapter, I discuss the overall performance-management framework for transformational outsourcing. Chapters 8, 9, and 10 address the management of transitions for people, leveraging capabilities, and endings and renewals, respectively. Again, I will focus on issues that are particularly important for transformation.

Metrics

Executives normally use metrics and incentives as a mechanism for establishing accountability and control. Whether they are working with people inside their own organization or with outside partners, they use metrics to focus behavior and incentives to motivate it. But transformational outsourcing presents a unique challenge. The more far-reaching and ambitious the outsourcing agenda is, the more blurred the lines of accountability and control become (see Exhibit 7.2). For well-behaved operations, control remains important, but strategic partnering requires more. Because of its bet-the-ranch character, transformational outsourcing needs commitment.

Exhibit 7.2. In transformational outsourcing, accountability doesn't match control.

At the senior level of the organization, this means relaxing the tight linkage between accountability and control. Executives go beyond best practices to use metrics and incentives to keep their interests tightly aligned and to support deep, continuing commitment on both sides. They establish new metrics to complement their operational ones, craft a compelling set of incentives, and use lower-level metrics in an entirely new way. Executives who operate at this cutting edge have loosened their white-knuckle grip on control and use metrics and incentives to foster commitment.

New Metrics for Transformational Outsourcing

Although a recent survey conducted by the Economist Intelligence Unit reveals that an astounding 82 percent of the respondents do not measure their outsourcing provider's performance regularly, effective outsourcers recognize the importance of setting targets and measuring progress against them. For the high-stakes game of transformation, this practice is even more critical.

When the goal is business transformation, the ultimate metric is how much value is created. To capture their strategic aspirations, organizations measure enterprise-level outcomes. For example, Archer Financial Group (not its real name), a global financial services company, set its sights on doubling its operating margins and stock price through transformational outsourcing. The Spanish bank that changed from a small mortgage lender to a full-service bank counted assets under management. Family Christian Stores went after revenue growth. Thomas Cook tracked profitability.

Leaders focus on outcome metrics where possible (see Exhibit 7.3). Outcome metrics show up on the bottom line. They make up the externally relevant results that drive transformation in the first place, such as market share, profitability compared to others in the industry, stock price, and so forth.

However, it can take months or years for good performance to show up in outcome measures. In this case, output metrics make good proxies.

Exhibit 7.3. Examples of different types of metrics.

Type of Metric	Examples
Input	• Hours of labor per transaction • Skill levels of people on staff • Payroll cost • Customer inquiries received
Output	• Number of transactions completed per labor hour • Percentage of deadlines met • Number of customer inquiries addressed per day • Number of new products implemented
Outcome	• Percentage of customers retained per year • Sales of new products • Win/loss record • Profit per customer • Market share

Instead of counting how many hours it took to complete each order, a photographic company asked its outsourcer to count how many orders it completed each hour. This small change in the way they kept score helped focus the vendor on speeding up throughput. Similarly, Family Christian Stores stopped tracking the uptime of store computer systems, and instead looked at whether or not its provider delivered the weekly replenishment orders to stores by 8 a.m. every Monday morning.

When executives move from outcomes to outputs, however, they must explicitly lay out their assumptions. There is no room for faulty logic here. The story of a poorly performing financial services company will illustrate. If you ask this company what drives good performance, executives will tell you it is having the right people and the right culture. (This is actually an input measure, but the point is still valid.) They go on to explain the ways they attract good people and create a culture that enables good performance. But if you look at their results, it turns out that this company underperforms others in its industry (see Exhibit 7.4).[2] In other words, their logic about what creates good performance doesn't work. Since they haven't tested their assumptions, they don't even know where the flaws are. So executives that use input or output measures as proxies

Exhibit 7.4. Financial services firm underperforms its competition.

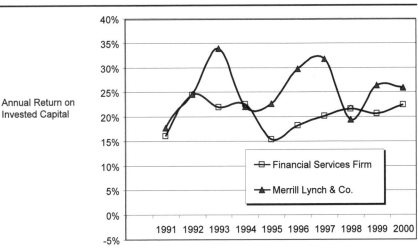

Source: Jane Linder and Brian McCarthy, "When Good Management Shows: Creating Value in an Uncertain Economy," Accenture Institute for Strategic Change management report, September 2002, p. 7.

for outcomes should take the additional step of validating their performance logic.

In some circumstances, however, even outputs may defy clear measurement. In these cases, executives evaluate critical inputs. For example, the success of Thomas Cook's transition from dispersed financial outposts to a compact, streamlined shared service center depended utterly on the operational leadership and competence of the individual its provider placed in charge of the initiative. The Thomas Cook team looked very carefully at this person's credentials and prior track record—input qualifications—before agreeing to proceed. On an ongoing basis, they carefully review their provider's personnel decisions for pivotal positions in the center. If there were a hiring or promotion error in one of these slots, it would eventually show up in output and outcome measures, and it would be remedied. By evaluating key people up front, however, Thomas Cook prevents these problems rather than taking the time to solve them later.

In addition to enterprise outcomes, these organizations track metrics that reflect progress on the essential process of deep organizational change. Executives recognize that successful transformation hinges on building and sustaining forward momentum. To keep this factor front and center, they measure speed. For example, the Thomas Cook team keeps a close watch on whether the provider's projects are meeting milestone dates. Slippage endangers the benefits flow, but more important, it calls the credibility of the entire transformation program into question. In Thomas Cook's case, the parent organization had concerns about the wisdom of cosourcing in the first place, and the affected employees were reluctant to move from an organization with which they identified strongly. If executives had allowed the momentum of the transformation to flag, the countervailing forces would have gathered strength.

Tom Boardman, the CIO of San Diego County, California, during its late 1990s stem-to-stern overhaul, reiterates the importance of managing momentum. "Time is the enemy," he states. "You want to go fast. If you go slowly, the people against you have more time to get organized. It took us less than a year from RFP to contract, then we gave our provider only three months to get operations settled down."

The San Diego County case also brings us back to the stakeholder analysis we reviewed in Chapter 5. Using that analysis, we have a good idea what our critical stakeholders want from the transformational initiative. Executives should establish metrics that provide evidence of visible progress to each important group. This approach keeps all the important constituencies on the supportive side of the ledger. Boardman cites this as an issue in the San Diego County story. Their initiative included outsourcing all information-technology infrastructure, including mainframe, mid-range, and desktop computers; help desk and break/fix services; telephones and networks; Web hosting; and core applications like e-mail and back-office systems. By reducing the cost and improving the reliability of its IT foundations, the county government reasoned it could begin allocating resources to appealing new Web-based services under the compelling banners "On Line, Not in Line" and "No Wrong Door." These spelled out the intention to have constituents doing everyday business with the government over the Internet instead of standing in line and to have every government office act as an entry point to the entire portfolio of county services.

Although the IT infrastructure outsourcing hit a few bumps, it delivered the intended cost and reliability benefits by the end of the first year of the contract. Boardman reflects that this accomplishment was substantial, yet did not help them create all the momentum they needed. At the end of that high-intensity year, he stated: "We deliberately decided to fix the infrastructure and the back-office systems first to get the savings. But, at this instant, we don't look good because there's nothing but infrastructure to show for our efforts. The citizens can't see anything. It takes more energy and more air cover than it should to keep going."

Use Metrics to Counteract the "Miracles Syndrome"

Metrics help communicate executives' objectives and expectations. If the outsourcing partners have any lingering misunderstandings about what they are trying to accomplish, this process dispels them. And it also helps set clear expectations for the initiative broadly throughout the organization. This helps executives counteract what I call the "miracles syndrome." An organization that could not manage an initiative on its own expects miracles when it pays another company to do it. This syndrome infects many outsourcing relationships, but it is more prevalent and more malicious in high-intensity activities. Why? Because the company lacks the expertise even to appreciate, let alone to surmount, the management challenges their initiative requires. And since they are paying for the service—and they feel entitled to expect performance—they naturally find themselves in the world of unrealistic expectations.

In order to overcome this debilitating syndrome, executives take the time to understand their partner's task plans, staffing levels, and deadlines in excruciating detail as a precursor to setting performance metrics. The purpose is not for the company to manage outsourced activities at a task level, but to gain an intimate grasp of the work. That way, they will be able to use interim performance results interactively to diagnose issues with their partner, rather than as a blunt instrument for reward and punishment.

Use Detailed Metrics to Build Trust, Then Simplify for Focus

For complex operations, executives start off with detailed metrics, then simplify measurement as they build trust. By working out detailed service-level agreements at the outset, they tee up critical discussions about roles, responsibilities, process interfaces, and expectations. Then they narrow the number of discrete metrics they track over time and move toward measures with broader impact in order to minimize administrative demands and raise their focus. The first to go are metrics that proved too difficult and time-consuming to measure. After several attempts, the senior vice-president of procurement at a UK transportation equipment company removed engineering efficiency from his outsourcer's list of target metrics for business-process improvement. It simply proved impossible to quantify the result.

As Thomas Cook gained traction with its shared-services center, it shifted from measuring a cornucopia of service elements in the finance process to a few overarching factors. According to Neil Hammond, Thomas Cook's director of strategic sourcing and IT efficiency, "Working out our service-level agreement for the finance and accounting process became the mechanism for defining the responsibilities. We ended up with too much detail at first, but that was a necessary part of the evolutionary process." As the operation was changing hands and being consolidated, the detail was important. It provided a structure for the two organizations to talk through the issues about who had responsibility and where the handoffs would take place. After watching the detailed metrics together for four months, the partners developed a solid understanding of the enacted process.

After the detail did its job, the obvious next step was to simplify. The two organizations identified and focused on six to ten key outputs. These included producing accurate and timely monthly financial statements, paying suppliers on time, and managing accounts receivable. "There is a great deal of activity underneath an outcome like getting the balance sheet right," Hammond continued. "For that to happen, a whole chain of events and processes has to work." Thomas Cook would never have gotten to the right level of understanding and effectiveness by aiming for the high-level targets at the outset. At that point, the measures were too abstract. First, both sides had to get comfortable that the details were under control.

Use Metrics to Take a Reality Check

Transformational outsourcing leaders, then, use new metrics to track enterprise outcomes and to sustain momentum for the people carrying out the initiative and the critical outside stakeholders. They also use new metrics to manage the boundaries of the transformation.[3] In other words, at least once a year they take a step back from what they are doing to take a reality check. They ask themselves the painful question, "Is this difficult thing we're doing still a good idea?"

For example, after years of outsourcing to cut costs, a global telecommunications service company we'll call GiantTel launched a bold new agenda. It partnered with a large telecom equipment company to transform its entire business. In a $1.4 billion, ten-year initiative, GiantTel outsourced its world-class, circuit-switched voice operations to InfraCom (not its real name) and additionally signed up the telecommunications equipment company to build the infrastructure powering GiantTel's new strategy: It sought a wholesale migration to Internet Protocol (IP) transmission services. GiantTel recognized that managing a transformational agenda required a deep, committed relationship—and the metrics and incentives to support it. The partners rolled up their sleeves and spent months envisioning their future and the potential paths to success. They developed an aggressive plan and a set of metrics to gauge their progress toward the ultimate goal: generating wholly new revenue streams from IP offerings. In addition, they set up an annual "early warning system" to take a cold-eyed look at the market and the competition. This approach enabled GiantTel to adjust direction if the assumptions underpinning its strategy came unwound.

Enterprise-level targets, indicators of momentum, and reality checks are important new measures of transformational outsourcing success. Leaders of these initiatives also use more traditional, lower-level metrics. However, they use these not to hit threshold goals, as conventional outsourcers do, but to communicate expectations, build trust, and drive continuing progress.

Conventional Metrics Motivate Continuing Progress

Supporting a transformational outsourcing initiative requires more than new metrics. Partners must also use conventional measures, but they use these in a way that is tailored to the objective of transformation. Importantly, the focus changes from hitting baseline targets to turning in the best possible performance. While many companies set stretch targets as well as minimum service levels in outsourcing deals, stretch goals take center stage in a transformational-outsourcing initiative. "Metrics tell you where to look to make things better," says a veteran business process outsourcer. "We don't treat them like positives or negatives; we treat them like information."

Transforming companies do continue to target basic service levels, but they hand off the responsibility for tracking these operational statistics to the outsourcing vendor itself. As part of taking on one telecommunications company's legacy voice operations, the outsourcing provider collects detailed statistics in areas like customer satisfaction and dropped calls, assesses its own performance relative to targets, and reports failures and its plans for improvement to its partner. This structure gives operational metrics just the right emphasis—worth measuring, but not the central focus of executives' attention. It also underscores the trust that this kind of relationship entails. One relationship manager explained, "People often ask me how I can let [my provider] report the performance statistics to us. What if they omit an error or lie about the data? Well, they report every single failure to me. If they didn't, the relationship would be devastated. I know they wouldn't do anything to spoil the trust we have."

Transforming executives are less interested in reaching some kind of operational steady state than they are in making continuing—even step-change—progress. A quick review of Thomas Cook's balanced score-card[4] shows this clear emphasis (see Exhibit 7.5). Executives take quarterly readings on these metrics to measure the provider's overall performance. It has five components: service levels, process improvement, improvement in quality and standards, the provider's cultural fit, and innovation. Only one of these factors is a conventional "state" measure—service level. Cultural fit sets a boundary condition for Thomas Cook's provider. The outsourcing partner must be listening to business needs and responding collaboratively in the eyes of key process clients to score well on this metric. If this is not true, executives reason, it is a major obstacle to the high-performance partnership they want. The other three factors on the scorecard are not states, but rather "rates" of improvement. A Thomas Cook executive explains: "Service levels are almost a given. We expect our provider to meet them. We use the other metrics to make sure we are making progress on the transformational agenda."

Companies that transform through outsourcing often use conventional metrics to diagnose issues and opportunities in their provider's processes. Leaders also apply companion measures to their own side of the house. The most sophisticated organizations take a relationship physical each year that assesses how both partners are contributing to success. Why?

Exhibit 7.5. Thomas Cook measurement approach.

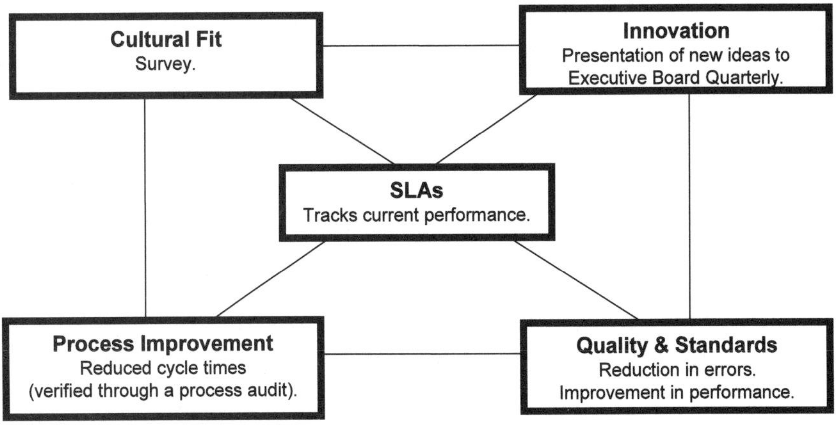

Source: Thomas Cook.

Frequently, the performance of the retained processes has a significant impact on the outsourcing provider's ability to work effectively. For example, NS&I retained new product design, but outsourced development and operations. By designing a complex product that was difficult to administer, NS&I could inadvertently sabotage its provider's ability to improve costs. The two organizations quickly learned to involve people from development and operations in the early product design discussions to head off these problems.

Results-oriented executives keep an external, competitive edge on their metrics through benchmarking with other organizations. By monitoring the external landscape, they learn how their own operation measures up to those of the leaders in the field and how to take advantage of innovations that others have pioneered. Peter Bareau of NS&I comments: "One fascinating thing we did was to benchmark retail debt financing around the world. We formed a 'club' with the US, UK, Canada, Ireland, and others to keep a broad perspective on what good performance looked like."

Benchmarking is not the only way these organizations stay tuned to the state of the practice. Many executives take regular field trips to other public- and private-sector operations to share insights and practices. They also welcome outside visitors in the same spirit.

Incentives

Transformational outsourcing requires that executives set new metrics and use conventional metrics in new ways. It also demands a specialized approach to incentives. The bonuses and penalties that often accompany conventional outsourcing have a role to play, but they take a different shape. Money should not change hands for hitting—or missing—everyday service levels and project milestones. That would distract both sides from the larger agenda. What some organizations do instead is simply share the revenue that results when they are successful. For example, a heavy equipment manufacturer has strategic partnerships with a few companies that provide critical subassemblies for its products. Instead of paying for these subassemblies as pieces, the company gives its partner an agreed-on percentage of the revenue from each equipment sale. This inspires both partners to take responsibility for making sure the joint product or service fills a market need at a price customers can afford.

Committed partners also share risk by betting their own money on the outcome. Both partners put resources at risk, and they both share the benefits when their strategy pays off. Remember the Spanish bank? It asked an outsourcing partner to help it implement new systems and processes to change it from a small mortgage lender to a full-service bank in less than one year. How did the outsourcing provider get paid? It received a percentage of the bank's assets under management. The more successful the bank became, the more benefits accrued to its partner.

Transforming executives do offer their outsourcing partners "interesting money" as a reward for significant or surprising accomplishments. Thomas Cook has a million-pound ($1.66 million) bonus awaiting its provider if the latter can provide a step-change improvement in the shared service center's cost structure by the end of the third year of the contract. GiantTel agreed with its provider that it would pay the entire development cost for the new Internet protocol network when it was "ready for revenue."

Some executives insist on charging their providers penalty payments for missing service levels or project milestones. Most would agree, however, that the purpose of this mechanism is to make sure providers pay attention to minimum standard levels of performance. In transformational outsourcing, if the vendor isn't paying enough attention, the initiative has already failed. Furthermore, a penalty payment is cold comfort when what executives really want is delivery of a critically important service. A more useful role for penalties in transformational outsourcing is to compensate the company for a catastrophic failure. Neither partner welcomes this outcome, but the penalty provides some protection for the company's shareholders.

Transformational outsourcers ensure that real incentives flow directly into the hands of key individuals. Leaders put the entire weight of both companies behind these initiatives by linking transformational outsourcing performance to bonuses, raises, promotions, and recognition for the individuals involved. For example, TiVo gave its outsourced customer care agents the product to use in their own homes and provided direct incentives to individual agents to motivate them to "think like a TiVo customer."

Money is not the only useful form of incentive in transformational outsourcing. The participants take motivation from other incentives that touch them emotionally. For example, committed partners put their names on the line. They announce their intentions and stake their reputations publicly on their ability to deliver the results they project. As one CEO quipped to his board, "If this doesn't pay off, I'll never work again in this industry. And neither will our partner."

I used to work in an organization that was led by inexperienced executives who believed that "management is measurement." No seasoned leader would make this mistake. Companies in committed relationships believe that relying on metrics and incentives alone can even undermine their intentions. Veterans of sophisticated outsourcing initiatives stress that success is all about people. And that means managing not only what they do, but how they feel.

Sustaining a High-Commitment Relationship

In the high-stakes transformational-outsourcing game, partners sign up together for goals they can't guarantee with organizations they don't control, and they bet their careers on the outcome. It requires unflinching commitment to an outcome that may be years away and a partner to share the journey. Although the potential rewards are enormous, unexpected shifts in technology or the competitive landscape could call for midcourse corrections at any moment. Executives forge strong relationships to see them through this whitewater ride. One CEO told us, "I work side by side with my counterpart at [the partner company] to ensure that we anticipate and confront change as it happens."

When executives reflect on the secret to effective outsourcing, they all reach the same conclusion: Trust is vital. However, most executives, even outsourcing veterans, built trusting relationships intuitively—with varying levels of success. And, like culture, trust is not built directly; it grows as a result of experiences. Transformational outsourcing leaves no room for error in this critical activity.

The conventional wisdom about managing outsourcing relationships guides executives in exactly the wrong direction when it comes to transformational partnerships. If leaders focus only on establishing clear accountability, specified service levels, and disciplined change control, they will miss the forest for the trees. These concerns have their place; they are important features of a healthy operation. But they fall far short of the tools executives need to manage intimate partnerships. If they focus only on these contract management tools, a company's executives are actually encouraging their outsourcing provider to act less like a partner, not more.

To achieve the level of flexible, intense guidance that transformational outsourcing demands, executives establish a foundation of clear expectations, a structure of mutual benefit, the capability to do what must be done, and regular feedback. Then they activate a positive cycle by managing relationships deliberately with four types of intense communications: contract negotiations, a track record of performance, strategic governance, and personal relationships (see Exhibit 7.6).

Contract Negotiations

In transformational outsourcing, executives use contract negotiations to make sure they have the right conversations. At the beginning of the ini-

Exhibit 7.6. Use intense communications to sustain commitment.

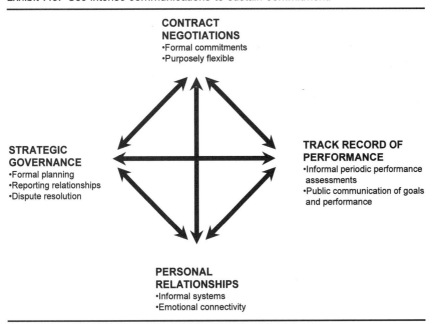

CONTRACT NEGOTIATIONS
•Formal commitments
•Purposely flexible

STRATEGIC GOVERNANCE
•Formal planning
•Reporting relationships
•Dispute resolution

TRACK RECORD OF PERFORMANCE
•Informal periodic performance assessments
•Public communication of goals and performance

PERSONAL RELATIONSHIPS
•Informal systems
•Emotional connectivity

tiative—and every time they revisit the model—they discuss key objectives and measures of success, how to make sure both partners have skin in the game, and how to deal with the big transitions. The process could not be more different from the kind of dickering over contract compliance that conventional outsourcing frequently inspires. Instead, these frank discussions set the tone for an open and honest dialogue. As one government executive remarked, "The relationship started when we agreed up front that our business partner deserved to make a fair margin." And delegating this process to an aggressive legal team may get you a better price, but it may also lead to a poorer relationship.

Strategic Governance

Keeping a transformational outsourcing relationship on course means jointly managing strategic execution as the transformation plays out. The CEO of one major UK grocery chain and its outsourcing provider's lead partner have offices on the same floor so they can meet frequently. They jointly report to the board of directors every second week to keep the high-stakes agenda on track. At Family Christian Stores, the outsourcing provider's lead partner functioned as the CIO and participated as a full member of the CEO's direct staff.

Effective governance starts at the top of the company and extends throughout the organization. Some outsourcing providers stress the importance of account management—point people who coordinate the relationship. For transformational outsourcing, good governance looks more like a "zipper than a funnel," according to Mont Phelps, CEO of Netivity Solutions, an information-technology outsourcing provider. Individuals at all levels of the relationship actively work together at the interface.

Formal communication processes also help structure solid connections. Operating managers communicate daily to monitor activities and resolve issues. Business unit executives meet monthly to assess progress and make course corrections. Senior executives address strategic direction in quarterly sessions. Every company does this the same way. So what makes some governance structures much more effective than others? Often it's the informal communication that makes all the difference. An executive at a U.S. laboratory that is noted for its ability to manage strategic partnerships effectively routinely posts individuals from her organization to two-year appointments at the partner's site. These people develop strong informal bonds with their colleagues that prove invaluable. When a difficulty or dispute arises in the collaboration—which it always does— the on-site person can use the informal channel to raise and possibly even resolve the issue. If it has to go through the structured process, the extra weight it carries can be divisive. Even if the issue cannot be resolved informally, it can be socialized. Then, when it does come up at the formal meeting, some of its heat has already been vented.

In an environment where accountability runs high, but control is elusive, transformational leaders substitute visibility for ownership. Companies open their books so their outsourcing partners can see their costs and margins. They open their boardrooms so partners can see—and influence—their strategies. And it goes the other way, too. A company that signs up for transformational outsourcing wants to know that the partner on which it is utterly dependent is making a fair and reasonable profit for its effort.

Track Record of Performance

Business partners build credibility through performance. No matter how effectively both parties articulate their vision at the outset, things get cloudy fast. Both partners will need a way to crystallize and communicate the progress they've made as they go along. Some track the cumulative benefits that have accrued as a result of the partnership. Others publicize their insights in jointly authored articles and speeches. Still others pause periodically to capture the progress in writing. These narratives not only document the headway companies are making, but provide a way to highlight roadblocks, rally support for course corrections, and refocus on the ultimate objective. It's not just the fact that they have set and met promises, but the way they use this information that makes demonstrated performance a lever for relationship management. As one executive remarked, "We periodically remind each other that what we have accomplished has been both difficult and significant. It helps motivate us to press on together."

Personal Relationships

In the end, outsourcing partnerships are about people. A successful software services entrepreneur said something to me recently that I think captures this point superbly. He was reflecting on his company's earlier attempt to expand from systems integration services into packaged software products. He said, "When you're selling a product, you sell the product first, your company second, and yourself third. When you're selling a service, you sell yourself first, your company second, and the service third." Transformational outsourcing is a service in every sense of the word, and its success relies on the specific individuals who champion the initiative. In British Petroleum's long-standing arrangement for back-office services in the North Sea, the two people who originally crafted the relationship have stayed involved, even though their company assignments have changed several times. They attribute the initiative's success and longevity, at least in part, to this mature personal relationship.[5]

What do we mean by a personal relationship? "We're not talking about hot tubs and Champagne," quips one senior vice president, "but the personal side of these business partnerships makes all the difference." Executives from both sides spend social time together, but the real bonds develop as they work shoulder-to-shoulder to transform the company. At its best, this personal chemistry builds at all levels of the business partnership—from the leadership to the individuals on the front lines of radically changing business processes.

Managing the Tension

When performance is on track, communications are easy and trust builds naturally. Every executive who has gone through a transformational outsourcing experience would admit, however, that relationships are not linear. They are rocky. Just as good progress welds them, setbacks of all sorts threaten them. Leaders create and sustain a sublime tension between the centrifugal relationship forces that pull people together and the centripetal forces that drive them apart. The former nurture community, but threaten to make a team insular; the latter foster discord, but provoke valuable insights. Leaders keep their organizations on the creative edge by balancing the two. How?

• Effective executives are prepared to give before they get. They start off by trusting to establish a positive environment.

- They approach issues with their partner the same way they would with a valuable long-term employee. They wouldn't think of firing this person or taking him or her to court to remedy a performance problem. They approach their partner with the same attitude.
- Leaders take the personal responsibility to make the relationship work. Executives on both sides of outsourcing deals—even those who set out to develop strong partnerships—are often surprised by the amount of personal energy and commitment these initiatives require of them. Many describe a defining moment at which they arrive in frustration at the almost overwhelming issues that threaten to sabotage their plans. Instead of retreating to their corner to blame their counterpart, they decide that the onus of making the relationship work is on their own shoulders. From that moment forward, transformational outsourcing has a chance to succeed.

Notes

1. Unpublished Accenture survey, January 2003.

2. Jane Linder and Brian McCarthy, "When Good Management Shows: Creating Value in an Uncertain Economy," Accenture Institute for Strategic Change research report, September 2002.

3. Robert Simons, "Strategic Orientation and Top Management Attention to Control Systems," *Strategic Management Journal* 12 (1991), pp. 49–62.

4. This performance measurement concept was first developed by the management of Analog Devices.

5. Jane Linder, Alvin Jacobson, Matthew Breitfelder, and Mark Arnold, "Business Transformation Outsourcing: Partnering for Radical Change," Accenture Institute for Strategic Change research report, July 2001.

CHAPTER 8

Managing People Through Transitions

In most cases, transformational outsourcing impacts people. Some may lose their jobs, or at least their current responsibilities. Some will be asked to move to a new employer. Even those who are not personally uprooted may have to accept a new way of working. In the managerial fight for competitive success, this part is the hand-to-hand combat. It's challenging, emotionally charged, and personally wrenching. There are no managerial techniques or approaches that completely eliminate the pain. But there are many that help to minimize it both for the individuals who are dislocated and for those who remain behind. These can be invaluable in helping an organization move on from a difficult transition to a prosperous future.

A recent story from National Savings and Investments shows that these difficult experiences can have positive outcomes. As you will recall from the story in Chapter 1, NS&I retained only 120 people from its original staff of about 4,200; the rest were transferred to its outsourcing provider. Over the next three years, more than 2,000 of the people who were transferred either accepted voluntary redundancy or were re-employed elsewhere as the operation was streamlined. These deep cuts were necessary to position the resulting organization to succeed, and some may have found them more palatable than the insidious incremental downsizings that had been going on for 15 years. However, these justifications didn't make the experience any easier for the individuals involved.

In 2003, the NS&I executive team held a one-day off-site meeting to communicate its strategy for the coming three years, to which every member of the staff was invited. As the employees of National Savings and Investments filed into the hotel ballroom in early April 2003, they could feel a palpable buzz. The UK government organization had executed a stunning transformation over the past three years, and the CEO had drawn them all together to discuss the organization's new strategic agenda. After he had laid out the organization's future plans, individual directors led breakout groups to discuss various aspects of the strategy presented.

We're talking about a government agency here, so you might be imagining a staid and stuffy day of "talking head" presentations. Nothing could be further from the truth. Steve Owen, Partnerships and Operations Director, led his breakout group in a silver-spangled top hat and tails. Several other key executives appeared in humorous costumes that even the most garrulous participants were reluctant to describe for me. Here's what happened in one of the sessions:

As the director began to lay out elements of the organization's future plans, an unfamiliar individual in the second row complained loudly about the quality of the ideas. This went on for several minutes—the director presenting and the heckler throwing verbal darts. Finally, an exasperated government employee in the audience stood up and said to the heckler, "If you will only keep your mouth shut, you might learn something."

The heckler was an actor, hired by the senior management to give voice to some of the issues they thought might be concerning their staff. They had decided that it was more important to get these things out in the open than to let them fester. The vocal employee's visible and unqualified support for the organization's leadership was more than they had hoped for. It earned her a bottle of Champagne from the CEO.

The point of the story is that painful transitions can have good consequences for people as well as bad ones. Remember Skip Stitt's comment?

Point out the people who will have their streets paved for the first time in 60 years and the neighborhood with a crime problem where the additional police will go.

He points out that executives should focus just as much attention on the initiative's winners as its losers. While initially reluctant, the government employees in Indianapolis got as much out of the change as the constituents. By asking employees to compete with the private sector to run various government processes, Stephen Goldsmith's administration created an entrepreneurial environment that unleashed creativity, improved motivation, and expanded opportunities for people.

In this chapter, I talk about setting the agenda for transitioning people, communicating about the changes, dealing with unions and with the media, preparing for and executing transitions, and addressing the specific challenges and opportunities that transitions present.

Setting the Agenda for People

Many managerial choices change people's lives. The decision to transform an organization and the decision to do it through outsourcing are both examples. Most executive teams need some time to work out their positions in these sensitive areas, and it's impossible to do so in an open forum. Why? Because when the decision to outsource is announced, employees want to know—in the same paragraph—how it will affect them. If the executive team has not prepared this analysis, they should hold their announcement until they do. If they have no choice but to go ahead without this information, they should be able to state when they will have definitive answers to employees' questions.

In one U.S. state, for example, a government IT executive tells the story of a previous administration's abortive attempt to outsource the state's information-technology function. As a member of the audience, she listened as the IT leadership went through their presentation about how they intended to structure the initiative and what they would be doing. They announced that they would require the winning bidder to hire all of the state's IT workers and keep them on for at least a year. She recalls that at the end of the presentation, someone in the audience stood up and said, "I understand the fact that it will take a year to get the contract finalized and that everyone will have one more year of employment after that, but my concern is for the people on my staff who have two more years to go before their pension plans vest. You will be moving them to the private sector just as they would be vesting. How will you be dealing with those people who have put in so much time with us?" The answer came back, "We haven't really thought about that." She reflected in disgust, "They did a lot of work behind the scenes, but when they made the announcement, they had not even taken care of the really predictable issues. How could they get this far without thinking these things through?"

The example underscores the importance of having a complete story to tell when outsourcing is announced. The baby probably won't live if it is delivered an organ at a time. Executives do need some "behind the scenes" decision making to pull this together. If they are new to the process, they also need a way to bring in expert guidance so they can craft a well-thought-out approach without risking information leakage by soliciting input from employees.

Thomas Cook used its bunker meetings this way. Only the senior leaders in the organization were involved—the CEO, group finance director, group business transformation director, HR director, and corporate communications director. Each week for about eight weeks, this small team spent an entire day or two sorting out what they needed to do to transform the company. They not only agreed to use outsourcing to help accomplish their aggressive objectives but they also designed a new structure for the organization and attached individual names to new responsibilities. As part of this process, they had to determine exactly which roles and functions would remain inside the company and which would be taken on by the outsourcing partner. The implications of this strategic choice—where to draw the line—trickled down through the organization as individual names went on the "retained" side or the "outsourced" side of the ledger.

This process of naming names is full of land mines. Any organization that has integrated an acquisition or conducted a layoff has picked its way through the issues. Setting up transformational outsourcing is no different. Executives begin with an approach for making decisions about who goes and who stays. In Thomas Cook's case, the principle was to retain the strategic thinking for finance, HR, and information-technology functions in a lean staff. NS&I used a similar principle. It retained strategy, product design, and relationship-management functions. This is a common way to divide internal and outsourced roles. Organizations that retain no strategic capability often find they don't have the internal expertise to manage their relationship with their outsourcing provider effectively.

Setting the dividing line does not completely solve the problem of who goes where, however. When it comes to deciding about individuals, executives have difficulty following the rules. They tend to protect their favorites. Instead, as these choices are made, the team must ask itself whether the chosen people have the values, the talent, the experience, and the energy to manage the new organization. If they do not, the organization will not benefit from keeping them on either the retained or the outsourced side. Delaying that decision by transferring these individuals to the outsourcing partner simply undermines success.

The leadership team also has a responsibility to the people whose lives will be affected by the decision to transform through outsourcing. That responsibility is to set an agenda for people with the principles and values that will guide how individuals are treated during the change. This is not a responsibility that can be delegated to the outsourcing provider.

I am not arguing for a particular set of principles and values, although I know the choices I would make personally. I am just asserting that the principles be laid out clearly so the employees understand the rules of the game. They are grownups; they can then make their own decisions. For its part, the leadership team should give these principles the weight of commitments—or commandments, if you don't mind the religious overtones. If they promise to be open and honest, they should not be caught hiding bad news or rewriting history. It just won't sit well with those whose trust must be reearned.

Executives should take account of the current economic and business landscape as they decide what terms and conditions will apply to the transfer of people to the outsourcing provider. A government IT executive in Australia, for example, chose what they call the "clean break" model when his organization transferred all of its IT workers to the private sector. With this approach, employees receive a generous redundancy (or severance) payment when they leave their government posts because they are not transferred directly to employment with the outsourcing partner. The alternative approach would have eliminated the redundancy payments, but arranged for the transfer of employment. In this situation, the executive reasoned, the market for IT skills was strong so the workers would have no trouble finding new jobs. Many went to work for the outsourcing partner immediately, and they pocketed their redundancy checks as well.

The UK's TUPE laws (transfer of undertakings protection of employment) restrict executives' choices about the terms and conditions of transferred employees. These laws require that employees of a business sold as a going concern retain their existing employment terms and conditions under the new ownership. This applies to transfers that result from outsourcing as well as from mergers and acquisitions. If it is necessary to reduce the workforce shortly after outsourcing, it becomes incumbent on the employer to consult with the affected employees prior to their transfer to the outstanding provider. The intention of these laws is to protect employees' rights and to take the fear out of transfer for employees. It also takes the responsibility for setting personnel-transfer principles away from company leadership and encourages them to shuffle the responsibility for these difficult decisions onto their outsourcing partner.

Michel-Marc Delcommune, the CFO and executive director of Magyar Oil and Gas Company, a Hungarian energy company, compensated transferring employees in an unusual way. He recognized that employees were moving from the energy sector to the services sector and that pay scales in the latter were significantly lower. To keep employees from bearing the long-term consequences of this pay gap, he calculated redundancy payments that reflected the net present value of their reduced career-long earnings.

One extremely successful way to address people's concerns about outsourcing is to deal with them in relevant groups rather than taking a one-size-fits-all approach. And some of those relevant groups may include only one individual. For example, a company might establish three broad groups based on pension-plan vesting. One group contains employees who have no vested pension rights. These employees could keep their years of service when transferring to the outsourcing provider, and could apply toward vesting in the provider's plan. A second group that is already vested could keep its current pension rights or transfer full vesting to the provider's plan. Additional years of service would accumulate in the latter. Individuals who are on the cusp of vesting could be retained in the organization until that point, then transferred as above. Executives should apply the same kind of logic to health care benefits, vacation, and every other part of the employment relationship. Further, they should think through these issues at the outset or they risk negotiating a rat's nest of inequitable, piecemeal arrangements.

Goldsmith's administration used this approach in transforming Indianapolis, and they added one other feature that gave employees a comforting sense of control in their changing world: They told all employees who were transferred to an outsourcing provider that they had the option to return to government service—not necessarily to their old job, but at their prior terms and conditions. This safety valve allowed employees to put aside their fears and give the new employment arrangements a try. The only individual who ever took Goldsmith up on his offer through 60 outsourcing deals was a union steward.

Establishing a principled structure for transitioning people from one company to another is essential. Extensive and intensive communication helps people step across with confidence.

Communicate, Communicate, Communicate with Employees

When the decision is to outsource, there's no such thing as too much communication. The first thing employees want to know is, "What about me?" And they want to know in very specific, concrete terms. Will they have a job? How will their pay and benefits change? What will happen to their retirement plans? The chief financial officer of a large central European energy company outsourced all of information technology, finance, and accounting to a provider that created and operated a shared-services center. This experienced executive was well aware of the need to communicate with the affected employees, and he took the steps he thought were necessary. Despite careful attention to this issue, it was not enough. Individuals were able to get back to work and focus on the project only when they had been given comparative pay slips for their current job and their new role at the provider's company. This was the level of detailed communication that individuals needed to feel comfortable with how the terms of their employment would be changing.

Of course, handing out pro forma pay stubs may answer the most critical questions, but it doesn't answer all the questions. Workers want to understand enough about their new employer to be able to make an informed and proactive choice to move. NS&I's outsourcing provider went to great pains before it had even won the contract to present itself to the affected employees. In this case, the company's strong brand and world-wide reputation made it very appealing as an employer. Long-term employees had to leave the government service, but the fact that they were joining a respected company and would still be contributing to the success of their former employer helped ease the pain of the transition.

Road shows are an important part of a concerted campaign to communicate with employees; they should be followed up by one-on-one conversations between the individual and the new supervisor. Some outsourcing providers also make "buddies" available to prospective transfers. These are individuals who originally worked for another company but were transferred to the provider as part of an outsourcing initiative. These people can reassure transferring workers about both the process and the opportunities it can provide. Again, the entire purpose of this process is to give individuals the means to make choices. The sense of personal control they get from this process helps them adjust more quickly to their new work situation.

Once employees get clear, if not pleasing, answers to their questions about personal status, they will raise their sights a bit. They will want to know why this is happening. In some ways, this question is easier to answer for transformational outsourcing than for more conventional outsourcing initiatives. The organization's financial and competitive situation should provide a compelling motivation for dramatic change. And the more external the driving factors are, the more it helps. An external driver gives the initiative legitimacy, while avoiding the implication that the current leaders' missteps created the organization's poor performance in the first place. This helps workers rationalize their situations and add their support to the cause.

Thomas Cook's initiative gained some legitimacy from the September 11, 2001, terrorist attacks. Every employee immediately grasped that this unconscionable act would undermine travel sales for some time to come, and that the company would have to adjust. When executives lack such an obvious driver for change, they must make their own reasoning tangible to employees. This requires walking an emotional tightrope. On one hand, executives must convince employees that an outside provider can make the extensive changes the company needs. On the other hand, executives are not likely to win the staff's support by insulting their abilities in comparison. An NS&I executive recalled that what convinced the senior team that outsourcing was the only answer was "the specter of how it would've been if we had to do it all ourselves." But the public-sector process for gaining approval for outsourcing requires a detailed comparison of the expected costs and risks for both options: outside provider and in-house initiative. He continued, "This cost comparison is a very sensitive thing. If you give people the perception that you're enhancing any of the costs to favor outsourcing, or impugning their ability to do the work in-house, they will revolt. In the end, we very significantly underestimated the cost and risk of doing it in-house. But you have to strike the right balance to keep people on board, without being overgenerous to the idea of in-house being effective."

One more word of caution is appropriate here. The executives in some companies are not skilled at delivering unpleasant messages. Many don't have the courage to be open and honest when the news is bad. To soften the impact, they give in to the temptation to make promises to the employees that they are later unable to keep. Nothing can sabotage a change initiative faster than having the leadership demonstrate that they cannot be trusted. And employees would rather know the truth about what is likely to happen to them, even when that truth is painful.

What you have to say is important, but how you say it is even more important. When most executives communicate, they focus on sending out the right messages. What they really need to attend to is not what they are sending out, but what employees are receiving. This means structuring communications that are more likely to be understood and internalized. For example, when executives want employees to learn more about the outsourcing providers competing for a contract, they ask the providers to make presentations. Instead they should opt for more memorable and engaging experiences. They should structure workshops where employee teams have the opportunity to play the role of the outsourcing provider companies and try to convince each other that employees would be better off if their particular company won the bid. This would motivate employees to find out more about the bidders, and the information they sought would be what was most important to them. This kind of simulation would not only help get the messages across, it would provide invaluable feedback to executives about the bidders.

This is only one example of a whole category of communications approaches that are designed to ensure that messages are received and remembered.[1] These include everything from case study discussions and story-telling to field trips and war games. Effective communicators make learning active. You will want to ask employees to give the presentation, not listen to it; write the book, not read it; act out the new process, not hear about it.

Communicating with Other Stakeholders

Some transforming executives recognize how important it is to communicate with employees, but they pay less attention to other critical stakeholders. What they really need is a concerted communications campaign that covers all the bases. This includes addressing the concerns of investors, customers and community leaders (see Exhibit 8.1).

Outside Investors

Outside investors are probably the easiest to deal with, so let's start there. A study in August 2000 by Stern Stewart showed that investors reward companies that outsource. They looked at the stock market performance of 27 companies that had recently signed major IT outsourcing contracts. On average, these companies outperformed the market by 5.7 percent, measured by stock price, for the four-month period surrounding the announcement. Sixty-two percent of the companies in the sample showed a positive impact from announcing outsourcing in the short term.

If we can extrapolate from these results to outsourcing in general, we can conclude that investors are positively predisposed to outsourcing. That makes communicating with them somewhat easier. Executives can lay out the business case, the financial projections, and the timing in a fairly straightforward manner. That said, executives should realize that financial analysts can discount earnings that result from nonrepeatable financial engineering. For example, when J. Sainsbury and Accenture formed a joint venture to manage the supermarket chain's IT activities, analysts were less than effusive about the quality of the earnings improvements. One report in May 2001 downgraded J. Sainsbury stock and said: "The Sainsbury and Accenture joint-venture vehicle was set up on 12 November 2000 to procure and build a totally new IT system. However,

Exhibit 8.1. Stakeholder interests should drive the communications agenda.

Stakeholders	Power/Influence over Outsourcing Initiative	Example Interests
Employees	Can withhold or share process knowledge and/or effort.	• Job security • Career opportunities • Pay and benefits • Work satisfaction
Investors and Owners	Can approval or veto outsourcing initiative; fire or retain senior leadership.	• Solid business case • Transaction risk • Strategic benefit of outsourcing
Customers	Can continue business relationship or take their business elsewhere.	• Product/service continuity • Product, service, price, value improvements
Community	Can make tax and regulatory conditions hospitable or inhospitable.	• Job creation and economic development • Environmental impact • Traffic impact
Management	Can support or resist outsourcing initiative.	• Changing skills required • Company's growth potential • Personal career opportunities • Probability of success

six months on, there are many aspects of this deal that we find unclear, potentially misleading to investors, and of a real concern to us is how future IT costs are being manipulated to provide substantial increases in profits in the next few years. How," the report wondered, "is £35 million [$58 million] in cost savings achieved before any real IT investment has actually been made?"[2] Regardless of the real impact on earnings, analysts' and therefore investors' perceptions are colored by complex, non-transparent financial arrangements. In the post-Enron era, it behooves executives to stand up for innovative initiatives that make good, long-term financial sense and to communicate these clearly and openly to shareholders.

(Just to bring the record up-to-date, it has been two years since Sainsbury's outsourced almost its entire IT function, and the company is seeing real cost savings that will amount to more than £200 million ($332.8 million) a year. In addition, it is also beginning to tap the new levels of flexibility and innovation that were an important part of the transformational outsourcing agenda.[3])

Community

A second important outside constituency is the larger community that gives a company its physical context. This means politicians and special-interest groups. One NS&I executive remarked: "We ran a very big campaign in all the operations sites to let people know that outsourcing would not only be good for the customer and taxpayer, but it also would create jobs. At the local level of Parliament, the thing they're most interested in is how many jobs will be in that constituency, not who they work for." Although the Newport Systems staff that would be dedicated to NS&I was expected to drop, the partnership actively encouraged the provider to bring new work into the operational centers. Executives anticipated that this new work would absorb many of the excess employees.

Politicians have less influence over transformational outsourcing in the private sector, but that does not mean that local community leaders should be ignored in a communications campaign. They will be especially interested in movement of jobs and tax revenues. They may even be willing to make concessions that will change the financial appeal of one bid or another, depending on how these issues fall out. Executives will want to include community leaders in the communications agenda and solicit their participation in creating the best overall partnership for the companies and the community.

Customers

Customer communications require a great deal of judgment. Customers can react strongly to news that a company is having financial difficulty. One executive involved in a transformational outsourcing initiative recounted, "You have to be careful. You don't want the information going out in the press. One of the retailers in our area suffered from this problem; when consumers thought the company was in trouble, they took their business elsewhere. We didn't want our customers to think we were in dire straits. It's hard to strike the right balance between being honest with our employees and not letting news of our difficulties get out." This company decided that it was essential to communicate openly with employees. The senior leadership took workers into their confidence. They explained the potential consumer reaction to them and asked them to support the company by keeping confidential information confidential. It worked. The company's temporary financial troubles and its outsourcing initiative were not covered by the press.

Owners

Owners and parent companies also require special handling. In most situations, they have to approve outsourcing initiatives, and they have a complex set of appetites and interests that color their views of these types of initiatives. For example, Thomas Cook AG is owned by public companies with obligations to outside investors. It has an overall strategy that gives it competing priorities for both capital and management attention. The individuals making decisions at the parent board level have their own attitudes about outsourcing and risk profiles. Yet they had to be convinced in order for Alan Stewart's initiative to proceed.

Peter Bareau faced a similar structure at NS&I with the UK Treasury. He commented: "Early on, I realized that we had to involve the Treasury. All the big decisions are ones that the Treasury makes. The Treasury officials advise the ministers, so it is absolutely critical that these [decisions] carry their support. They are involved in big decisions on procurement, but also all the decisions on annual plans and targets, the amount of money we're going to raise, and new products have to be agreed with Treasury. We propose the plans, but they have to agree."

Executives structure relationships with their owners that range from contractual to committed. The way they communicate with owners depends on the type of relationship they have and they type they want. For example, Peter Bareau changed the management board structure and invited the Treasury officials onto the board. He involved them in his strategic planning and in his team's process of deciding to outsource. He deliberately cultivated a collaborative relationship. In fact, if you look at NS&I's annual report, you'll see photographs of Treasury officials standing alongside the organization's executives.

Alan Stewart also had an arm's-length relationship with parent company executives, but played his cards differently. Instead of inviting them into his decision process, he crafted a compelling business case for outsourcing and used it to convince them to approve the initiative. Ultimately, he had to put his own job on the line to overcome the board's concerns. This difficult process had a happy ending, however. As Thomas Cook turned in the results they had contracted for, management credibility grew, and their relationship with the board improved. This sets the stage for a different communications approach for the next phase of Thomas Cook's strategic agenda.

Dealing with Unions

Because of their role, unions can be particularly tricky to work with. Their stated role is to protect the interests of workers. Many unions define these interests by setting them in opposition to management and defending them with an adversarial approach. This approach is exactly like contractual outsourcing, with each side hammering the other to stick to the terms of the contract while flexibility and mutual benefit often suffer. In some cases, the individuals charged with managing the relationship on both sides have additional agendas that make the engagement even more dysfunctional. For example, some managers focus on crushing the union rather than getting good work done; some union officials focus on aggrandizing the union rather than protecting the interests of the workers. These inflexible, adversarial agendas stand in the way of positive incremental change, almost guaranteeing that organizations lurch from transformation to transformation. Again, executives should consider the kind of relationship they have with unions, and the kind they want, when addressing union issues in transformational outsourcing.

As we discussed earlier, transformation makes the most sense in the face of big threats and opportunities. In these cases, unlike the situation with smaller, incremental changes, the initiative's probability of success is lower, but the rationale for proceeding is much clearer. Basically, the organization has little choice. However, union leaders, especially staunch adversaries, may try to ignore these compelling forcing functions. In the U.S. government, union leaders:

> . . . aggressively and consistently oppose . . . innovative outsourcing approaches. [Although] where such approaches have been pursued, such as the National Security Agency, the Army, and the Navy, the benefits to the affected federal workforce have far exceeded anything that could have been done under A-76,[4] including if the workforce had been retained in-house. In each of those cases, the workforce was treated as a critical asset and was rewarded accordingly.[5]

A veteran of Indianapolis's intensive and successful outsourcing during the 1990s continues:

> The myth that outsourcing is bad for public employees is one of the greatest fabrications ever. We looked at our wastewater utilities seven years after we signed the outsourcing contract with a private sector company and found that the difference in total compensation for the people who left versus the people who stayed was very dramatic. The average compensation for the people who went to the private sector was 28 percent higher than for people who stayed in public-sector jobs. In addition, on the private side the rate of accidents, the time lost due to injuries, and the grievances were down while the pay raises, the incentive compensation, and the pension contributions were higher.[6]

Just having outsourcing in the mix can improve opportunities for workers. In Indianapolis, the unions vigorously opposed privatization of public functions, but because of the fiscal and political mandates given to the new mayor, they had little chance of success. As a result, they turned their attention to competing against private-sector companies for the work. Ultimately, unionized public-sector workers "got their costs down and productivity up and outbid private companies for over two dozen contracts"[7] out of the 65 that were signed over six years. The experience of competing for and winning the work helped change the public-sector culture in Indianapolis. Workers recognized that good ideas paid off, and the entrepreneurship this stimulated was both satisfying for workers and beneficial for the public.

This growing body of evidence that outsourcing can benefit the workforce creates a rift between union leadership and the workers they represent. In cases where the employees see opportunities for growth in their chosen professions and a willingness of their future employer to invest in their training and development, they can begin to sense union opposition to outsourcing as barring their way. In one such situation, an employee confided to the HR director: "Don't mind the unions, they're not representing us."

Although managers are frequently reluctant even to consider outsourcing because of the threat of union backlash, outsourcing veterans would agree that these issues are surmountable. Peter Bareau recalls: "Some initiatives have been deterred for fear of industrial action. We were the guinea pig because it was the largest outsourcing the government had ever done, and we did it without industrial action." Successful executives bring union representatives into the conversation early—generally not into the bunker meetings, but certainly before they make organization-wide announcements. Involving unions at this point conveys an intention to work cooperatively with them. It also gives the union representatives an opportunity to set up their own negotiations with potential outsourcing providers. The union may want the provider to recognize it so unionized employees will be able to retain their membership, for example.

Of course, a comprehensive communications campaign does not stop when a contract is signed. Nor does it end when employees have transitioned to the outsourcing provider. It should be part of day-in-day-out management of important stakeholder relationships.

Preparing for Transition

Transitioning people and work from one company to another presents a huge opportunity for misadventure. Ideally, the work transfers smoothly and almost invisibly; in reality it is often fraught with problems and missteps. It is the first real activity of the outsourcing initiative. And as such, it can color people's perceptions about the wisdom of the whole process for a very long time. In addition, those perceptions are sticky. Employees don't lose the sour taste in their mouths after a poor start, even after many issues have been rectified. One company reported that it was receiving explicit complaints on its satisfaction surveys one full year after a nasty start-up problem had been completely resolved.

It almost goes without saying, but before executives start a transition, they will want to put the right management team in place. If critical management changes have not yet been made, now is the time. One executive recalls, "Quite early on, after the initial strategy, after we designed the outsourcing approach, we asked all the existing management team to rebid for their jobs. That was radical, there was some pain, but we had to do it because with the existing structure we couldn't execute the change we needed. They rebid, and we had a process of competition. The previous team was not unprofessional; they are just entirely associated with the old way of doing things."

By this time in the process, executives will have made one of the most important transition decisions: whether to move the work process "as is" or whether to move to a new process and/or system as the work is handed over to the provider. This is an important decision because it affects the complexity of the transition process. Companies and their providers almost always underestimate the complexity of the work. When technical uncertainty is stacked onto political and emotional uncertainty—all managed under financial constraints—things are more likely to go wrong. From a technical perspective, the lowest risk option is to transfer the work as is. Next best is to transition to an existing operating system and process even though it may be different from the current one. The most risky option is to implement a new, untested system and process as part of the transition (see Exhibit 8.2).

What would make executives take these technical risks? They have to trade them off against more compelling risks that push them in the opposite direction. Political and financial risks most often revolve around time to achieve benefits. The more time-compressed the transition process is, the faster companies begin to achieve the results that set them on this course to begin with—assuming, of course, that the transition is managed effectively. So from a political and financial standpoint, faster is better.

Exhibit 8.2. Technical risk increases as the transition spans more process change.

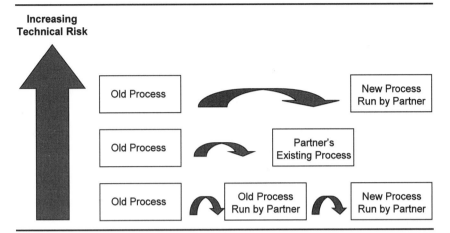

This is a perfect time for an explicit risk-management process. Most companies and most outsourcing providers do not use this approach, but they should. If the outsourcing provider does not come with a risk-management approach based on its own experience, the company should borrow the scheme it uses for evaluating new product or capital investment risk.

A systematic project-management approach is also a very good idea overall. Many systems of this sort exist, but my personal favorite is Speed to Market's Concerto. Instead of just capturing all the task-level details for managers, it helps focus attention on the bottleneck activities. Companies report very good results with on-time program delivery using this tool. Of course, tools by themselves don't do anything. The executives who are accountable for the outcomes must decide they will use these tools to achieve their ends. So executives have a task plan for transition along with a risk-management and a program-management process. My intention is not to cover the details of outsourcing transition here. I just want to focus on the issues that are particularly important for transformational outsourcing.

If the object is transformation, the work process is going to change a great deal. If a company is going to transfer the work as is, it must document the old processes in detail. This process description should provide enough information so that the work can be done completely and accurately, even if the current employees do not transfer. In most situations, the company and its outsourcing partner would like to know which employees are not likely to move with the work so they can pay explicit attention to that part of the documentation.

If a new process is being implemented at the same time the work is being transferred, executives will want to take a different tack. They should collaborate with the provider to develop a detailed—underscore detailed—process and information flow for the way work will be done. Then they should map each data element, form, calculation, responsibility, decision, and handoff in the new process to its source in the old process.

When this is considered complete, the two organizations should run a rehearsal of each work process, conducted by the individuals who will be doing the work after the transition. Readying the organization for this event will involve training, but an action focus will give people every incentive to make sure they get what they need to know. Plus, this dry run will identify disconnects, missing data, poorly defined responsibilities, and timing issues. When these are cleared up, executives will want to stage a successful dress rehearsal before they allow the work to transfer.

Executives will complain, but the rehearsal should include the management process as well as the detailed transaction process. Why? With apologies to designer Mies van der Rohe, God is not only in the details, she is in the interfaces. Like passing the baton in a relay race, processes are most likely to break when roles and handoffs are unclear, where timing is tight, and where personal relationships are distant or nonexistent. A good rehearsal exercises all the interfaces.

Outsourcing provider organizations that offer multiclient shared-service centers frequently establish model offices so that new clients can rehearse both transaction-level and management-level processes with real data before they go live to iron out the interfaces. This model has working versions of all the systems that the service center will use to process the work. For example, before declaring the Chunnel from Britain to France complete, its program managers staged a simulated disaster to help fire, police, and ambulance crews prepare for their responsibilities. One thousand tunnel workers and their families pretended to be train passengers who were evacuated in a rehearsal of the tunnel's emergency security procedures.[8]

Worker transfers heighten the challenge in an otherwise complex transition process. People can feel angry and betrayed because they have to leave their employer of choice and separate from colleagues. Yet they are being asked to hand over all their specialized knowledge and then work especially hard to make the process happen. Even if they do have a job on the other side of the transition, they may be anticipating a more stressful environment and possibly a fight to survive more layoffs. Natural antipathies get in the way of the collaboration that is essential to transition work smoothly. Executives frequently supplement open and honest communication with quid pro quo incentives and stay bonuses. These kick in when knowledge and work have been transferred effectively to the outsourcing provider.

By the way, the new process documentation is more than just a transition tool. It is the starting point for a living library that should be audited annually for completeness as part of standard operating procedure in the outsourcing relationship. This not only provides the basis for thoughtful process improvement, but enables a company to change providers or bring work in-house if the partnership fails.

Cutting Over and Settling Down

With a good plan, good process documentation, good training and knowledge transfer, and good rehearsal, transferring work processes to the provider organization should be relatively painless. That does not, however, mean problem-free. No matter how much experience outsourcing providers have or how diligently they prepare for transitions, problems will occur. Successful outsourcing providers do two things right here. First, they set up processes to dispatch the problems quickly and effectively.

Many set up a war room for the most intensive first weeks of the transition. This is common practice for postmerger integration, important product launches, big system implementations, plant start-ups, and many other complex activities. The war room should be staffed by knowledgeable managers and lead workers who can allocate resources and get colleagues' attention so that unexpected problems can be resolved at their root cause. Even after the need for a war room for daily problems abates, executives will want to staff it and use it for the first time through key processes like quarter- and year-end closings and new product launches, as well as for subsequent transitions.

In terms of activity, the transition is a particularly intense time. More operational processes and issues will be noted than can be resolved immediately. Experienced outsourcing providers use triage principles to categorize the problems and implement a "parking lot" for issues that have to wait.

Research shows that new organizational systems and processes will gel over three to four months.[9] Whether their work is streamlined and effective or full of dysfunctional work-arounds, people will settle into patterns. Transformation asks a great deal more of them. It will require them to provisionally settle, then break the patterns again and again to achieve extensive performance improvements. It is not continuous change. Instead it is a series of change packages or releases. The outsourcing partners must set the metronome that creates momentum from this cycle. If it ticks too slowly, routines become entrenched; if it ticks too fast, workers burn out. So in conventional outsourcing, the partners schedule and manage their transition, then settle into a new phase of slow, continuous improvement. In transformational outsourcing, on the other hand, they must plan beyond the first transition—to the series of change releases that will follow right on its heels.

Thomas Cook's task plan shows how transformational outsourcing differs from its single-transition cousin (see Exhibit 8.3). That initiative released a series of change packages over 20 months. NS&I's metronome ticked off facility moves, new product introductions, and system implementations for over three years. As a result, both organizations have mastered not just a new process at the end of one transition but also the capability to make transitions. This particular and precious, hard-won learning is what makes the journey worthwhile.

A well-managed change release program can also help a company manage waves of workforce transfers. Executives report that while the first group of employees to transfer often feels anxious about moving to an outsourcing provider, they quickly see the investments their new employer is making in training and tools. Soon-to-be transferred workers hear good reports from those who have gone before, their fears are allayed, and they actually feel eager to make the move. This shifts the emotional energy of the process to support forward momentum.

Exhibit 8.3. Transformation program release plan.

2002:	June	July	Aug.	Sept.	Oct.	Nov.	Dec.	Jan.	Feb.	Mar.	Apr.	May	June	July	Aug.	Sept.	Oct.

R1A: Distribution Finance
Business Case Plan
Actual

R1B: Tour Ops Finance
Business Case Plan
Actual

R1C: Airline Finance
Business Case Plan
Actual

R1B: Payroll
Business Case Plan
Actual

R1B: HR Administration
Business Case Plan
Actual

R2: ESS and Flexible Benefits
Business Case Plan
Actual

R3: Procurement
Business Case Plan
Actual

R3: Enhanced Financials
Business Case Plan
Actual

Source: Thomas Cook.

Lessons and Implications

- *Don't just send messages; make sure they are received.* Executives repeat that there's no such thing as too much communication before and during the transitions associated with transformational outsourcing. In addition to committing to a comprehensive campaign that addresses the needs of all the relevant stakeholders, executives should begin to use communication approaches that help people hear, understand, and internalize the news.

- *Manage the risks.* Orchestrating work-process transitions and worker transfers is a complex and difficult process. Systematic risk-management approaches won't take away all the uncertainty, but they can improve the odds of success.

- *A few experienced hands can make all the difference.* Executives should resist the temptation to be pennywise and pound-foolish with staff allocations during transitions. Add a few extra experienced hands at the doer level to keep critical processes flowing.

- *Set realistic expectations that the transition may bring disruption.* When processes change, they change for the whole company. Let everyone know that issues may arise and get involvement from individuals inside the company who will have to work differently as a result. If insiders do their part, everything else will work more smoothly.

- *Manage the pace and the momentum.* Transformational outsourcing entails extensive change over an extended time. If executives explicitly manage page and momentum, their companies will master not one transition, but the ability to execute change.

Notes

1. Jane Linder, "Spark Learning with Engaging Experiences," Accenture Institute for Strategic Change research report, March 1999.

2. Mike Dennis, "Beware the Black Swan," SG Equity Research, May 30, 2001.

3. "Case Study: Going Gangbuster at Sainsbury's," *Retail Week*, April 25, 2003.

4. A-76 is the U.S. government circular that governs most outsourcing. It stipulates that government employees have the opportunity to compete with the private sector for the right to perform functions that are declared noninherently governmental. Private-sector firms must first win this competition before they can be awarded outsourcing contracts.

5. Stan Soloway, "Buy Lines: Straight Talk about Fed Employees, Competitive Sourcing," *Washington Technology* 17, No. 24 (March 24, 2003), www.washingtontechnology.com.

6. Personal interview, September 18, 2001.

7. William Eggers, "Interview," *Government Technology*, September 1997, www.govtech.net.

8. "Curtain Up on Eurotunnel," *Glasgow Herald*, April 30, 1994, p. 10.

9. M. Tyre and W. Orlikowski, "Windows of Opportunity: Temporal Patterns of Technological Adaptation in Organizations," *Organizational Science* 5, No. 1 (February 1994), pp. 98–118.

CHAPTER 9

Leveraging Capabilities

A transformational outsourcing initiative can look and feel like a snake that swallowed a gopher. The gopher looks tasty, but immediately after the meal, the snake's body is stretched and distorted. Digestion takes some time, and during that time, the snake isn't good for much else. Once the gopher is digested, however, the snake isn't the same. It's bigger and stronger.

For most companies, the transition process that comes with outsourcing holds many benefits. Managers learn how their processes work, and they make vast improvements. They use their partner's distance and expertise to make organizational changes that they never would have done on their own. They establish valuable new skill sets, operational assets, and relationships that they can use to fuel growth in their businesses. And they create organizational momentum: they lift their companies off the dime or out of the downward spiral and get things moving in the right direction. As transforming companies move through their planned transitions, they put the support structure for their new business models in place—the capabilities, physical assets, know-how, and relationships that they need and the appetite to use them. We talked about designing business models in Chapter 5; in this chapter, I want to talk about how organizations actually enact their models and leverage their new tangible and intangible assets to prosper.

As we discussed earlier, companies hold different aspirations for their transformational initiatives. Some executives just want to put their companies into a new competitive position. Others want also to establish an entirely new growth trajectory. Executives' aspirations color the intensity with which they leverage the new capabilities they have. Let's talk about three general approaches they take:

1. Actually using the new tangible and intangible assets they have developed
2. Exploiting the new assets to get more out of them than originally envisioned
3. Expanding the partnership to find additional ways the partners can collaborate to create even more value

We will also want to talk about the strategic failures: those situations in which the transformation initiative helped a company build assets and capabilities that ended up being poorly aligned with its strategic needs (see Exhibit 9.1).

Actually Use the Assets You Have

Transformational outsourcing establishes new operating assets for a company—not ideas for assets or theories about how they might work, but working organs. Effective companies fully incorporate these into the way they do business in order to get value out of them. This sounds obvious, but stop for a minute and reflect on all the management initiatives like Total Quality, Six Sigma, and ERP (enterprise resource planning systems) that were implemented but failed to deliver the value your company anticipated. The gap between what you expect and what you get does not usually come from a failure to implement a tool; it comes from a failure to use it. Why? Using a new tangible or intangible asset—a capability, relationship, or physical asset, for example—means changing the way the organization works to take advantage of it. That means taking new assets for a road test, pushing their limits, analyzing the results, and trying again.[1] In this process, both the new asset and the organization adjust to each other. And this process relies on close interaction between the outsourcing partners.

Exhibit 9.1. Three levels in leveraging joint assets.

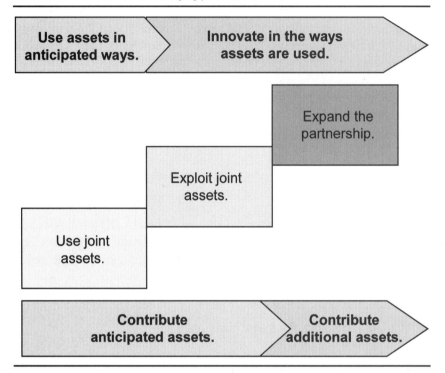

For example, in 1999, Magyar Oil and Gas Company (MOL), central Europe's largest integrated oil and gas company, adopted a strategy of growth through acquisition. At that time, it already controlled more than 120 separate companies, each one operating with relative autonomy. The senior leadership team decided to use outsourcing to dramatically improve the pace, the process, and the results of its acquisition agenda. Initially, it outsourced nonindustry-specific transaction-processing activities in finance. This included accounting, taxation (other than excise tax), treasury back office, management reporting, and external reporting, along with the information-technology systems and infrastructure to support these processes. Since then, it has also moved the energy trading back office under the outsourcing agreement. After three years, the company has streamlined its focus, integrated control of operations, reduced finance and accounting costs by 40 percent, and developed a capability for change.

Michel-Marc Delcommune, the CFO and executive director of MOL, explains that the company's strategy depends on his ability to get financial control of new acquisitions quickly and effectively. Outsourcing has accomplished that. He especially values the separation between the responsibility for achieving performance and the responsibility for measuring that performance. He points out, "In the post-Enron era, it's valuable to have the back office reporting centrally so you can make sure it is operating with the highest ethics. The head of trading didn't like this decision, but no one can oppose it today."

This is one way MOL makes use of its outsourced functions to achieve managerial ends. Delcommune describes others. He says some people in the company could have created a shared-service center and could have achieved some of the cost reductions and organizational consolidations that outsourcing brought. He argues, however, that an in-house team would have implemented a center "in a frozen envelopment." In other words, the process would have been stuck in 1999. He asserts, "Because our company is growing, we have asked [our provider] to change the organization seven times in three years, and they have done it. We don't even ask them if they can; we know they will." In short, MOL uses its outsourced shared-service center as a lead player in the organizational changes it needs to drive growth.[2] Finally, Delcommune argues that the entrepreneurial sparks have started to fly in the company as a result of the outsourcing. "Seeing the deal in action has opened managers' eyes to all sorts of possibilities. It's made them more commercially aware," he says.[3]

This is a powerful force that outsourcing offers by its very nature. Workers are no longer buried in a back-office cost center that is disconnected from the performance of the enterprise. They have moved to the face of the organization. They deal directly with the customer, and that makes all the difference. Take your own pulse on this question. Whose request is more likely to motivate your best effort—your boss's or your customer's?

Managers are often surprised by what they can do with a new asset. Recent research shows that as executives gain more experience with outsourcing, they raise their aspirations about the ways they can use it to create value.[4] In a recent study on global government outsourcing, we found that organizations that target higher-value objectives are actually more likely to be satisfied with the outcomes than those that aim only for cost cutting.[5] These progressive executives learn that they can achieve their managerial objectives, and that the impact exceeds their expectations. Ian Ailles, the group finance director at Thomas Cook, describes this experience enthusiastically: "Cosourcing makes visible the cost and implications of decisions." He asserts that employees become accustomed to working around the process glitches internal operations often have. But when a company hands the same operation off to a third party, it can no longer ignore the inefficiencies. And you get benefits—even new insights—by repairing these process problems. Ailles found that welding the cracks in the pipe led his company to make different decisions about what they offered to customers. They could see how much it cost to offer each type of service, and they began to trim the unprofitable services from their line. Managers could begin to understand the implications of their actions and what decisions cost. Ailles continues: "I knew we would get this benefit from cosourcing, but I had no idea how powerful it would be."

NS&I gives us another example of how an organization can use its new capability to prosper—and what it takes to do so. Before outsourcing, NS&I had introduced three new products in eight years. It intended to use transformational outsourcing to dramatically improve the company's record on product innovation. As the timeline in Exhibit 1.9 in Chapter 1 shows, Newport Systems actually completed the technical work for NS&I's first new product on its watch in the same month as it took over the operations—only four months after signing the contract. In the next seven months, it launched two additional new products and five new product variations. These accomplishments do not happen automatically. NS&I's product designers and Newport Systems's product developers pooled their expertise and their effort to drive this result. The capability they created together was—in every sense of the word—a joint asset. And these accomplishments showed that they actively used it to drive NS&I's performance.

Exploit Operating Assets in New Ways

Some organizations make a concerted effort to wring more value out of their new tangible and intangible assets than they can get just by using them. These organizations leverage those new assets to create new revenue streams or to further improve the operating characteristics of their businesses. This is one common way organizations extend their business models effectively: They take an asset that supports the current business model and use it to edge out into new arenas.

Using a jointly created asset this way presents some unique opportunities and some unique management challenges. NS&I foresaw the potential for attracting new business with the operation it transferred to Newport Systems, but it went one step further. As part of its contract with Newport, NS&I arranged to share in the benefits if Newport could use staff and other assets for third-party work. If Newport is able to use staff employed on NS&I business for other clients, NS&I receives a rebate. If Newport sublets space in a service center to another company, NS&I is entitled to 50 percent of both the net rental profit and the improvement in spending on its own operation. This gain-sharing arrangement reflects the partners' commitment to exploit their joint capability to improve their businesses, both separately and together.

The decision to open a single-company center to other clients should not be taken lightly. It is easier than turning an in-house center into a for-others operation, but it still raises important service-policy issues. The management teams of the original partners must sort out issues such as how priorities will be set when resources are scarce, how intellectual property will be shared, and whether staff will be dedicated to particular clients or pooled by function. In addition, they will want to mock up the first year's gain-sharing report so people on both sides can come to grips with how the benefits will be distributed.

They should expect to encounter new pressures. Since the assets will be shared among several clients, the outsourcing provider will have opportunities to improve operating costs by moving to standard technologies and work processes. Together, the partners should evaluate the trade-offs in swapping a customized, dedicated unit for one that is standardized and shared. The questions in Exhibit 9.2 can assist in this analysis.[6]

Extend the Partnership to New Arenas

A good relationship opens new doors. Once partners master the art of working together, it only makes sense for them to explore other opportunities to combine their skills and assets in valuable ways. Most start simply. They extend the outsourcing partnership to other parts of the company's business where it might be profitable. MOL started with finance and accounting and later incorporated the back office for the en-

Exhibit 9.2. Should we have shared or dedicated assets?

	People		Physical Assets		Technology Tools	
	Low	High	Low	High	Low	High
Value of sharing in getting access to advantaged assets—lower cost, higher quality, or both	1......3......5		1......3......5		1......3......5	
Ability to improve costs by sharing assets	1......3......5		1......3......5		1......3......5	
Value in the ability to leverage unique expertise in acquiring and managing assets by sharing	1......3......5		1......3......5		1......3......5	
Value in the ability to handle fluctuating demand by sharing	1......3......5		1......3......5		1......3......5	
Ability to invest more in shared assets to maintain or improve asset quality	1......3......5		1......3......5		1......3......5	
In addition, how important and difficult is it to integrate standardized assets with the organization?	1......3......5 High	Low	1......3......5 High	Low	1......3......5 High	Low
Total						

1 – 12	13 –17	18 – 30
Favor dedicated assets.	Weigh other criteria.	Favor shared assets.

Adapted from: Jane Linder, Susan Cantrell, and Scott Crist, "BPO Big Bang: Creating Value in an Expanded Universe," Accenture Institute for Strategic Change management report, August 2002, p. 7.

ergy-trading function. Thomas Cook is considering expanding its relationship with Accenture to include additional processes like procurement and yield management for its airlines. These extensions carry their own compelling business cases, but they also take advantage of the strong, trusting relationships that partners have established. Trust takes some of the coordination risk out of these ventures.

To expand the initiative's scope to entirely new arenas, most partners do not issue an entirely new request for proposal. They just work out the details with their current partner. This approach saves the time and cost of managing a multi-bidder sourcing process, but it can also eliminate the parts of the process that enable all the right discussions between the partners. Prudent leaders document the process, identify the stakeholder issues, evaluate business model implications, and envision future scenarios.

Then they negotiate a written agreement that documents their aspirations, their principles in managing the process, their financial arrangements, and their management process.

Thomas Cook has developed a template for this kind of agreement to institutionalize the approach for each organization that participates in the overall outsourcing partnership. While the details may vary, creating this kind of standard operating procedure reinforces good practice and makes continued partnering easy. It also places the responsibility for defining roles and accountabilities squarely on the managers who are setting up the agreement. When these arrangements are negotiated centrally, companies are not likely to get the same level of engagement and ownership from local management as this approach provides. The learning that is accumulated over multiple iterations of the process can also be incorporated into the template.

In each of its agreements, Thomas Cook takes the time to include a preamble. This section outlines the way the partners intend to work together. By acknowledging that a provider will not be blamed when issues are caused by the company and by outlining how disputes will be resolved, the two organizations can avoid endless legalistic specifications about how to handle every transactional detail. Neil Hammond, director of strategic sourcing and IT efficiency for Thomas Cook, explains: "Everyone is concerned about what happens if things go wrong. But you don't want to document all that detail. You should be trying to deal with that on a relationship level. Sometimes it will be one company's fault, sometimes it will be the other's. So we say that if it's clearly our responsibility and we fail, the supplier won't be held to blame. It is a statement of intention."

Of course, setting up a relationship and a process for the first time, and bringing a new organization into it, are two entirely different things. The first involves an extensive design process—the partners are starting from scratch. For the second, the existing relationship and operating assets create a huge pull of gravity. Why would a company want to set up a separate processing center when it already had one in operation? But managers of the newly entering organization will almost certainly claim that the existing center or process or relationship does not fully meet their needs. They will ask for the latitude to do some things differently. This issue will appear as a tactical consideration, but it is not. Deciding how much process consistency the enterprise needs and in what areas is a long-term strategic call. If the senior team has not yet established this policy, it should. Otherwise, the organization is inadvertently choosing to operate with a cornucopia of inconsistent processes.

A small number of companies that are transforming through outsourcing reach even more deeply into their partnership for innovation. Fifteen percent of the companies among our examples go beyond extending the partnership to new processes or functions within the company. They deliberately search for business opportunities that combine the partners' expertise or assets in innovative ways. Thomas Cook provides an especially good example. This organization started with a two-part agenda: to fix the old and to create the new. The executive team realized they could return the company to profitability by cutting costs and streamlining processes, but they could never achieve their growth goals this way. Moving from third to first in the UK travel industry would require more innovation.

Thomas Cook explicitly invited their transformational outsourcing partner to take that journey with them by making innovation part of the partner's quarterly performance evaluation. They put bite in the invitation, but not just for their partner—for themselves as well. How? They obligated their partner to appear before the senior executive team each quarter with a presentation of innovative ideas. This motivated their partner to attend to this issue, and, equally important, it guaranteed that the executive team would find time on its busy agenda to listen. The team would evaluate the quality of the ideas, and that assessment would influence the partner's bonus for the quarter. So in one stroke of the word processor, Thomas Cook established a mechanism for engaging with its partner—at the right level of the organization—that would generate a discussion about innovative business ideas each quarter.

For example, Thomas Cook's partner has an expertise in emerging supply-chain technologies—specifically radio frequency identification tags. The partners are considering how these might be used to improve baggage handling for vacation travelers. Thomas Cook knows every customer's hotel before he or she gets on the airplane. It could use this technology to scan the luggage and have customers' bags delivered directly to the hotel. In the low-margin packaged holiday business, this could improve the customer experience enough to be an important differentiating factor.

These two partners are looking beyond their own local skills and expertise as sources for new business opportunities. For example, a sub-

sidiary of Thomas Cook's outsourcing partner provides airline reservation and passenger financial-transaction-processing services. This
organization already counts 40 airlines as its customers, and it might provide some benefits to Thomas Cook Airlines as well.

Finally, Thomas Cook is looking at its multinational outsourcing provider as a market for its services. Reasons Thomas Cook's group business
transformation and operations director Marco Trecroce: "Seventy-five
thousand Accenture employees worldwide have to get their holidays
somewhere. It may as well be from us." If this arrangement works out,
Thomas Cook will take its place beside a selected list of other vendors
who offer their products and services directly through the internal Accenture portal.

The extent to which these ideas turn into good business for Thomas
Cook remains to be seen. But the company's approach puts it way ahead
of most other transforming organizations that hope for product and service innovation while they reward operational excellence.

The Failures

Not all transformational outsourcing initiatives are successful. Every
company in our universe of 20 examples proceeded through implementation with enough success to call the program effective up to that point.
None was perfect, but the processes and the systems that the partners
intended to put in place were actually implemented. Where, then, do these
initiatives fail? In using the capabilities the partners have created to
achieve their strategic aims. Out of 20 examples, it's too early to see the
results for three of them, and three (15 percent) ultimately failed to meet
their strategic goals.

By the way, this is a remarkably small number when it is compared
to other types of large organizational change initiatives. Whether we're
talking about acquisitions, alliances, major systems implementations, or
even conventional outsourcing, the statistics are fairly consistent. Fifty to
75 percent of the initiatives ultimately fail to achieve their objectives.[7]
Compared to other big organizational moves, then, transformational outsourcing is remarkably successful.

But let's talk about the failures. There is one dominant reason for the
three failures. These companies accomplished the organizational transformations they set out to make, but the changes they made did not—or

were not perceived to result in competitive success. While none of the implementations were problem free, tactical setbacks were surmountable.

The real failures were issues of strategy, not of execution. For example, in 1997, the group chief executive of a large insurance company in the UK laid out an aggressive strategy for driving growth through door-to-door agents. He knew this would involve investments in information technology, but he was skeptical that the IT organization had the capability to deliver. Two major development projects had incurred frightening budget overruns before being canceled. He concluded that the company needed an infusion of expertise to develop the new tools its strategy required. He contracted with an outsourcing partner to take over and run daily information-technology operations, to improve IT processes and services, to ready the company for the millennium, and to launch a major program of strategic development.

Through three years of effort, the information-technology capabilities of the company were dramatically improved. Operations were streamlined and brought under control. Y2K-related improvements were made on time so the company passed into the new millennium without incident. And the new systems for supporting door-to-door agents were implemented. Unfortunately, by the time this work was completed, the company had changed business direction. Instead of outfitting 2,000 agents with new technologies, it laid them off and announced that it was withdrawing from direct sales. In other words, the outsourcing initiative did what it was designed to do: clear away the barriers to growth. However, by the time they were cleared away, the game had changed. As a result, the strategic impact of this transformational outsourcing initiative was minimal.

A start-up Web exchange that prefers to remain anonymous also failed to achieve its objectives through transformational outsourcing. Again, the culprit was strategy, not execution. The exchange was launched by a consortium of large oil and chemical companies in the late 1990s to provide a portal for online procurement in these industries. The consortium's intention was to preempt any pure Internet upstart from taking all their business, and as we all recall, the heat was on to do it quickly. At the outset, the company planned to connect buyers and sellers in both tendering and auction processes. In order to get to market quickly and scalably, the exchange's executives elected to outsource finance and accounting, human resource management, customer contact, and information technology. They reasoned that the only way to create a capability to handle high volumes of transactions with complex pricing quickly and effectively was to rely on established operations available through outsourcing.

Unfortunately, the transaction volumes the exchange anticipated never materialized, the pricing never became complex, and the way business was conducted among oil and chemical companies never changed much. The exchange had implemented all the capabilities its parents thought it needed; it just never used most of them. An executive explained: "It was not a problem with the outsourcing; it was a problem with the business model. The business model we took to market did not hold. If we knew then what we know now, we never would have done it."

The third failure is the Spanish bank. Recall that it was a Spanish subsidiary of a bank headquartered in the UK. After five years of losses as a narrow-line mortgage lender, the Spanish CEO took a hard look at his options. He concluded that he should either sell the bank or transform it into a full-service operation to enable it to compete head-to-head with the other institutions in its market. Given only nine months by headquarters to show improvement, the CEO lined up a transformational outsourcing partner and started to work.

On a local level, he succeeded. The bank stopped hemorrhaging red ink and broke even within two years. However, his growth strategy sent his organization off on a direction that was at odds with that set by headquarters. He wanted to continue to grow as a full-service bank, and the folks at the top wanted to consolidate and refocus on mortgages alone. Eventually they fired the Spanish CEO and sold the subsidiary. Again, the transformational outsourcing initiative was effective, but the strategy it enacted was not perceived to be the right one.

What can we conclude from these three stories of failure? Transformational outsourcing can be dangerous. But that danger is very different from the one executives usually face with big strategic change initiatives. Normally, they do not implement the changes they intend. In fact, I would hazard to say that many executives are so accustomed to getting less than they set out to achieve that they barely consider the consequences of actually succeeding.

Transformational outsourcing is different. The changes executives initiate will be made. The organization will transform. Like being beamed out to some unexplored planet, however, executives must be inordinately thoughtful when they set the coordinates lest they find themselves surrounded by hostile aliens when they get there. Most strategic maneuvering takes effect incrementally. This pace gives executives more time to judge competitive response and tweak the direction. Transformational outsourcing involves a bigger, faster leap forward. As we said in Chapter 5, executives will want to look before they step out.

How to Leverage Capabilities

After every combat exercise, the U.S. Army uses its well-publicized After Action Review process to establish a causal connection between what people did and the results they achieved. It starts with some very pointed questions like: What did we intend to achieve and what did we actually achieve? It then invites participants to review what they did that led to the outcomes and what they could do to improve those outcomes.

Executives can borrow this approach to improve their ability to get value from transformational outsourcing initiatives. They should:

- *Set the agenda for leveraging capabilities at the outset of the initiative and revisit it regularly.* The business model design and scenario planning processes described in Chapter 5 will enable executives to take up these questions in detail. Executives will want to repeat the process when competitive and marketplace changes shift the landscape. These reality checks will keep the company's strategy on course and bring key stakeholders into the process at the same time.

- *Adopt metrics and incentives that keep both partners focused on increasing the return on the relationship over time.* Whether these spark waves of innovation or just encourage a company to use its new capabilities, these diagnostic and motivational tools should align the priorities for both partners.

- *Establish the organizational machinery to act on opportunities.* Executives will want to integrate responsibilities for innovation and value improvement into the established roles and governance structure for the relationship. That way, it will become part of the everyday management of the partnership.

- *Open the doors to cross-fertilization.* Give employees on both sides the means to navigate through each other's organizations. When they know they can easily figure out whom to talk to about a new idea, they will. Enabling serendipitous innovation throughout the partnership is just as important as driving directed innovation.

Notes

1. See Marcy Tyre and Wanda Orlikowski, "Windows of Opportunity: Temporal Patterns of Technological Adaptation in Organizations," *Organizational Science* 5, No. 1 (February 1994), pp. 98–118. Dorothy Leonard also talks extensively about the mutual adjustment between an organization and its new technologies in *Wellsprings of Knowledge: Building and Sustaining the Sources of Innovation* (Cambridge, MA: Harvard Business School Press, May 1998).

2. Personal interview with Michel-Marc Delcommune, February 2003, and public presentation by Antoine Parmentier, MOL Accounting and Tax Director, September 6, 2002, at the European Outsourcing Summit. See www.malekigroup.com.

3. CFO Europe, "Finance's Finest," April 2002, www.cfoeurope.com.

4. Unpublished Accenture survey, January 2003.

5. Jane Linder and Thomas Healy, "Outsourcing in Government: Pathways to Value," Accenture Government Executive Series research report, May 2003.

6. Jane Linder, Susan Cantrell, and Scott Crist, "Business Process Outsourcing Big Bang: Creating Value in an Expanding Universe," Accenture Institute for Strategic Change research report, July 2002.

7. One study, for example, found that three-quarters of managers in firms surveyed believe that outsourcing outcomes have fallen short of expectations (E. R. Greenberg and C. Canzoneri, *Outsourcing: the AMA Survey* [New York: American Management Association, 1997]). Another study found that 20 to 25 percent of all outsourcing relationships fail within two years and that 50 percent fail within five (Marq R.Ozanne, D&B Barometer of Global Outsourcing, 2000). M. Clemente and D. Greenspan find that merger and acquisition transactions fail more than half the time (*Winning at M&A* [New York: John Wiley & Sons, 1998]). According to the Gartner Group, half of all strategic alliances fail to deliver the desired results.

CHAPTER 10

Ending and Renewal

Transformational outsourcing initiatives ultimately end. That is as it should be. The company achieves the changes that it sought, or it runs out of time. These changes pay off strategically, or they don't. No matter which of these paths a company follows, it must wrap up its transformational initiative and enter a new strategic phase. When the initiative has failed, the outsourcing partner is usually tossed out along with the senior executives who orchestrated the initiative. That's a definite end. In addition to the clear and obvious failures, some companies' results fall in the gray area. In these cases, the organization must decide whether to push on or pull the plug. Again, it may need to adjust the relationship in the process.

A wide variety of stakeholder changes can also interfere with a transformational agenda. The company's transformational champion, or vital member of his or her team, can leave. The outsourcing provider's key people can be replaced. Either of the partner companies can experience ownership changes. In the public sector, elections can empower a new political administration. In some cases, these changes can make it a whole new ballgame.

Finally, when executives have achieved their transformational objectives, they shift to operating the business rather than turning it inside out and capturing value from new capabilities. Of course, every business must keep changing to compete, but the nature of this change, well, changes. Sticking with sports analogies, it's like the difference between the Kansas City Royals and the Yankees. The Royals' longtime owner died and left the team under the direction of a nonprofit committee divided by in-fighting and acrimony. Predictably, the team's performance tanked. When David Glass bought the team in May 2000, he had a turn-around on his hands. For three years, he cut deals to bring more money into the franchise, brought in new management, and invested in new capabilities. The Yankees, on the other hand, are currently at the top of their game. They are building on their strengths, shoring up their weaknesses, and keeping their eyes on the challengers. It requires an entirely different balance of creating new capabilities and capturing value from existing ones. There's no guarantee that these two teams won't find their positions reversed in a few years. That doesn't change the point: Dominant organizations manage change differently from those in a turn-around situation.

Every transformational outsourcing relationship will change its character at some point. Exits, endings, and renewals are processes, not events. They work better if they are both planned for and managed well. This chapter talks about how to do both.

Recognizing Failure

Three out of the 20 transformational outsourcing examples on which this book is based are counted as failures by their executives. As we noted in Chapter 9, all three were failures of strategy, not failures of execution. (Since failures of execution are common in conventional outsourcing, this success rate highlights the value of sponsorship from the top.) The possibility of failure, even if it is small, raises some serious questions we should answer:

- How do executives know when their initiative is failing?
- When should they pull the plug?
- How can they spot doomed initiatives early so they can quit before they start?

- If the partnership fails, who does the work?
- How is that transition best managed?

Diagnosing Failure

In transformational outsourcing initiatives, senior executives pay a great deal of attention to implementation. As a result, their implementations succeed. They are often so absorbed in overseeing the transition to new systems, new organizations, new processes, and new facilities, however, that they do not pay nearly as much attention to changes in their company's competitive environment. When they emerge from implementation hell, they can find that the landscape has shifted underneath their feet. What they originally set out to do is no longer what they want.

The obvious remedy is to review strategic assumptions periodically during the implementation-intensive years of the initiative. But this is easier to recommend than to do. Why? The transformational outsourcing initiative is like a stone rolling downhill. It has direction; it has speed; and it has momentum. It needs these characteristics to succeed. To stand in front of it without killing yourself, you have to drain out some of its energy. This imperils the entire program.

This is the time for war games. With the help of the company's strategy and competitive-intelligence experts, the senior executive team of each major business unit should participate in a daylong competitive role-play at least once every six months—more often in a faster-moving industry.

Here's how a simple war game works. The company's managers form teams. One team takes the role of the company, and the others play the competitors. Colleagues from the outsourcing partner company should be included on each team. Groups of real stakeholders—customers, financial analysts, distribution channel partners—play themselves. Parent company executives and, in the public sector, influential politicians can also be brought into the process. Whether they participate as part of the competitive teams or judge the company as stakeholders depends on how close their relationships are with company executives. Putting them on the teams brings them into the inner circle; giving them a stakeholder role accords them respectful distance. It's a choice that management should address in designing the experience.

In an open forum, each team has a chance to present its value proposition to the stakeholders. This should include products, services, price points, profitability levels, company growth, and other key characteristics of the company that make it appealing. The company's own team portrays itself as if it were already transformed. The other teams use competitive intelligence and their own industry insights to portray competitors as they would portray themselves if they were in the room.

After hearing all the company and competitor value propositions, the stakeholders rank the companies. Customers base their rankings on which company they would most like to buy from; financial analysts consider how highly they would recommend each company to their clients; channel partners assess how likely they would be to carry and promote each company's products; parent company executives and politicians rate their willingness to support the organization given this competitive context.

A facilitated discussion among all the participants follows the ranking exercise. As stakeholders explain the logic behind their rankings, company executives will learn whether their transformational initiative is likely to have the strategic results they envision. As a by-product, they will gain an in depth understanding of competitors' positions and likely moves. To complete the exercise, the executives should summarize what they learned and what they intend to do about it. This will give them the opportunity to adjust their strategic direction if necessary, to shore up gaps in their value proposition, and to improve stakeholder commitment. If the company's transformation is on a path to failure, this will provide enough early warning to correct the course.

When to Pull the Plug?

The only viable time to abort a transformational outsourcing initiative is before it starts. Remember, we're not talking about conventional outsourcing programs that never make it onto the CEO's radar. The company's very future rests on the success of the transformational outsourcing initiative. Failing carries huge consequences. So before company executives—and their counterparts from their outsourcing partner—sign up, they must acknowledge that failure is not an option. They will do whatever it takes to make it work.

In earlier chapters we have talked about stakeholder analysis, business-model design, scenario planning, partner selection, and risk management as ways to reduce uncertainty and ensure success. Some companies take one additional step. They take a hint from the recent U.S. requirement that chief financial officers personally certify that their companies' financial statements are fair and accurate. They ask key executives to register their personal commitment to success as they sign the contract. This represents each individual's promise to make the initiative succeed. In my experience, executives find it easy to nod their heads in the right direction. When they have to sign their names, they get much more serious.

When the initiative hits a rocky patch—and it will—someone will remind the group that they all committed personally. This will help keep them from defensively retreating to their corners to point fingers and lay blame and, instead, to work through the challenges they face.

If executives cannot satisfy themselves that the initiative will succeed, they should not go forward. The governor of Connecticut did this in mid-1999.[1] The governor and CIO of Connecticut had decided to outsource the state's entire information-technology capability with an objective of reducing cost, improving capability, and driving economic development. They managed a careful tender process, evaluating bids from several multinational providers and the Connecticut State Employees Association, the union representing many of the workers who would be affected. After an extensive tender process, Connecticut chose a vendor and began detailed contract negotiations. The contract negotiations broke down at the eleventh hour over financing. To make the deal politically feasible, the governor needed the outsourcing provider to absorb costs in the first three years of the contract that the state would repay in latter years. The provider was reluctant to invest, asking instead for its cash flow to be more even. The difference was a deal-breaker. After all the effort, the two organizations simply walked away from the table.

Reacting to Stakeholder Changes

Transformational outsourcing initiatives may not fail in execution, but they always have hiccups. Many other authors have covered the day-today project management and people management challenges extensively.[2] I want to focus on one particular type of hiccup that is especially important for transformational outsourcing: a change in one of the initiative's key stakeholders. When new individuals enter the game, they must be brought on board. Without their support, the initiative will be placed at substantial risk. For example, the outsourcing provider could be acquired. Company executives would want to make sure the new parent would continue to encourage the provider to honor its commitments. If, instead, it sets a new corporate direction, this could undermine the long-term relationship on which the transformation depends.

For example, a European IT outsourcing provider—let's call it Snowden, Ltd. (not its real name)—had been actively crafting private finance initiatives in the central UK government in the late 1990s. A Japanese information-technology company acquired majority ownership of Snowden in 1990, but the company was allowed to operate independently. Faced with steep operating losses in the unit in 2000, Snowden's parent decided to step in. Snowden had not participated in transformational outsourcing deals, but its work was important to government clients, and some of its obligations were complex. When parent company management reviewed Snowden's contracts, they found that a number of private finance initiatives did not meet their standards for profitability.[3] Parent company management immediately sought to renegotiate these. And government executives found themselves unexpectedly pressured to provide higher fees.

Executives with open-book relationships were better able to navigate this disruption. According to one Snowden client:

> We have always tried to work in an open relationship where challenges and problems that need to be faced are dealt with in an open and frank manner. Each side recognizes the value of opening their books to the other party. When we face a problem, for us as customers or them as suppliers, we put our heads together and see how best to resolve it in the interest of both parties. We put our investment in the positive development of the partnership, rather than defense of respective positions.[4]

This executive encouraged his counterparts at Snowden's parent to continue in this kind of relationship, and together they worked out the financial issue. This executive continues: "For a while, we were uncertain about their commitment to the relationship. Those issues have been cleared away. The relationship is now in a strong and growing position."

Our small universe of transformational outsourcing cases does not have any examples in which the company changed ownership during its transformation. Leaving hostile takeovers aside, this shows that selling out and taking the initiative to transform seem to be mutually exclusive leadership choices. If a CEO decides to commit to a program of transformation, he or she is not shopping the company at the same time. The cognitive dissonance would simply be too great.

Public-sector initiatives are buffeted by changes in political administration. In some governments, top executives of departments and agencies change with every election. This leads them to take a unique approach to transformational outsourcing—one only found in the public sector. (We will talk more about this in the next chapter.) British Commonwealth countries avoid this dilemma by giving public-sector executives employment contracts for terms that make sense for the challenges they face. In these governments, when the administration changes, executives leading transformational outsourcing initiatives must bring new policy makers on board to keep their base of support solid. Peter Bareau at NS&I cleared this hurdle. Egos notwithstanding, we don't have any examples of a new administration trying to stop or undo a transformational outsourcing initiative.

On the surface, we might think that replacing key individuals in the company's leadership team presents the greatest threat to the continuity of a transformational outsourcing initiative. According to our limited data, this seems not to be true. In 20 examples, we have two cases in which the CEOs left in the middle of the transformation. In both cases, they oversaw the implementation of new capabilities, and they made sure their organizations used them. But they did not wait around long enough to capture all the strategic benefits these would deliver over the coming years.

In both cases, the new CEOs who took over set different priorities from those of the original transformational architects. In one, the change of leadership is very recent, so the ultimate impact is unclear. The other company, an intermediary organization that matches buyers and sellers of commodity products, has been highly successful. Here's the story.

In 1986, this company, let's call it Agora plc (not its real name), moved its business from a face-to-face market to distributed trading using remote computer screens and telephones. To accomplish this, it implemented a large information-technology infrastructure. By 1992, the costs, service issues, and inflexibility of this relatively undisciplined systems environment were stretching management's ability to cope. For example, information technology represented 30 percent of the organization's expenses and 20 percent of its staff, yet a seemingly simple systems change was estimated to take nine months to complete and cost £1 million ($1.66 million).

The CEO worked with a multinational technology company to create one of the earliest transformational outsourcing initiatives. He championed the radical notion that he could improve the cost and reliability of information-technology operations by outsourcing IT and use the funds that would be liberated to invest in flexible new capabilities. He started this all rolling with a five-year outsourcing and consulting arrangement. By 1993, he had resigned over an issue with the board on IT performance. His replacement lasted until 1995, when he, too, resigned over the board's lack of support for the new electronic-trading capabilities he wanted. His successor was able to preside over the implementation of these capabilities, which totally changed the way the company did business.

By 1997, Agora cut fixed IT costs by 40 percent and reallocated these funds to building a flexible contracting and information service. Despite two additional CEOs, neither of whom found information-technology issues important enough to merit his personal attention, the company can introduce new products and services more nimbly and cost-effectively. It stands at the forefront among its direct competitors in products, service, and efficiency. Approximately half of Agora's staff currently works for the outsourcing supplier.

How could all this happen amid disruptive changes in leadership? I am reluctant to grant all the credit to the outsourcing provider, but I cannot think of any other plausible explanation. Every time Agora replaced its CEO, the transformational outsourcing initiative hiccupped, but it did not stop. The provider's consistent focus enabled it to push ahead; Agora was the beneficiary. Does this mean I recommend undertaking these initiatives without CEO leadership? Absolutely not. It does mean that, with the right outsourcing partner, one visionary CEO can set an initiative in motion that reaches well beyond his or her term in office. For owners and investors, this surprising result holds great promise. They can rely, at least in part, on the leadership of the partner company to shoulder some of the burden of strategic execution. It's like having a buddy with whom to go to the health club. When your motivation for working out flags, she provides enough energy for both of you, and vice versa. As a result, the time frame over which you can sustain a healthy agenda extends dramatically, and the trajectory improves (see Exhibit 10.1).

Thomas Cook: Lift Off

An update to the Thomas Cook story illustrates how this works on the front lines.

Manny Fontenla-Novoa, an up-through-the-ranks executive, stepped into the CEO's position at Thomas Cook in January 2003, with his eyes open. He said, "Thomas Cook is an amazing organization. It has more than 150 years of proud history. I want this to be the best and most successful period of Thomas Cook history so it will be around for the next 150 years. This is not a stepping stone to something else for me; this is it. This is our time."

Exhibit 10.1. Partner leadership helps sustain strategic progress.

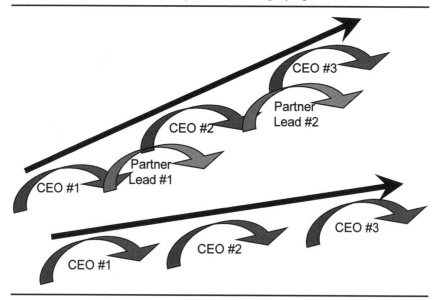

His predecessor had spent the prior 18 months engineering a much-needed financial turn-around. But Manny recognized that bringing costs in line was only the first phase of the dramatic and lasting transformation they sought. To lift the organization from third place in its industry to the top spot would require that they grow faster and more profitably than their competitors.

No mean feat, that. The industry, it seemed, had suffered more than its share of setbacks. Just as Thomas Cook laid plans to take the Florida vacation market by storm, the September 11, 2001, terrorist attacks and the following anthrax scares intervened. Following this shock, global travel volume plummeted, and discretionary vacation travel was hit the hardest.

Over the past year, the company had restructured from independent vertical businesses—airlines, tour operations, and distribution—to a single coordinated operation. A few lingering elements of the consolidation were still in process, but the leadership team had implemented consistent financial processes, consistent human relations practices, and consistent rewards and incentives to focus all of Thomas Cook's 13,000 employees on the good of the whole.

By mid-2002, vacation travel peeked out of the shadows, but the Iraqi conflict and the SARS threat drove it back again. In addition, sluggish economic conditions across Europe made customers especially price-sensitive. As a result, vacation travel was changing. The straightforward packaged vacation market of the past was fracturing into components. People wanted short breaks as well as longer stays. They wanted to take advantage of a discount Internet airfare as they pieced together their plans. And they wanted more flexibility than ever before in designing their own itineraries.

Focus on the Front Office

To drive profitable growth, Manny wanted to take full advantage of the back-office consolidation that the company had implemented through its cosourcing agreement with Accenture. More important, however, he wanted to place his focus squarely on the front-line business. He began by rebuilding his management team.

Glenn Chip, a colleague of Manny's from the tour operations business, stayed in place as the head of the Thomas Cook airline, but Manny appointed a new finance director and director of HR. He also asked Russell Margerrison to take responsibility for yield. Margerrison had joined tour operations finance just in time to help implement the SAP general ledger and transfer the operation to Accenture. In Margerrison's new role, he managed all the prices—for vacations, foreign exchange in the retail network, fees for third-party travel agents, insurance companies, car hire, and airport parking lots. He explained, "If I price too high, sales can't sell the holidays [vacations]. If I'm too low, margins slip. Plus I have to operate within the competitive market. We have pulled this activity together to a single location, and we now change prices on a daily basis."

Manny also brought in outsider Chris Onslow as his managing director of sales. With a background in retail, not travel, Chris took responsibility for everything that faces the customer—all the channels from the shops and foreign exchange bureaus to the direct TV station, Web site, and business-to-business activities. Onslow admitted he was initially reluctant to join Thomas Cook, considering it too much like the BBC and Barclays and not enough like Virgin. Ultimately, Manny's vision and passion convinced him his perception would soon be wrong, if it were not already.

Getting into the Thick of It

Manny and his team charged the organization to get their hands dirty. As an operating executive who had "zigged and zagged his way up through the organization, touching everyone on the way," Manny intuitively understood the intimate, emotional connection between customers and staff that drove profits. He asked his team to improve profits by 50 percent for each of the next two years.

The first challenge was to make sure the previous administration's improvements were bedded down and operating sustainably. Tim Barlow, Manny's new finance director, was not completely satisfied with either the level of financial control or the management information coming out of Accenture's shared-service center. Barlow was particularly eager to strengthen the practice of paying suppliers only from official invoices and segregating duties to prevent fraud. He began holding regular meetings with the Accenture team to address these control issues and to develop a new finance dashboard that would give management up-to-date access to a daily profit-and-loss statement. Barlow explained, "The biggest obstacle to improving the center was getting people to recognize we had a problem. Once the previous management acknowledged the issues, it became easier to put improvements in place. Now I am exploring the opportunity to transfer more of my retained team to the center as well as giving the business directors timelier, more relevant information."

As the new team took over, however, the back office was in much better shape than the front. Without much ado, Onslow renamed his four contact centers to be sales centers. He explains: "I wanted to change the mind-set from 'taking calls' to 'selling holidays [vacations].' We now have targets for flow, targets for conversion, daily targets, personal targets, infinitely more targets." He also launched a sweeping improvement program to implement retail centers of excellence in his 650 high street shops. He asked each of his 27 regional managers to identify one store in the center of their regions to be their model. In that store, the manager would implement best practices. The staff would know how to open the store, what the window card should look like, how to approach a customer, and how to do effective training. When this store was operating at this high standard, it would be certified by the executive team as "Fit for Trade #1" in its region. As the manager rolled these practices out across the region, the model store would begin pushing best practices to the next level to become "Fit for Trade #2." Onslow recounted: "This approach gives us both consistency and improving profitability forever. When you are in a business our size, you have a big problem if your poster is wrong. This way, you never roll out your mistakes."

Onslow was not the only member of the executive team who was involved with the centers of excellence. Both to give the model stores the benefit of top management attention and expertise, and to connect top management more closely to the business, each of the top 27 executives in the company adopted one of the centers as his or her personal charge. "The stores grow up as a result," Onslow explained. "The first thing that happened is that performance went down. Sales went down; morale went down. The only thing that went up was pressure to perform. People were ringing up to complain that they couldn't stand to be monitored every day. They said it was ridiculous to think their entire staff would know the brochure. But we got through that, and now people are excited about the direction we are taking. We launched this program three months ago, and the model stores already have a nine-point sales differential over the others."

Improving retail sales was necessary but not sufficient to drive the company's transformation. Historically, the vertically siloed Thomas Cook had a tidy profit record at retail and in its airline, but these were more than offset by losses in tour operations. The new vertically integrated organization required much more coordination among the parts. Glenn Chip, managing director of Thomas Cook Airlines, laid out some of the challenges: "The airlines are a factory. What's best for us is the lowest seat cost per kilometer, so if we can do things in a standard way and minimize change, we will be more cost-competitive. But that doesn't tell the whole story. If we have capacity on routes where there's no demand, that's not good. We have to be flexible enough to see what the market wants and provide that efficiently. It might drive cost in the airlines, but it will improve profits overall."

While the sales side could respond immediately to yesterday's profit-and-loss report, the airline had to manage capacity that was relatively fixed for a season. With overall travel demand depressed, the airline's ability to sell excess capacity to charters was limited. Chip's challenge was to optimize the route structure based on demand and profitability, with a careful eye on fixed-cost allocation and contribution to overhead. In addition to coordinating with the Thomas Cook tour and retail operations, Chip had to work with parent company executives in Germany to plan how the airline would operate as a pan-European system. He explained: "We are trying to establish what can sensibly be centralized to drive out the costs that customers don't care about, like adopting common aircraft types and common maintenance procedures." To make sure the organization kept its priorities straight, Chip reminded his colleagues: "Our customers are not sophisticated businessmen; they are families on holiday [vacation]. It's our job to give them a holiday [vacation] experience. We should drive costs down to compete with the no-frills airlines, but not to the point where we become a 'no thrills' airline." Nadine Jones, acting director of HR, added: "We are not selling a shirt or a toaster that you carry out of the store; we are selling a dream."

To orchestrate the next stage of Thomas Cook's transformation, the executive team was hungry for better management information. Barlow was working on a daily P&L to help operating managers throughout the company adopt a profit focus. Margerrison, the director of yield, sponsored the introduction of a revenue-management system to enable his analysts to manage prices with day-to-day responsiveness. Onslow added: "Eventually I would like to send every member of the sales staff a sheet in every pay envelope that says: 'Here's how you did this period on the P&L.' I want to drive accountability to profit; not margin or market share or any of those other things we have measured in the past."

The executive team's passion for better information extended deep into the organization with a new initiative called "eXcelerate." Its objective was to provide a knowledge base and simulation-based training program to bring every sales associate rapidly up to the level of the best person in the business. Onslow explained: "We wanted to take the wisdom of someone with 25 years of experience and implement that in formal training for our new associates. And we wanted to bring the experience of everyone who travels with us back to our sales centers."

Working with Accenture, the executive team crafted a sales simulation to coach an associate through the sales process, helping him or her identify customer needs, recommend vacation destinations, and close the business. If the associate failed to offer the best vacation option or missed an opportunity to add a rental car to the package, the system was designed to take the associate back to the point in the conversation where he or she had made the error. "It's a fabulous tool," Onslow remarked, "more like a one-on-one coach than short-lived classroom instruction."

The training system was based on a detailed map of the sales process as well as an extensive knowledge base about vacation destinations and experiences. To build the knowledge base, Thomas Cook asked everyone in the business, including the customers, to send a postcard when they traveled. A customer might write, "On my trip to Malta, I found a romantic little church. I got engaged." With this kind of information a sales associate who had never been to Malta could help a customer imagine the possibilities.

The executive team recognized that the cosourcing relationship with Accenture had been instrumental in helping them design and implement the next phase of the company's transformation. This included upgrading management information across the board as well as developing the new sales training systems. Onslow noted: "The cosourcing relationship is cleverly set up to be measured in part on innovation, so Accenture comes to us with tools like eXcelerate." Manny added: "The great thing about this is that we are doing it on a profit-sharing basis. Accenture is prepared to earn money based on the improvement we get from using the tool. That gives us a massive benefit."

Passion for Change

If the first phase of Thomas Cook's transformation helped the company taxi down the runway in the right direction, the second phase aimed for lift-off. As Manny and his team set their sights on making the coming years the best time in Thomas Cook's history, they recognized the importance of their unique management approach. While they had plenty of short-term targets, their real aim was to create a lasting, successful business. That meant building from the foundation, not just polishing the external appearance.

To reach their high-performance goals, the executive team unwound some of the pay and performance tactics that were in place when they took over. They opted instead for programs to reward, recognize, and encourage their people. Nadine Jones explained: "Whatever we do today, our competitors will copy tomorrow. How do we move ahead, then? We have to make sure our people are unique. They must be the best motivated, the best trained, the most obsessed with the customer, united as one team, and intensely proud of who we are and what we do. Manny is the right leader for us now, and Accenture is helping us every step of the way."

Manny summarized, "I am passionate about this organization. I have always felt that the teams we have in the field are the best in the industry. They do things every day that go beyond the call of duty. I have the support of the organization, which is fantastic. It spurs me on, and I would never take it for granted. Our job is to inspire and lead these amazing people to achieve. We want to be the company of choice, full stop, and now we have real forward momentum."

Phase Change at an Operational Level

A transformational outsourcing initiative may never face strategic failure. It may never have a stakeholder hiccup. But it will certainly change its operating character at some point. When the new capabilities that executives sought through transformation are in place, they turn their attention to operating, not implementing. The organization takes smaller bites of change—relentless incremental improvements rather than big, radical shifts. Operating managers, rather than change champions, take the lead.

This is all normal. It does not call for a new contract with the outsourcing provider. But it does require the leadership on both sides to agree on a change in emphasis. For example, Thomas Cook measured its cosourcing partner on meeting deadlines and cultural fit during the transition to the shared-service center. They exacted no financial penalties for missing service levels during that time. When the emphasis shifted to operations, the service-level standards, performance penalties, and push for incremental improvements kicked in.

Executives do not stumble over this transition. They see it coming; they plan for it; they carry it out successfully. And executives who are only trying to reposition their organizations can declare victory. The companies that are looking for a better strategic trajectory, however, can fall prey to complacency at this stage. In a global study of national governments' outsourcing experiences, for example, we found that only 10 percent of the executives were extremely satisfied with the level of innovation their outsourcing providers offered. Less than half ranked their satisfaction above neutral on that score.

Executives in our universe of examples use six different mechanisms to stimulate and refresh their operating relationships with their outsourcing partners in order to stay on the trajectory they worked so hard to achieve. These mechanisms follow in order of disruptiveness, starting with the least:

1. *Changing the Faces.* Companies and their outsourcing partners rotate their senior operational staff to bring in fresh blood and fresh ideas. For many outsourcing providers this is a deliberate strategy to develop their people by exposing them to a variety of engagements.

2. *Strategic Planning.* The two partners jointly review their strategic position and aspirations and lay plans to move forward. This is a great opportunity to bring in outside perspectives—with independent consultants, academics, or strategists from the outsourcing provider's staff.

3. *Benchmarking.* Companies use mid-course benchmarking to ensure that their performance is keeping up with leaders and to spot practices

that make sense for their operation. Benchmarking can be time-consuming, but large outsourcing providers can smooth the way by establishing the process within their own constellation of clients. Benchmarking has the potential to be eye-opening when it is used to stack up an operation against the best in class. I think it is just as valuable when it is used to provide an annual ranking. When formal benchmarking seems too distracting or costly, companies can substitute a more qualitative effort. They can schedule a series of "field trips" to high-performance companies to share perspectives and management lessons.

Regardless of which approach they use, companies and their outsourcing partners must establish the organizational follow-up to make use of what they learn. That means naming individuals and teams responsible for moving the needle on selected measures and releasing them from other duties so they can make this effort a priority.

4. *Renegotiating the Contract.* Most often, companies and their outsourcing partners renegotiate their contracts when the financial picture changes substantially. But, as we discussed earlier, the process of renegotiation brings both executive teams into a detailed discussion about goals and objectives, responsibilities, incentives, and the way forward. If the partners have devolved into stale routines, a discussion that impacts their wallets may be just what they need to reengage. Again, the process is costly and disruptive, and both sides must be vigilant to make sure the lawyers don't take over. However, executives can use it to shake their partnership out of its lethargy.

Thomas Cook put an explicit break in its seven-year cosourcing contract after the third year to allow for renegotiation. Executives reasoned that their shared-services center would be operating stably by then and that they would want to consider making another step-change. Their options could include consolidating operations across Europe or moving the center to a low-wage rate country, for example.

5. *Retendering.* Retendering a transformationally outsourced activity means calling it quits on a committed relationship. Whether or not the incumbent wins the bid, a retender implies that the level of mutual commitment has relaxed. Our universe of 20 examples includes only one that involved retendering. More than six years after a major energy company catalyzed change by outsourcing back-office functions ex-

tensively across the enterprise, it retendered one of its earliest contracts. Performance had slipped, and the company simply wanted to get cost-cutting back on track. By this time, executives had accomplished their transformational objectives, and the outsourcing relationships had changed to focus on more modest goals.

6. *Repatriation.* Repatriating a process ends the relationship by bringing the outsourced capability in-house. This can even be part of the original plan when the transformational outsourcing is intended to launch a start-up or clear roadblocks to growth. All of the failures among our examples, and two of the successes, brought their outsourced operations back in-house after these were transformed.

In all of these cases, the transition back to the company was managed quite differently from the transition in the other direction. Instead of an aggressive, big-bang handoff to highly experienced management, operations returned in-house in a slower and more deliberate manner as the company brought in skilled employees who could assume the responsibilities. In at least one case, the outsourcing provider received incentives based on the company's increasing level of self-sufficiency, as measured by the decreasing number of outsourced workers on the job.

How does a company decide which of these renewal options is right? It depends completely on the partnership's strategic intent going forward—not the operational performance, but the strategic intent. As we discussed in Chapter 9, if the partners can leverage their joint and collective assets to drive future innovation and growth, they should find a mutually satisfactory way to manage the operational activities. This does not mean operations should continue as is; it just means the partners should agree on how best to manage them. And, if they see no strategic promise in partnership, they can safely sever it over issues of operational efficiency.

Making Room for Endings and Renewals at the Beginning

There is no such thing as a good exit in the middle of transformational outsourcing. Executives will want to exit before they start or find a way to make the relationship work. After the partners have executed the transformation, however, the relationship can change its character. At that point, if the partnership holds no continuing strategic promise, executives can consider retendering or repatriation.

To prepare for this eventuality, executives will want to do several things. First, as they make the decision to transform through outsourcing, they should decide whether or not they would cut off the option to bring operations back in-house. They should think through this decision as if it were irrevocable. NS&I, for example, decided it would never again own the operations it outsourced. It could conceivably change partners, but it could not repatriate the processes. Thomas Cook reached the opposite decision. While it does not anticipate bringing its co-sourced center back in-house, it has not ruled out the possibility. This decision makes a difference in the retained staff. Every company will want to retain the ability to set strategy, but Thomas Cook will also want to keep high-level operational executives on staff. These individuals will work jointly with the outsourcing partner's staff during the transformation, but would form the kernel of an in-house capability if need be.

Second, executives will want to make process documentation audits a regular requirement of the initiative. At least annually, a knowledgeable internal or external auditor should review the process flowcharts, data descriptions, role and responsibility definitions, and key decision criteria to make sure these are up-to-date. This kind of annual review will give the partners a regular occasion to look for process improvements. And it takes the heat and emotion out of some of the tasks that are required to hand the process over to another operator.

Third, executives should incorporate provisions in their agreement to reset the partnership to adjust to phase changes. Whether these provisions take the form of structured breaks or opportunities to renegotiate the contract or whether they look more like collaborative strategic planning programs, they act like expansion joints in a concrete surface. They create room for a partnership to move instead of breaking under the pressure of change.

Finally, they should construct the financial obligation of ending the relationship to align with their partnership objectives. For example, the CEO of the Spanish bank recognized that his outsourcing partner would be making a substantial up-front investment in his company's infrastructure. He agreed to pay a very large penalty for terminating the agreement early to keep his parent company's ROI interests in favor of continuing. Organizations that may repatriate outsourced activities will want to avoid incurring a large cost for new software licenses in that eventuality. And they certainly will not want to pay a fee to obtain an up-to-date copy of their own data.

Notes

1. Jane Linder and Thomas J. Healy, "U.S. State and Local Outsourcing: Leadership in Value," Accenture Government Executive Series report, August 2003.

2. See Mary Lacity and Leslie Willcocks, *Global Information Technology Outsourcing: In Search of Business Advantage* (New York: John Wiley & Sons, 2001); Maurice Greaver, *Strategic Outsourcing: A Structured Approach to Outsourcing Decisions and Initiatives* (New York: AMACOM, 1999); Simon Domberger, *The Contracting Organization: A Strategic Guide to Outsourcing* (New York: Oxford University Press, 1999); Steven M. Bragg, *Outsourcing: A Guide to Selecting the Correct Business Unit, Negotiating the Contract, Maintaining Control of the Process* (New York: John Wiley & Sons, 1998).

3. Gareth Morgan, "Spending Watchdog Slams Court IT System," *Management Consultancy*, May 28, 2003, www.managementconsultancy .co.uk/News/1132304.

4. Personal interview with UK government executive on January 8, 2003.

CHAPTER 11

Managing Transformational Outsourcing in the Public Sector

Increasing demand for services, global fiscal pressures, and a public-sector capability crisis add up to irresistible pressure for governments to do more with less. In response, some government executives are turning to outsourcing. Through outsourcing, they save money, extend their capabilities, and improve the services they provide to citizens and businesses, and many government executives are eyeing these potential benefits hungrily. In the UK, agency and department heads must include an analysis of private finance alternatives for every major investment. If anything, the liberal administrations in New Zealand and Australia have pushed outsourcing even more strongly than their Whitehall cousins. And as one of his top five priorities, President Bush has set escalating targets for agencies to market-test noninherently governmental jobs.

But outsourcing also generates controversy. The results are mixed—some outsourcing initiatives fail to produce the expected results—and many executives see it as a means of indiscriminate government downsizing, an abdication of accountability, or simply a risky financial maneuver. Labor unions feel particularly threatened by it.

Some government organizations have even wiped the word *outsourcing* from their lexicon. For example, several states have laws that prohibit outsourcing. These states still hire private companies to do public-sector work, but they don't call it outsourcing. And federal executives would rather talk about "competing" jobs rather than outsourcing them. The terminology implies that government employees and private companies have equal opportunities to win the work. British Commonwealth countries "market-test" or "contest" functions to convey the same message.

Process constraints and political exigencies unique to government make outsourcing especially challenging in the public sector. For many, outsourcing works more like a political football than a sensible management tool. One executive wonders, "Why is it so hard to do the right thing?" However, a small number of standout executives are using outsourcing to truly transform the way their governments operate. These executives have achieved dramatic improvements in public-sector performance. This chapter talks about how.

Outsourcing in Government Is Growing

Outsourcing in the public sector is growing (see Exhibit 11.1 for more information on how outsourcing is defined in the public sector). Solid numbers are hard to come by—at least in part because executives in different countries don't even share the same definition of the term—but the trend is unmistakable. By the end of the 1990s, governments around the world had transferred more than $1 trillion in assets to the private sector.[1] From this base, outsourcing in the U.S. government is expected to double over the next five years.[2] A recent International Data Corporation (IDC) report shows outsourcing spending in both U.S. federal and state and local governments growing at faster rates through 2005 than in any other industry segment—15.7 and 14.7 percent per year, respectively. The projected growth in government outsourcing in Europe is even higher—17 percent per year through 2004.[3]

What makes up this boom? Some government somewhere has outsourced just about every public function you can think of, from running schools to collecting taxes (see Exhibit 11.2). This chapter focuses on the administrative and information-technology functions that government organizations require to operate and fulfill their public missions.

Executives expect outsourcing to improve both the cost and the per-

Exhibit 11.1. What do we mean by outsourcing in the public sector?

My definition of outsourcing is the same for the public sector as for the private:

Purchasing ongoing services from an outside firm that an agency or department currently provides, or most government organizations normally provide for themselves.

This excludes short-term project work and contracting out for jobs where the government tells the supplier how to do the work, and it also stops short of privatization. The diagram below illustrates the activities that are within and outside of this definition.

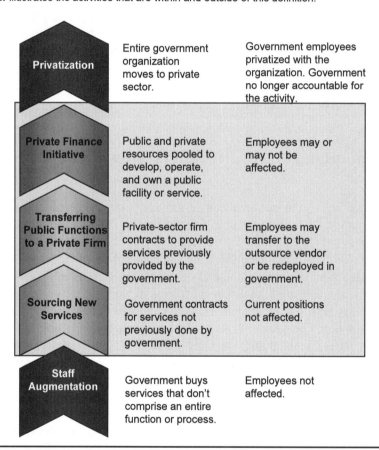

Privatization	Entire government organization moves to private sector.	Government employees privatized with the organization. Government no longer accountable for the activity.
Private Finance Initiative	Public and private resources pooled to develop, operate, and own a public facility or service.	Employees may or may not be affected.
Transferring Public Functions to a Private Firm	Private-sector firm contracts to provide services previously provided by the government.	Employees may transfer to the outsource vendor or be redeployed in government.
Sourcing New Services	Government contracts for services not previously done by government.	Current positions not affected.
Staff Augmentation	Government buys services that don't comprise an entire function or process.	Employees not affected.

Exhibit 11.2. Governments have outsourced a wide variety of functions and processes.

Function	Outsourced By...
Military Training & Training Facilities Operation	Defense Procurement Agency (UK), Royal New Zealand Navy, Royal New Zealand Air Force
Construction of Military Facilities	US Department of the Navy
Immigration Control	Singapore Immigration Registration
Tax Collection	State of Arizona (US)
Welfare Administration	State of Wisconsin (US)
Policing Services	Los Angeles County (CA—US), City of San Diego (CA—US)
Background Investigations	US Federal Bureau of Investigations (FBI)
Fire Services	City of Scottsdale (AZ—US)
Correctional Services	Province of Ontario (CAN), State of New South Wales (AU), State of Texas (US), The Home Office (UK)
Parking Enforcement	London Borough of Brent (UK), City of Chicago (IL—US)
Water & Wastewater Systems	City of Indianapolis (IN—US), City of Taipei (Taiwan), City of Atlanta (GA—US), State of South Australia (AU)
Transportation (highway, bridge construction & maintenance)	State of New Mexico (US), Province of Ontario (CAN)

Traditionally Governmental Functions

formance of their organizations and to create distinctly better value for taxpayers. And they have some justification for these high hopes. NS&I's results stand out as excellent value for money, according to the National Audit Office of the UK. And that's not the only example of successful transformational outsourcing in the public sector. In the early 1990s, Mayor Goldsmith turned around Indianapolis, using outsourcing to cut costs in some arenas in order to improve services in others. The U.S. military's Defense Logistics Agency questioned its ability to survive as an organization before it reengineered its supply chain through outsourcing.

Outsourcing in the Public Sector Is Particularly Challenging

These results look very appealing, but many government executives and policy-makers are reluctant even to consider transformational outsourcing. Why? The public-sector environment makes it particularly challenging to choose this option and even more challenging to manage it effectively. Government executives are often buffeted by a set of powerful influences and political forces that make it inordinately difficult for them to succeed (see Exhibit 11.3).

We have seen how important it is to establish a clear purpose and business case for the transformational initiative. But most government organizations lack good, outcome-based measures of success. Profits and return on investment play this role in private-sector, for-profit companies. What would the corresponding measure be for a court system or child welfare agency? Executives could aim to reduce crime or child poverty, but they certainly do not influence all the factors that contribute to these results.

Even if goals are rock-solid, some governments' accounting systems don't give executives a way to assess performance against them. Australia, the UK, and New Zealand have implemented accrual accounting practices that support their ability to match investments with the returns they generate. The U.S. and other governments lag behind in this arena. Their accounting systems measure cash outflow rather than offering management-

Exhibit 11.3. Constraining forces funnel executives toward suboptimal outsourcing decisions.

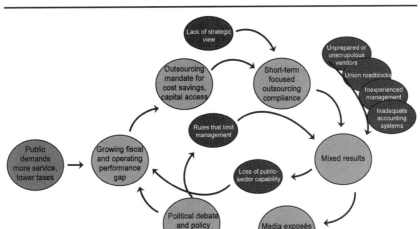

type accounting reports that take a more comprehensive view, such as total cost of ownership or multiyear project benefits.

Cost is one metric that *can* be tracked—although with some difficulty—but public-sector organizations are structured to take such a short-term view of savings that this measure can do as much harm as good. In Australia's ill-fated cluster program, outsourcing was mandated for groups of government agencies, but these groups were not allowed to choose a provider unless they were promised a 15 percent year-on-year cost improvement. They could not consider other benefits unless the proposal reached this threshold.

Shifting from a short-term focus on cost to a search for value can pluck executives out of the frying pan, but drop them unceremoniously into the fire. Higher-value outsourcing initiatives often involve more complexity and flexibility and require deeper skills to manage outsourcing relationships effectively (see Exhibit 11.4).

As new administrations are elected, leaders swing the public agenda from bigger, more capable government to smaller, less intrusive government and back again. With long-term objectives subject to sudden change, agency executives are reluctant to enter into long-term agreements that commit them to one policy agenda or another.

Exhibit 11.4. Increasing scope and complexity make outsourcing more challenging.

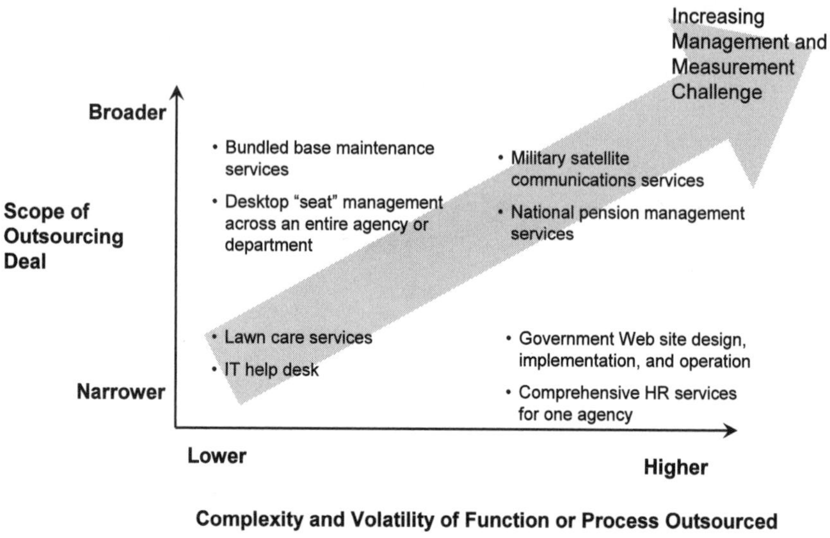

Increasing Management and Measurement Challenge

Broader

Scope of Outsourcing Deal

- Bundled base maintenance services
- Desktop "seat" management across an entire agency or department

- Military satellite communications services
- National pension management services

- Lawn care services
- IT help desk

- Government Web site design, implementation, and operation
- Comprehensive HR services for one agency

Narrower

Lower

Higher

Complexity and Volatility of Function or Process Outsourced

Some governments' checks-and-balances political structures undermine the strong leadership roles that transformational outsourcing requires. In the U.S. federal government and some so-called weak-governor states, any substantial initiative is immediately subject to partisan political infighting. Leaders must be willing to spend their time and limited political capital on outsourcing in order to push it over these structural hurdles just to strike a deal. And leading the ongoing relationship with outsourcing providers to ensure continued progress requires sustained political supervision.

Procurement procedures that were designed to ensure fair, transparent processes can be cumbersome, time-consuming, and unwieldy as a result. A U.S. CIO remarks: "The [U.S.] government has not had a great track record of adopting best commercial practices because laws and regulations get in the way." In the United States, for example, some regulations require work to be conducted in a particular way rather than allowing the outsourcing provider to operate most efficiently. And conducting the competitive process to evaluate whether jobs should remain in-house or be outsourced must be completed in a specified time frame. If managers do not complete it by the deadline, they must start all over again, from the beginning. An executive from Canada explains that his country's procurement process requires him to consider all bidders, even those that are clearly incapable of performing the work. Despite this national government's lead in using outsourcing progressively,[4] a UK executive calls their procedures "tactical at best."

Some governments' incentive structures inhibit risk-taking. While the outsourcing track record varies from country to country, the price of failure is uniformly higher than the reward for success. For example, after the UK outsourced its railway track infrastructure, a series of train wrecks pointed out serious service-quality issues, and the government subsequently declared the outsource supplier bankrupt. Even attempting to make big strides can elicit strong counterforces. A U.S. defense executive described a sorely needed initiative to regionalize military operations to drive out expensive duplicative functions: "Budget pressures drove consolidation; they just couldn't afford business as usual. The regional base commander was a champion for change. She energized the workforce, and they were making wonderful progress consolidating 300 physical locations down to a handful. As these things often happen, she got reassigned, and the new person didn't have the same fire in his belly. When the backsliding began, who got tarred with the failure? The first base commander. No wonder no one wants to take on projects like this."

Yet short political cycles make it essential to move quickly. One U.S. state executive explains: "Why do we see big successes in the UK and New Zealand? They have a parliamentary government with no adversarial relations between the executive and legislative branches. Today our [U.S.] legislators give money to the executive branch doled out in little chunks with micromanagement."

Finally, workforce issues loom large. Many government workers belong to unions. One U.S. executive states: "If it's a new outsourcing contract, the unions will bring everything in their power to bear against you." An executive from the UK continues: "It's like the poacher and the gamekeeper. The people being transferred will never buy in because they feel dumped on the scrap heap."

Under pressure to "do more with less," governments search for ways to provide needed services, cut costs, and find new sources of investment capital for infrastructure. Outsourcing looks like an answer, so leaders issue mandates designed to achieve measurable results before their political time runs out—that is, urgently. Unfortunately, this short-term forcing function skews outsourcing initiatives toward the lower end of the value spectrum. Specification-driven procurement processes favor narrow tenders that often don't invite innovative solutions. And a strong emphasis on visible cost savings over value attracts vendors who bid low, but intend to make up their margins on inevitable out-of-scope work. As a result, executives often end up paying more than they expect as unanticipated work creeps in and getting too little of the service they really need in a dynamic environment. In this context, it's not surprising that public-sector outsourcing has mixed results, which make it even less appealing.

Conventional Wisdom Imposes Blinders

The conventional wisdom about what and how to outsource appears to be designed for a stable, well-defined environment. But it is the wrong recipe for a world in which technologies, priorities, finances, and citizens' demands are more volatile. One government executive snorts: "The model doesn't work. It never worked." Conventional outsourcing principles advise executives to outsource noninherently governmental jobs and noncore processes so they can focus attention on more important matters. But clearly identifying work by these categories isn't so easy. The answer depends on an organization's strategy, and it can change quickly. In the United States prior to September 11, 2001, for example, airport security was a noncore, nongovernmental activity. President Bush would argue it still is. According to Congress, however, it isn't, so U.S. airport security workers have been federalized. Robert Bowley, director of the UK's Passport Agency, states: "We still talk about the core/noncore distinction but the reality is more fluid and strategic."

The bit about executive focus isn't solid, either. Executives report that they spend as much time and effort managing outsource vendors as they did when the operation was in their own shop. One manager who has carefully measured this cost claims it amounts to 8 to 10 percent of the contract value on average. Sixty-two percent of the public-sector executives that were interviewed count continuing, concerted executive attention to leading the relationship throughout the contract as a critical success factor for outsourcing.

Conventional wisdom about what to outsource isn't helpful; additionally, conventional wisdom about how to outsource leads executives astray.

The outsourcing textbook calls for avidly negotiated, tightly specified contracts that penalize vendors for failing to meet stipulated service levels. But airtight contracts don't offer the flexibility executives need to adjust to changing conditions. These contracts also set up an adversarial relationship that inhibits joint problem solving. In the words of one executive: "If you have to go to the contract to manage the relationship, you have already failed." Through agency consolidation, for example, a UK government organization inherited a problematic outsourcing deal. The executive in charge explains: "The outsourcing provider was required to rewrite, then run, an application, and they were losing money on the deal. When we operate an agreement and the supplier is taking a huge loss, we can't just walk away from responsibility for that. It's bound to affect their service, and we'll suffer the consequences. We altered the terms of the deal so the supplier could earn a fair return."

Leaders Embrace Transformation

Despite the challenges, leading government executives around the world are using outsourcing to achieve dramatic improvements in their agencies, their governments, and their public/private value models. They create markets, collaborative partnerships, and equity commitments to nurture a thriving public/private value network that improves government, serves citizens, and fosters healthy enterprise. The results range from massively more effective organizations to stunning improvements in economic value. Executives who have structured transformational outsourcing projects generally follow one of two paths: They make a market for services or they make lasting commitments to transform the value equation.

A Blueprint for Transformational Outsourcing in Government

As their arsenal of outsourcing approaches grows, some public-sector executives are learning to construct new operating models that parcel up value and risk in advantageous ways. These deals can involve creative financing like joint ventures and private finance initiatives, and they can extend public-sector activities into whole new arenas. These ventures work like breeder reactors—they don't just capture value, they also stimulate its growth. Government executives use two forms of transformational outsourcing to redesign the way the public sector works: they make lasting commitments to transform the value equation like private-sector companies and, in what appears to be a unique approach in the public sector, they make a market for services.

Use Outsourcing Partnerships to Transform the Value Equation

Government organizations can use outsourcing to make an effective market for services when the services are relatively independent or modular. In other words, executives can outsource the copy center to one vendor and the wastewater treatment to another without worrying about how they will interact. When a government organization needs a radical improvement in systemic performance, executives take a different tack. They use committed outsourcing partnerships to transform critical processes and create new operating models.

To radically change an organization's performance, executives outsource functions and processes that are essential to the mission through a long-term, strategic commitment. The UK's National Savings and Investments stands as a premier example of stem-to-stern transformation through outsourcing.

Government executives also outsource to eliminate roadblocks to growth. They create new operating models by turning costs into investments and generating new sources of revenue. In the United States, 17 states have joined with a private company to build and operate state Web portals without spending taxpayers' money. NIC, Inc., earns revenue from fee-based online services such as providing motorists' driving records to insurance companies. It generates enough money to pay for operating and maintaining the state's Web site in the bargain. The government of Ontario, Canada, has joined with Bell Canada to operate and maintain the province's mobile communications towers. Ontario funds this capability by enabling its partner to use the towers to offer revenue-generating services.

The government of South Australia, identified by *Outsourcing Jour-*

nal as having the best government outsourcing relationship of 2000, framed a transformational approach that, to date, has been unique to the public sector. I'll call it the quid pro quo model. The government aggregated the mainframe and mid-range computers and wide area networks of 100 agencies to attract a top-drawer IT infrastructure outsourcer. In return for the business, the vendor had to offer an attractive price and commit to providing economic development for the state. The low-price bidder didn't win—government executives chose the vendor with the best economic development proposal—but the savings have been substantial. More important, the vendor's operation in the area has more than tripled, spawning new support businesses and providing millions of dollars in value to the local economy.

Establishing and sustaining a transformational commitment means government executives must go beyond contract management to master relationship management. Because of its strategic importance, transformation requires leadership at the highest levels of both public- and private-sector organizations. It demands fresh thinking about how services, risk, and value can be unbundled and an intense, committed relationship between public and private partners can be developed to deliver on enterprise outcomes. To use this approach, executives come to grips with a series of management issues. They find ways to measure outcomes and outputs. They aim for outcomes, then work with their partner to craft an agenda to reach them. When they cannot get at outcomes, they use outputs as proxies. What's the difference? *Outputs* are measures of service delivered, while *outcomes* are the consequences of excellent service delivery. For example, an output might be processing child-support payment requests within 24 hours; the corresponding outcome would be reducing child poverty. Targeting outcomes enables both public- and private-sector partners to align in doing whatever it takes to achieve the ultimate objective.

In addition, these executives measure critical inputs. For example, they carefully assess the key individuals who will be leading the charge on the outsourcing provider's team. If these people don't inspire confidence, government executives ask for replacements. These high-profile initiatives cannot afford missteps, and penalty payments don't come close to making up for the political flak that executives will take if they occur.

Executives look for a strategic ally, not an outsourcing vendor. They use procurement processes that give outsourcing providers the latitude to make innovative proposals. They assess vendors' capabilities and ideas, then choose a supplier who will work with them to do whatever it takes to accomplish their objectives. While some government executives retort that their procurement laws prevent establishing this kind of relationship, others have found a way to do it (see the case study, "Making a Lasting Commitment," below).

Case Study: Making a Lasting Commitment: UK Department of Social Services

In 1995, the UK Department of Social Services (DSS) turned to the private sector to supply support processes it believed were not critical to its mission: data center and technical support services for large systems. It retained applications development in-house because of this activity's centrality to the department's mission. After a thorough analysis, DSS awarded the contract to a large, global company and transferred 1,500 employees. The results were good. A DSS executive recounts: "The service has been perceived to be good, there were no horror stories about the money, and the people we transferred have had all the advantages we anticipated."

By 1997, however, DSS was embarking on a major new strategic agenda to modernize the welfare system. The executive reports: "At the start, we didn't quite know what we wanted the partner to do, so our first step was to identify a company to work with. We advertised in the official journal of the European Commission for a strategic partner to forward welfare reform." DSS selected its data center vendor as the lead service provider and began to craft a partnership to develop and operate a new child-support system. "The degree of risk transfer we were seeking was hard to obtain on a development project in isolation," the executive continued, "so we rolled up a broader deal. We combined the operational work from 1995 and added the in-house development capability. Fifteen hundred more people transferred to the outsourcing vendor, and they became our partner for delivery of all new systems."

> DSS's remaining organization concentrates on two functions: ongoing management of the department's commercial relationships and negotiating new deals. It's still early in the transformational partnership, and results are still to be determined. But DSS is clearly counting on its outsource partner to play a major role in implementing the modernization strategy: "Our 1995 contract was for noncore business. Now we want a much broader relationship. We want [the vendor] to assist in driving forward with this major strategic change. It represents a whole set of expectations."

In direct opposition to adversarial contracting practice, they insist on creating a financial model that makes a profitable business for the private-sector partner and compensates them for the risk they assume. To attract investment, government executives recognize they have to offer their partners appealing rewards. Prestige and the ability to provide a reference can bolster the value proposition, but these alone will not be enough. Conducting the analysis to build a robust model will have an additional benefit: Executives will understand what value has to be created, where the business risks lie, and who has to carry them.

To achieve high-level outcomes in a volatile environment, executives understand they need to drive innovation at the top. Both partners will want a hand on the strategic steering wheel to bring their unique skills and expertise to bear. Performance improvements accrue as the partnering relationship deepens, not just at contract renewal time. Executives will want to lead a regular, active governance process to stimulate new ideas and drive innovation.

In addition, executives will not want to underestimate the leadership challenge. If anything, executives need to focus *more* attention on effective operations, not less. An NS&I executive remarks: "Some managers think their problem will go away when they outsource. It never does. We knew we were just swapping one management challenge for another."

Make a Market for Services

As part of their transformational efforts, some government executives create a "contestable" market for services. This approach works in an environment characterized by multiple independent services, and is built on a foundation of market testing practices, but it goes well beyond. Executives who undertake this kind of transformation step back from the everyday, "one deal at a time" perspective to establish an overarching agenda to aggressively promote innovation through competition in each separate service.

Executives who use it:

- Change their own mind-set from controlling functions to buying services.
- Shift fixed assets to private companies so government payments can come from recurring funds, not allocated capital.
- Recompete contracts relatively frequently to stimulate continuous improvement.
- Track performance metrics for every service, whether it is performed in-house or by an outsourcing provider.

For example, Steven Goldsmith, the mayor of Indianapolis from 1992 to 1999, argued that his city was in direct competition with its suburbs for citizens. Faced with a reduced tax base and the need to do more with less, Goldsmith opened more than 70 services to competitive bidding in six years. Regardless of whether the current employees or the private sector won the competition, savings accrued. Goldsmith redeployed these savings to improve the government's value proposition. He recounts: "We have reduced our operating budget by 7 percent, cut taxes twice . . . put 100 more police officers on the street, [and] invested $700 million to rebuild our roads, sewers, and other parts of the city's infrastructure."[5]

Australia's government makes service markets by institutionalizing choice. It allows government departments and agencies to choose any supplier, not necessarily the in-house organization. They also regularly measure the government's unit cost for producing its outputs through pricing reviews and post this information, along with benchmark data, for everyone to see. An Australian finance and administration executive elaborates: "When services were in-house, costs were not explicit. When you outsource, you get a market signal about true costs. It revealed to us that government had been overinvesting for generations in areas that were marginal." As a result, the size of the government workforce has been reduced by about one-third over five years. When they make outsourcing decisions, they explicitly consider how their awards will shape the vendor community to create a vibrant marketplace when contracts must be renewed. Instead of building and owning expensive infrastructure, the UK defense department makes a market for services in order to limit its investment in underutilized assets. Executives now buy flight simulator training, air-to-air refueling, ship repair, and equipment transport services from the private sector on a "per transaction" basis. In other words, they no longer pay to maintain and operate the flight simulator and to conduct training for pilots; they pay a fixed price for each pilot who can pass the flight test. They pay for fuel delivered down the pipe, not the equipment and people to deliver it. The UK chief of defense procurement explains: "I don't have to pay for excess capacity—the vendor can use it to serve other customers." By owning all the equipment, the outsource vendor controls all the components of performance and has every incentive to invest sensibly. This executive notes that his approach subtly changes the dynamics of demand: "There's a magic law in life—once you have to pay for something, you always want less of it." His organization improves cost significantly by managing demand in this way, and that allows them to increase resources to war fighters.

In the United States, the Defense Logistics Agency (DLA) also used this approach to transform its operation from mediocre to top-drawer. It uses a concept called "prime vendor" to outsource supply of military repair parts, medical supplies, and meals. Instead of purchasing and managing supplies itself, the DLA contracts with a supplier to take on this critical logistics function. The supplier is responsible for managing inventory and positioning it appropriately to fulfill demand quickly and reliably.

To make an effective contestable market for services, executives must sustain a competitive environment. Otherwise, when it's time to renew the contract, they will have only one viable vendor in the market. To transform their operations by making a market for services, executives adopt a very different set of practices than those described above (see the case study "Making a Market for Services: UK Defense Ministry," on the next page).

Case Study: Making a Market for Services: UK Defense Ministry

If an asset doesn't fight on the front line, the UK Defense Ministry considers outsourcing. This is a whole new way of looking at the provision of defense capability: Instead of the government's owning the capital asset, the government buys the service. Let's take an example: If they buy a Chinook helicopter, they have to train the crews. They know it's much cheaper to train on simulators, but when capital funds are short, it's normal to delay buying the simulator. So it may turn up six to 12 months later. Then they must keep it up to the same revision as the aircraft. It is staffed and maintained by people who would otherwise be on the front line, so the personnel are always changing. And they have to do it according to regulations, which can be unwieldy. The asset is almost always underused. Why? The ability to predict how much they need is difficult, and no one wants to be caught short.

This organization has learned they can do a much better job by outsourcing the service. They create a "take or pay" contract that stipulates they will pay for a certain number of trained pilots per year, whether or not they actually use this capacity. This kind of contract provides a solid foundation for the supplier to get financing for the asset. Today, that might represent 90 percent of the capacity, but over time it might decline to 50 percent as needs change. The outsource supplier takes responsibility for owning, operating, and maintaining the asset. The government no longer commits combat personnel to the activity, and they get other benefits as well. It saves the Defense Ministry 10 to 20 percent of the cost. Furthermore, that simulator turns up on time and gets maintained effectively because the supplier gets paid only when it turns out trained pilots.

As an isolated example, this is interesting, but not transformational. Extend the concept broadly across the Defense Ministry, and it fundamentally changes the way the organization works.

They use fast, flexible procurement processes to facilitate repeated contracting. When they use market forces to drive improvement, the real upticks come each time the contract is tendered. Executives set their sights on a tendering process that takes no more than three months in order to maintain a healthy pace. It should also encourage reengineering to tap into the opportunity for change.

We're talking about contracts here, not partnerships. Executives should manage the scope and complexity of each deal to minimize switching costs. The more complex and volatile the requirements are, the more difficult it will be to switch vendors when the time comes. Executives will want to craft deals with clear output requirements and explicit end-of-contract handoffs. In terms of the government's own managerial skills, making effective transitions comes to the top of the list.

Striking avowedly short-term deals can inhibit the outsourcing provider's willingness to invest up front. Using "take or pay" pricing can help. "Take or pay" refers to a commitment to pay for a specified volume of service regardless of whether it is actually used. For example, the UK commits to paying for two military equipment transport ships at all times, with an option to use four additional ships. Contracts to provide prison and hospital services often stipulate a basic number of beds required. Because of the risk of being replaced, vendors will be reluctant to invest in specialized assets without some volume guarantees. Executives will want to make sure their contractual exit clauses enable these assets to be transferred when and if they choose a new vendor.

In order to manage transformational service markets, government executives relentlessly measure performance. Without clear, specified outputs and visible measures of performance, they will never be able to line up a contest. They use pricing reviews, competitive benchmarks, and activity-based costing to track outputs during the vendor's term as well as at renewal time.

These government executives are transforming the way their organizations work by making a market for services. While many government agencies outsource some processes, what sets these executives apart is that they use this approach broadly and strategically. They're not just crafting deals, they're orchestrating an active environment of deal making that stimulates healthy competition and inspires an entrepreneurial attitude among public-sector staff that fosters continuous improvement.

This approach is categorically different from using deep outsourcing partnerships for transformation. Why have we seen it only in the public sector, and rarely there? It makes sense only when a wide array of the organization's activities can be packaged up as independent commodity services and purchased from any of several vendors. These must be well enough understood to be managed and coordinated by public-sector relationship managers. And they must operate in neat organizational silos to minimize the chaos and coordination costs that would mount rapidly if government executives had to orchestrate daily cooperation among multiple competing vendors. Also, this transformation model relies on the threat, if not the reality, of replacing vendors at will. So they must enter and depart like plug-and-play modules in a desktop computer. If every retender were extensive and difficult and every transition were time-consuming and risky, this approach would soon be swamped by the costs of administering it.

Making Transformational Outsourcing Work in the Public Sector

Transformational outsourcing can support government executives' drive to effect change. For it to work, they must have the latitude to shape the tool to the purpose. For starters, that means knowing how to match their outsourcing approach to the situation at hand. Public-sector executives must then execute their outsourcing strategies masterfully.

Enable Transformational Initiatives with Performance-Oriented Management

Performance-oriented governments master the everyday management practices that enable effective transformational outsourcing. Outwardly focused, progressive governments institutionalize good outsourcing management through activity-based budgeting, clear goals and objectives, and visible progress reporting. They master techniques for dealing with the obstacles that arise, from tough labor unions and changing political administrations to reluctant finance departments.

Some governments—notably the UK, Australia, and New Zealand—

have worked for the past decade to put these enabling management practices in place. The important components include overarching strategies and goals to guide their efforts and measures of success against which they can check their progress. At the execution level, they hire capable, practiced leaders with the authority to make sensible decisions to implement their plans and programs. They rely on sound financial systems that tell them how they're doing. And they have responsive processes for sensing the pulse of their constituents, taking the measure of their competitors, and addressing the threats and opportunities. Finally, they institutionalize accountability for results to put some starch in the process. These governments:

- *Query constituents to find out what they want from government.* Ironically, many public-sector organizations operate without ever asking directly what the public believes its needs to be.
- *Articulate a clear strategic mission and the measures of success that give it teeth.* They favor outcome measures, and publish annual public reports that document performance against them. Among other things, for example, the UK department of work and pensions has committed to reduce child poverty by 50 percent in five years and to eradicate it in ten. New Zealand posts its government performance on the Web. In the United States, the Government Performance and Results Act (GPRA) takes a step in the right direction, and substantive performance reports are increasingly in evidence.
- *Adopt accrual-based management accounting systems designed to foster accountability for outputs.* Australia has put accrual budgeting in place for the whole of government. The state of Virginia developed COMPETE, a computer program that compares government and private-sector proposals on an apples-to-apples basis because state financial systems don't provide comprehensive cost data.[1]
- *Solicit new ideas from potential vendors.* Use flexible procurement processes like Australia's Expression of Interest and the UK's Information Memorandum to solicit new ideas from public- and private-sector organizations that are competing for the work. This process allows government executives to consider innovative vendor proposals before they craft an official tender. The government agency issues a brief description of the service it is looking for, then reviews the responding ven-

dors' capabilities and experience. Then and only then the government puts its request for tender together. As a result, government executives can create a tender that incorporates the potential for reengineered solutions.

- *Seek executives who will achieve results.* Attract experienced executives with contracts that pay them market rates with incentives for excellence, and put civil servants to work under their able leadership. As Wilson Bailey of the New Zealand court system explains, "When we're looking for people, we ask what you have done. If you haven't done anything, you're not welcome in our organization."

Institutionalizing a performance-oriented management environment doesn't, by itself, make outsourcing work. It does, however, set the stage by preparing executives to manage transformational outsourcing effectively if they should choose to use it.

Match the Outsourcing Approach to the Situation

Both public-sector types of transformational outsourcing—changing the value equation and making a market for services—can produce stunning results. But each also requires a different approach (see Exhibit 11.5). Getting the approach wrong can sap the benefits from any outsourcing relationship. Executives will want to tailor every aspect of the deal to the

Exhibit 11.5. Match outsourcing approach to purpose.

	Make a Market for Services	Make Lasting Commitments to Transform the Value Equation
Primary Outsourcing Objective	Use competition to improve price/performance.	Achieve radical improvement in performance.
Outsourcing Relationship	Conventional.	Committed.
Ideal Deal Scope	Narrow.	Extensive.
Complexity	Low to moderate.	Highest.
Length of Contract	3 to 5 years.	5 to 10 years.
Source of Innovation	Competition among suppliers and ability to switch vendors.	Strategic market pressure.
Key Challenges	Vendor scope creep, intervendor cooperation.	Sustained high-level leadership commitment.

objective they are seeking: the length of the contract, the scope of the deal, the type of relationship you form with the vendor, and even the tendering process.

To put a transformational outsourcing initiative on the right track, executives:

- *Shape the outsourcing relationship to the objectives.* Set the tone for the relationship you want from the beginning. Manage the tendering process to invite the level of innovation, partnering, and commitment you need.

- *Select vendors that will work in the kind of initiative you envision.* Public-sector executives who design long-term commitments will evaluate vendors, at least in part, by their willingness to collaborate. An NS&I executive emphasized: "The most important thing for us was to find a partner whose business was being driven in a strategic direction that would converge with ours." An Australian public servant recalls a different experience: "We declined to be victims of [our vendor's] global processes—most of which were designed to avoid risk for them. We spent lots of time and contractual leverage to ensure we had a strong say about how our processes would work. We do not consider them a good faith partner."

- *Prepare for some disruption when political administrations change.* When the public agenda shifts, new policy directions can create havoc with existing outsourcing relationships. For example, agencies and departments with long-term capability partnerships might be asked to about-face to make a market for services—violating collaborative relationships by soliciting multiple vendors and retendering more frequently. The resulting disruption won't serve anyone well. To evaluate the last administration's outsourcing strategies, review the objectives they graciously committed to writing. If these have changed significantly, revisit the outsourcing approach. Tracking outcome measures will also help. Together with the new policy makers, executives can decide whether the existing approach is paying off. Peter Bareau from NS&I recalls: "A Labor government took over in May 1997, when the outsourcing process had just started. We had to ask the new ministers whether they were happy with what was going on. Fortunately they were."

Masterful Execution

Effective outsourcing needs more than sound strategy; it needs masterful execution. Leaders around the world shared their views of the critical success factors with us. Dealing with the workforce issues loomed large, but they also had some advice for ongoing leadership of the effort (see Exhibit 11.6).

Workforce Transition

Outsourcing almost always changes the way people in the organization work—sometimes dramatically. Employees may be transferred from the government payroll to private-sector jobs; they may be redeployed to other jobs in government; or they may be laid off. As a result, they may feel threatened, confused, and betrayed, and emotions run high. The government executives we interviewed mentioned workforce opposition and labor union issues as the most important challenges they faced. They recommended:

Exhibit 11.6. Critical success factors in effective outsourcing.

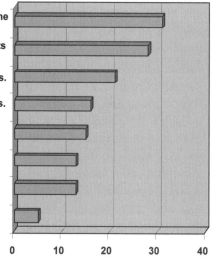

Actively lead the relationship throughout the contract.

Understand and communicate requirements and expectations clearly.

Maintain a partnering attitude on both sides.

Communicate actively with all stakeholders.

Execute transitions smoothly, including ensuring data integrity.

Measure and monitor performance.

Manage implementation risk explicitly.

Hire good legal and specialist support.

0   10   20   30   40

Number of Interviewees Who Mentioned This Factor (N=50, Multiple Responses Allowed)

- *Get employees and unions involved early.* You won't eliminate employees' feelings of uncertainty, but communicating early and often will help them navigate the process. Your communications agenda should explain the why, the when, and the how to employees and their union advocates. When you don't know the answer, provide a date when you will, and only make promises you can keep.

- *Create appealing transition packages.* Some government agencies negotiate soft-landing packages with the vendor—for example, the U.S. Navy and Marine Corps required their intranet outsourcer to provide pay raises, bonuses, and three years' guaranteed employment to ease the transition of government employees to the private sector. The UK Passport Agency converted casual contracts into permanent ones to create more security for workers. Mayor Goldsmith's Indianapolis team crafted a range of solutions to meet individuals' needs: those who qualified for pensions retired and were rehired; those who got a better pension plan from the vendor just moved; and those who would be disadvantaged by moving were redeployed in the government.

- *Give workers choices to allow them a sense of control.* Although it's not always possible, giving workers options can ease the transition. When the UK's Passport Agency outsourced data entry and printing, it first asked for volunteers. Robert Bowley, the agency's director of public/private partnerships, and his team asked workers what kinds of choices they would find appealing. Bowley commented, "We wanted to take the heat out."

Ongoing Leadership

Workforce transition isn't the only challenge that government executives face when they outsource. We don't have many transformational outsourcing initiatives to learn from, but we can borrow management lessons from well-executed but less far-reaching public-sector outsourcing engagements. To overcome obstacles, executives:

- *Get and keep key stakeholders on board.* To effect lasting change, support is essential. You'll want to identify the critical leverage points and find ways to bring them to your side. A UK government executive needed the UK Treasury Department to support a proposal to the Minister of Finance. She recounts, "They are very risk-averse. We worked through every objection tediously. It took time, but the challenge process made it a better deal."

- *Manage expectations.* Outsourcing makes implicit costs explicit and casual interfaces formal. The impact? Things that public servants used to get done by asking someone in the next cubicle now require a formal request or a manager's approval. Clarifying the new work process before it happens will make the new disciplines less contentious. The IT director for Australia's Department of Health and Aged Care launched a two-year change management program as part of the agency's effort to outsource IT infrastructure.

- *Pilot wholly new processes.* Both you and your outsource vendor will stumble over implementing functions and processes that have never existed before. Conduct an explicit, limited-scope pilot to sort out the staffing, operating procedures, training, systems, and connections to the rest of the enterprise. When one U.S. federal executive set out to implement nationwide call centers, she started with two demonstration sites. She recounts: "In order to roll these centers out all over the nation, we needed to understand how they would work."

- *Keep their hands dirty.* Public-sector executives can never delegate their accountability for outsourced activities. That means staying intimately involved, whether the issue is operations or strategy. One Australian IT executive notes, "Our partner brought standard work plans with them, but we refused to be rushed. When it took time, we took the time to do it right." New York State's deputy commissioner for child support enforcement says, "Three people from my staff are on-site in our partner's operation daily. We identify problems and suggest solutions—we monitor to make sure things are going well."

There's More to Be Done

The results from transformational outsourcing speak for themselves, and the leaders who have achieved these outcomes deserve our praise. But there's more to be done. The motivation for understanding how to make transformational outsourcing work in the public sector isn't just more effective outsourcing, it's more effective government. When executives around the world are asked to describe a "massively more effective government," many agree on the broad strokes of a vision. One Australian executive put it best: "Government services are information-rich. The developments with the Web and the convergence of information technology and communications provide significant opportunity for massive changes. Borders and distance become irrelevant when services are provided electronically." Forward-looking executives anticipate:

- *Informational Services Provided Virtually.* Many of the world's governments have placed this objective squarely in the crosshairs with aggressive e-government initiatives. Services like marriage licenses, business registrations, and motor vehicle transactions have moved to the Web en masse, and leading governments have gone much further. Singapore's Supreme Court, for example, notifies lawyers by Short Message System (SMS) messaging and e-mail about proceedings. It also uses a form of secure videoconferencing to enable them to attend court sessions without being physically present.[6]

- *Coordinated Solutions, Not Fragmented Services.* No matter what services the citizen needs, and what government organizations provide these, citizens and businesses will be able to get complete, orchestrated services that make internal government boundaries invisible. This coordination will apply to policy and regulation as well through consolidation and streamlined legal structures, tax collection, and security processes. As a U.S. state executive describes, "Fifty-eight California cities collect property tax with 58 different property tax systems. There ought to be one. The huge improvement will be aggregation." Canada already provides a Web site for benefits recipients that gives them a comprehensive picture of their entitlements; it spans across agencies and across national and provincial levels of government.[7]

- *Most Important, More Choice.* Citizens and businesses will be able to choose levels of service and pay accordingly. As with school voucher systems, they will substitute private for government-provided services. Ultimately, they may be able to choose services from governments outside their own geographic region. For example, the German postal system already competes with the U.S. postal service as well as UPS and FedEx for package delivery. The entrepreneurial Belgian Post has subsidiaries that provide direct marketing services, document processing and work-flow consulting, specialized distribution for publications, and software solutions for managing mail.

To move in this direction, governments will need an information architecture that enables them to synthesize data from disparate and widespread sources. This obligation becomes even more urgent as governments undertake transformational outsourcing initiatives. Why? As the number of different public and private organizations involved in service delivery grows, the need for coordination expands geometrically. Without a comprehensive understanding of the information jigsaw, governments will never be able to orchestrate good service delivery, either physically or virtually.

Progressive government executives are already laying the groundwork for this radically different information requirement. They are focusing on managing information, not infrastructure, and they are explicitly addressing the information implications of outsourcing. To get the right foundations in place, government leaders should start immediately to:

- *Build public-sector information management expertise.* They will need information and the ability to use it to survive in tomorrow's government. An executive in New South Wales, Australia, cautions: "We outsourced IT for an organization that manages children at risk. The department of finance drove the effort, and they were not discerning about where they drew the line. They never should have outsourced the database. We had to bring it back." Another Australian continues: "Whether you do core services in-house or out doesn't really make a difference. But there are some areas of expertise and data knowledge where you need the skills in-house."

- *Drive interoperability across government boundaries through information architecture.* A U.S. state chief technologist has implemented an information architecture that moves disjointed agencies and departments toward just enough consistency to be interoperable. "We now understand that we'll be judged by the same yardstick as the private sector when it comes to service delivery. How many Web sites do you have to visit to plan your vacation? One. That's how many you should have to visit to take care of the details of moving to our state."

- *Establish an information framework that enables outsourcing.* As part of strategic outsourcing initiatives, executives should work with outsourcing providers to define their information obligations. By keeping a company grip on the information in-house, executives can substitute visibility for control and comfortably lighten their touch on service operations. As the value network of outsourcing partners expands, governments will be well positioned to coordinate services and outcomes through an information hub.

* * *

Now more than ever, citizens are looking to their governments for leadership. We expect our public servants to institutionalize management practices that foster good decisions. We expect them to have sound relationships with private-sector companies to get the right things done right. And we expect them to have the information they need to orchestrate excellence over the long term. In today's fiscal pressure-cooker, some government leaders are turning to outsourcing to radically and rapidly transform the way they work. We applaud their progress. Now we want them to leverage their outsourcing experiences to drive step-change improvements *across* government agency silos. In the words of one thoughtful public-sector executive, "The large, traditional, infrastructure-heavy, investment-eating organization is the past; the lean, virtual business model is the future. Government has a bundle of cash flows and obligations and values, and you can shape them deliberately to get the outcomes you want. Outsourcing is one way to completely change the boundaries."

Notes

1. Yochi Dreazen and Andrew Caffrey, "Now, Public Works Seem Too Precious for the Free Market," *The Wall Street Journal*, November 19, 2001, p. 1, A10.

2. Cynthia Doyle, "Worldwide Outsourcing Market Forecast and Analysis, 2000–2005," International Data Corporation, May 2001.

3. Nick Wakeman, "Foreign Nations Outpace U.S. in Outsourcing," *Washington Technology*, August 28, 2000.

4. Jane Linder and Thomas Healy, "Global Government Outsourcing: Pathways to Value," Accenture Government Executive Series report, May 2003.

5. Stephen Goldsmith, "Can Business Really Do Business with Government?" *Harvard Business Review,* May-June 1997, pp. 110–121.

6. "eGovernment Leadership: Engaging the Customer," Accenture Government Executive Series report, April 2003.

7. Op cit. See www.canadabenefits.gc.ca.

PART IV

Transformational Outsourcing Horizons

CHAPTER 12

Transformational Outsourcing Horizons

Companies have had a terrible track record for implementing change. Seventy-five percent of major change initiatives, 70 percent of mergers and acquisitions, and 50 percent of alliances fail to meet expectations. Poor execution is widely recognized as the culprit. In a 2002 Harris poll of more than 300 major U.S. corporations, 66 percent of CEOs said leaders' skills at execution had to be improved "a great deal" for their companies to be successful in the coming decade. In fact, execution skills ranked second only to the ability to think globally on the "needs improvement" list.

Every industry has its own tectonic pressures that raise the ante. Whether they are facing globalization, industry deregulation or consolidation, increasingly demanding customers, disruptive technologies, or a fiscal chokehold, organizations must learn to make and absorb changes faster than ever before.

Most organizations have used outsourcing in some way. A 2003 survey puts that count at about 70 percent in the United States.[1] But only a select group of leading executives have recognized that outsourcing can be used to accomplish enterprise-level, transformational change. This small group has proved that organizations can make big strategic moves reliably and quickly with this approach.

We can expect to see transformational outsourcing grow. A 2002 survey conducted by the Economist Intelligence Unit found that more than 50 percent of the 232 global executives surveyed agreed that their organizations would need radical change over the next three years, and 75 percent of these were willing to work with a partner to implement it.[2] A 2003 *Wall Street Journal* survey of 325 U.S. executives goes further. Fifty-nine percent of these executives anticipate extensive change in their organizations over the next three years; 71 percent are already using outsourcing; and the vast majority expect to increase their use of outsourcing (see Exhibit 12.1). More than half recognize that outsourcing makes an organization more flexible, and 54 percent agree that it is an effective way to implement organizational change. The larger companies and the more experienced outsourcers dominate these groups.[3]

The conclusion? As they get more experience with outsourcing, executives are learning the tool's potential, and they are beginning to wield it for more strategic purposes. They won't be waiting for their organizations to hit the skids; they will be proactively shaping and reshaping their business models.

Start-Ups

In the current environment of tight venture capital and even beyond, we can expect to see start-ups that get off the ground quickly using an outsourcing provider's ready-to-fly operations and its capital. Instead of working the venture companies for financial support, then taking all the operating risk on their own shoulders, entrepreneurs will seek operating partners who can help in both domains. Entrepreneurial corporate executives will step in between venture capitalists and their start-up audiences, then use their own corporate strength to access cheaper capital. Strategy will still tell, but reducing the operating risk will change the rate of start-up success and improve the overall returns the partners share.

Roadblocks to Growth

Most of the readily available outsourcing services fall into a few narrow categories—information technology, transactional business processes,

Exhibit 12.1. Executives expect to increase their use of outsourcing.

What is the likelihood of your organization to contract with a third party to provide the following services in 2003 and 2006?

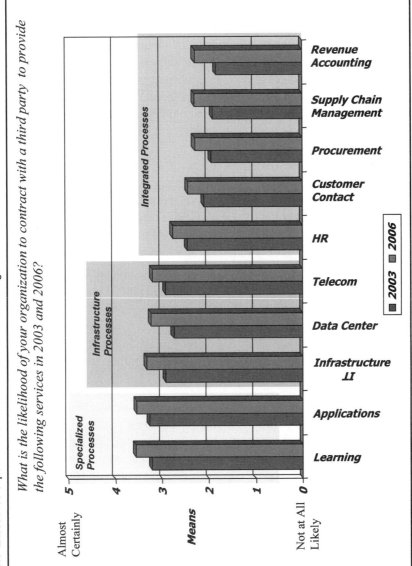

Source: Accenture survey of 325 U.S. executives, January 2003.

and well-defined specialty services such as wastewater treatment, executive education, prison and hospital management, and food service, for example. Organizations have been able to use outsourcing to remove roadblocks to growth only when their particular roadblock happened to fall into one of these categories. This will change. As strategic outsourcing gathers steam, providers will extend their offerings to broader and potentially more valuable types of capabilities. Then companies that find themselves *verklempt* will have ready partners for the capabilities they really need.

For example, in the past, EMC has sold storage hardware and storage-network management systems. As those products have come under margin pressure, the company has decided to move toward platform-independent data storage solutions. In a five-year pact, EMC and Accenture have agreed to create a new unit, the Information Solutions Consulting Group, which will use Accenture staff to help EMC customers streamline business processes and integrate hardware and software from different vendors into an effective storage environment. While EMC already has a 1,400-person professional services organization focused on its own technology, this new organization will be separate. "Just as EMC is creating platform-independent software through the AutoIS strategy, we are now developing a full range of consulting services for heterogeneous storage environments," says Joseph Walton, an EMC senior vice president.[4]

EMC describes the value proposition as follows: "Accenture establishes long-term relationships with their clients, delivering high-value technical solutions at much improved speed, scale, and cost. Accenture delivers an objective, expert solution to their customers' unique business problems. EMC products and services are becoming an integral part of Accenture's go-to-market strategy."[5]

The Accenture–EMC partnership illustrates the trend toward providers offering, and companies using, a broader array of strategically critical outsourcing services. We should expect to see growth-oriented companies evaluating outsourcing to build their capabilities in product commercialization, marketing analytics, postacquisition integration, and globalization, to name only a few.

Some of these new capabilities will emanate not from traditional outsourcing suppliers but from hands-on experts. For example, one of the world's largest consumer products companies recently out-licensed its reliability engineering know-how to a service company that will offer it on an outsourced basis. A senior executive explains: "We acquire businesses all over the world, and we have developed a toolbox of capabilities to get our manufacturing lines up to unprecedented reliability levels in a very short time. We signed a few deals to take that outside ourselves, but it is not scalable for us because it is extremely labor-intensive. So we found a partner who is in that business. It filled a need in their suite of manufacturing services so they're taking our process to market." He added: "I would salivate if we had an opportunity to offer our market research capabilities; we're world-renowned in that arena."[6]

These examples point to only two higher-level processes that now are available in the outsourcing marketplace. Watch this space for many more.

Catalyzing Change

Many of the companies catalyzing change are outsourcing to shed processes and operations that no longer give them a competitive distinction. BP is the poster child for this approach. But again, companies' choices have been restricted by the narrow range of services that have been available in the past. Progressive executives will push this opportunity more deeply into the operations of their companies. Instead of waiting for a debilitating shake-out or by distracting top management with a series of large-scale mergers to wring out excess capacity, companies will turn to outsourcing to reshape themselves before they have a stroke. And they will outsource their assets to an industry insider—a company that knows how to operate these assets better than anyone else.

We can anticipate seeing insurance companies outsource routine underwriting. They already lean in this direction with risk-sharing and reinsurance. Companies with high fixed-cost operations, like those in steel and aluminum, and oil and chemical companies can consolidate commodity manufacturing in this way. Chemical companies have been known to share operating assets like this: One insider tells a story of two competitors making customer deliveries from the nearest tanker, regardless of which company's product the tanker carried.

Banks also have precedent for using this approach. State Street's non-bank banking strategy illustrates this perfectly. Instead of competing head-to-head with other commercial banks for the next loan or corporate fixed-asset deal, State Street took a different tack in the mid-1970s. Tapping the opportunity created by the 1974 Employment Retirement Income Security Act, it parlayed its strength in technology and back-office services to a very profitable position in financial services processing.[7]

Telecommunications companies can use the same approach to improve the profitability of their networks. Through outsourcing, they can retire old capacity and improve the cost structure, and the entire industry will benefit. Cable & Wireless already stepped forward to outsource its voice network to Nortel. In 2000, C&W and Nortel signed a $1.4 billion deal through which Nortel would take responsibility for C&W's old voice operation while it also constructed its new voice-over-IP network.[8]

Radical Renewal

A small number of companies will continue to use outsourcing to execute stem-to-stern enterprise transformations. New CEOs will take over neglected organizations with board-level mandates for change and compelling deadlines. Legislatures will adopt policies that run seismic fault lines through the playing field. Disruptive technologies will change the game, and some executives won't notice until the final period that their team has the wrong uniforms on. The executives in these companies will recognize transformational outsourcing as a viable option for making the strategic changes that their organizations require for survival.

Some executives will use outsourcing to reposition their organizations; others will set their sights on a new competitive trajectory. Both of these objectives—repositioning and acceleration—stop short of tapping the full potential of transformation through outsourcing. The executives with the longest view will have an even more far-reaching objective for transformational outsourcing. They will want to use it once, and then never again. In fact, they will want to use it in a way that keeps their organization from ever having to transform again. They want to parlay it into an entirely new capability: the ability for fluid change. In other words, they want to liquefy the rigid walls around their organizational silos and create a capability to implement strategic change with sinuous grace (see Exhibit 12.2).

Exhibit 12.2. Dynamic organizations evolve from fixed units to fluid ones.

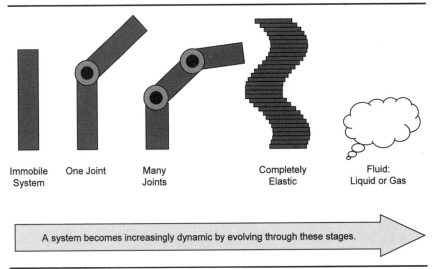

| Immobile System | One Joint | Many Joints | Completely Elastic | Fluid: Liquid or Gas |

A system becomes increasingly dynamic by evolving through these stages.

Source: TechOptimizer from Invention Machine, Inc.

Companies that stop short of this ultimate objective may achieve their radical agenda, but they may become hooked on transformation in the process. When their business models wear out or their performance flags, they will have to go through another lurching and expensive repositioning. If they can master the art of fluid change, they can escape this dysfunctional cycle.

Smaller Bites

Strategically flexible companies will use outsourcing to try out and adopt new business models more frequently, and in smaller bites. They may use outsourcing for transformation when their company has no better option, but they will also use it for innovation all the time. If transformational outsourcing makes a one-time radical improvement, we might call this approach fluid sourcing.

How would this work? Transformational outsourcing fills the gap between M&A activity and alliances in the CEO toolbox for strategic combinations (see Exhibit 12.3). It holds some advantages over both. Unlike

Exhibit 12.3. Outsourcing sits between alliances and acquisitions in the CEO's strategic toolbox.

| Alliance | Outsourcing | Merger/Acquisition |

an acquisition, executives need not buy a whole side of beef to get the tenderloin. They can secure precisely the operating capabilities and assets they need to execute their strategy—and ensure that the people with the know-how are leading them. In addition, because of the special structure involved in outsourcing, they are far more likely to actually achieve their objectives than with either an acquisition or a strategic alliance. So let's acknowledge that transformational outsourcing has earned a place in the CEO toolbox.

All of these techniques for revamping an organization's portfolio of capabilities share a common assumption—one that limits them. They equate one organizational unit with one way of working. In short, they assume that business models are constructed out of organizational building blocks. These must be well integrated to operate coherently, and they must be aligned with enterprise strategy, but they remain single-function operating modules.

This assumption fails to recognize the natural and inherent flexibility of people in organizations. Instead of seeing only the organizational structure, with its rules, roles, and boundaries, we should be looking first at the intrinsically variable capabilities of people working in groups and leverage their abilities to master multiple business model mind-sets.

Let me use an organic example. When researchers first started studying genetics, they believed that each gene produced one protein. In the early 1950s, however, as they began to crack the genetic code, they found a much more fluid process. Proteins are produced by variable and overlapping portions of the DNA structure. So each part of the genomic program has multiple roles to play. Sometimes a bit of genetic material works in combination with its neighbors on the left; sometimes it works with its neighbors on the right. (I'm oversimplifying here, but the concept is generally correct.) Each of these collaborations produces entirely different proteins. And furthermore, the impact of a protein in the body can change based on other proteins nearby. It's almost as if they work in teams. The mechanism is chemical, not mechanical, which makes an enormous difference in how it works and what it can do. I am suggesting that organizations can take advantage of the same kind of difference in speed, flexibility, cost, and innovation when they operate fluidly, not mechanically.

When executives need to implement change, most rely on their favorite lever, organizational structure. They spin off separate business units to pursue new product or service opportunities. Look at all the e-commerce subsidiaries that were created in the late 1990s. They also crash existing organizations into one another to try to get "synergy" from their collective capabilities. For example, a few years back, the textile business of a major chemical company tried to improve its focus from selling products to addressing customer needs by merging three separate fibers business units into a single, market-focused organization.

A few nimble companies have found another way. They change business models more fluidly without changing organizational structure, the way a good band switches from Bach to Back Street Boys with a tap of the leader's baton. How? They abandon the flawed assumption that one organizational unit has one way of working. Instead, they build on the principle that people working in groups can develop an extensive repertoire of working models, not through structures, but through mind-sets.

Models Are Mind-Sets

A working business model is a mind-set—a rich, tacit understanding of how all the pieces of an enterprise work together to create value. When an organization is at the top of its game, this understanding is shared broadly as "the way we do things," and the company operates with single-minded clarity. Take Mary Kay Cosmetics, for example. It hasn't changed its highly effective business model in decades, and managers up and down the chain know exactly how things work.

When markets change, however, the same mind-set can make a company seem completely out of touch. Especially when a company has been successful, business model mind-sets can get in the way of growth. One very profitable global-insurance company, for example, had tried several times unsuccessfully to tackle the low end of the commercial insurance market. A company executive recounts: "They failed because of their view of the world—their model. They knew very well how to manage difficult risks and work through high-end brokers. In the low end, the whole process is different—the way you market, sell, and underwrite. Instead of a raft of financial specs, reports, and a staff of highly paid underwriters, you need a few people and a computer. They just didn't know how to do this."

When executives change organizational structures, what they're frequently after are new mind-sets. By carving out new units, mashing existing units together, and redrawing the boundaries, they give their managers both the incentives and the space to reconstruct their mind-sets. For example, Teradyne's CEO decided that the product line was ready for a disruptive technology, and he set up an internal start-up to develop it: a handful of people with a radical charter, $12 million in investment funding, and a lot of autonomy. Freed from the company's established practices, they created a new product platform, a new market, a new price structure, and a new business model. Explains Hap Walker, manager of advanced development: "We would never have been able to do this within an existing division. Establishing an internal start-up let us focus people's full attention on the product and quickly free them from their existing mind-sets, rules, and traditions."[9]

Outsourcing has the same effect. Executives agree almost unanimously that their own organizations could never have accomplished what the outsourcing partner did. Peter Bareau justified the extensive changes in his senior team by saying the previous incumbents were "associated with the old way of doing things." MOL CFO Michel-Marc Delcommune explained that his own organization might have been able to implement a shared-services center, but it would have been "inside the old envelope," rather than ready for more changes.

Consider this. In some outsourcing initiatives, the individuals actually doing the work do not change at all. The people who were answering calls in the call center before the transition are still sitting there after the smoke clears. There may be fewer of them; they may have new tools and technologies. But what has really changed is that they are under new management and they are serving a customer, not a boss. They have moved to a new organization to get a new mind-set.

What many executives fail to realize is that a single organizational unit doesn't have to mean a single mind-set. Fluid companies avoid the cost and trauma of repeated structural change by inviting each organizational unit to master multiple mind-sets and the ability to switch among them at will. Let's first talk about how this works in general, then look at how it applies to transformational outsourcing.

Your Organization Already Knows How to Change Mind-Sets Quickly

Whether they know it or not, almost every organization has experience managing multiple mind-sets and changing them quickly. Some of these may not be as all-encompassing as business-model mind-sets, but they make the point.

What happens in your company when there's a hurricane, a flood, or a product-tampering threat? Most companies have crisis teams and planned approaches for situations like these. When disaster strikes, the members of the team switch hats, assume their responsibilities, and begin to manage the situation. In the military, soldiers know exactly what to do when the commander signals for "battle stations." And these transitions take minutes, not months.

People switch mind-sets when they switch roles, change tools, or step into a new situation. In the early days of artificial intelligence, for example, a CIO I know wanted to learn more about it. He took a course and hired an expert for his staff, but he knew he needed to get his hands dirty to really understand the potential of the new technology. So he bought two hats—a red one and a blue one. When he had the red hat on, he was in his CIO role and the AI expert reported to him. When he wore the blue hat, he was a member of a pilot AI project, and he reported to the AI expert. This is an unusual approach for an executive to take—many could not tolerate being so vulnerable to a subordinate—but this executive actually got the learning he was after.

I have another story about hats to illustrate how people change mind-sets when they change tools. This one takes place at midnight in the back office of a large East Coast bank. The bank had been on the acquisition trail for years. The signage had been changed on the front door of the latest conquest, but it had not yet been operationally integrated. That meant there were two separate systems running in the back office for processing the day's transactions. Management issued two hats to the people encoding checks and entering transactions. When they wore their red hats, they were doing the parent bank's work. When they switched to the acquired bank's transactions, everyone put on a blue hat to help keep things straight. No one would mistake this for the right way to run a bank back office, but it helped this organization function until the systems caught up with the signage.

Nimble Companies Drive Growth Through Mind-Sets

A few companies have learned to leverage the power of multiple mind-sets to frequently and fluidly change business models without changing organizational structure or undergoing transformational upheaval. For example, a large distribution company we'll call Zing anticipated dramatic changes in its market as its retail customers consolidated. Suppliers shifted more than 50 percent of their volume out of the channel and direct to the retailers, but Zing didn't miss a beat. They opened up a new line of business by offering to provide Internet retailers with pick, pack, and ship services along with a virtual store and database catalog support. Zing's vice president of business development said, "It was easy to offer these services for the products we already sell—videos, DVD, TVs, consumer electronics. Now we're expanding to other products as well. This is all very profitable."

What makes Zing distinctive is that it did not create a separate Internet division to tap this new opportunity. It runs lots of different strategic business units—the core distribution business, publications and advertising, Internet fulfillment, two e-commerce sites, and a business that specializes in the grocery trade—all with the same core people under the same leaders. Instead of dividing its business into multiple organizational units with one unit per business, Zing's leaders have chosen to cultivate multiple business model mind-sets, all of which reside in each of their employees' heads.

Zing's vice president explains: "We are growing phenomenally, but we haven't built a huge infrastructure by maintaining separate organizational units. This has kept our costs down, and has enabled us to prevent the layoffs that our competitors have been forced to undergo." Managing mind-sets instead of organizational units has also enabled Zing to adapt more quickly to a changing environment. "This way," explains the vice president, "we can more easily make the moves and experiment as we go." The result? Zing's two closest competitors have gone out of business, while Zing remains quite profitable.

In an example from another industry, Eli Lilly and Company has taken a fluid approach to innovation over the past two or three years. In the past it focused on vertically integrated operations: discovering, developing, and commercializing drugs that address unmet patient needs. With the spate of consolidations in the industry, Lilly has adopted an explicit strategic decision not to join in the fray. Instead, it aims to create an abundance of innovation—"having the stuff," as senior executives say. They reason that having distinctive intellectual property will give Lilly the strategic position to capture more of the industry's value than other companies will. And it plans to exploit its innovations through a holistic process it calls "discovery without walls." It will partner with universities, strategic partners, competitors, private research labs, and even individuals in a wide variety of ways to bring in new ideas, turn them into patentable products, and commercialize them.

Peter Johnson, Lilly's vice president of corporate strategy, explains the flexible process it will use to move resources to the right opportunities. He admits, "We're not terribly good at deciding what the big markets are going to be 10 or 15 years out. By the way, our competitors aren't very good at that, either. So we're trying to work with as many different and potentially valuable compounds as possible." In addition, Lilly is positioning itself as the partner of choice for collaborations of all types. That way it will have the broadest possible visibility and access to new discoveries, specialized development capacity, manufacturing resources, and commercialization capabilities. It will be able to move deliberately toward any market that shows promise.

Internally, the Lilly organization must be ready to shift gears from inside discovery programs to collaborative ones and even to out-licensing intellectual property. Each of these represents a different way of creating value—a different model. Senior executives will set the priorities and call the plays, and Lilly's multitalented workforce will switch hats as appropriate.

When Should You Use a Fluid Approach?

If your business environment is demanding and you're after growth, you'll want to consider managing mind-sets. You'll be able to change and add business models faster with this approach than with the one-organization, one-model limitation, and you'll also be able to experiment with new models without sacrificing profitability.

But managing mind-sets as opposed to organizational blocks does exact a cost. First, your employees may incur some switching cost as they shift from one mind-set to another. This is the same kind of deliberate transition we all go through as we wind down from work at the end of the day. In addition, attention management becomes even more challenging. Explains the vice president at Zing: "People often get frustrated because they have to constantly shift their attention between different mind-sets. If managers don't carefully help people focus attention where it belongs, this approach could be a disaster."

Finally, most individuals can master and use many different mind-sets, but developing a new mind-set often takes a great deal of attention. For example, a few years back, the CEO of a traditional newspaper decided to redirect his organization to consider itself a multimedia communications company. To accomplish this, he had to change the way they wrote stories. Instead of traditional, linear news stories, they had to produce a set of related vignettes that could run in the paper but could also be hyperlinked on the Internet. And they had to "accessorize" the pieces with video and audio clips as well as photographs and graphics. The CEO recognized that mastering the new mind-set would take effort. He first pulled the writers, editors, graphic artists, and photographers into a single bull pen so they could work together intimately. Then he asked them to write—and rewrite—every story in the new way, as a group, for a year. That was what it would take, he reasoned, for these experienced journalists to master a new way of working.

Building a Capability for Strategic Flexibility Through Outsourcing

To build a capability for fluid growth, you will need to broaden your portfolio of options by deliberately mastering and utilizing new mind-sets. Here's where outsourcing comes in. As we have seen, outsourcing is the fastest and most effective way to implement a new way of working in your organization. In one neat package, it combines the four components that are critical for adopting and using a new mind-set:

- A competitively viable and valuable joint business model—the strategic bit
- The management know-how, accountability, and resources to build the essential capabilities that support it
- The urgency and focus that comes from aggressive goals combined with an entrepreneurial spark that ignites when individuals work at the face of the company
- The sustaining momentum that visible success creates

The need to move large numbers of people across impermeable corporate boundaries, however, keeps organizations from taking advantage of these benefits. The disruption and managerial effort involved stands in the way of fluid change. This outsourcing assumption is a holdover from the mechanical world of organizational blocks.

Companies that aspire to strategic fluidity will establish deep, committed partnerships across organizations and move leadership control, not employment contracts, across porous boundaries. They will combine characteristics of strategic partnering with outsourcing in a new approach: *fluid sourcing.* Here's how it works. Deep strategic partnerships will provide an umbrella organization—perhaps crossing several companies. Entrepreneurs at all levels will lead initiatives and manage work that pulls in resources and expertise from the extended enterprise. They'll call cross-organizational plays. For example, in the late 1990s, a UK grocery retailer worked "mechanically" with a leading technology company to develop and implement new self-service technologies for shoppers. The grocery CIO contributed his knowledge of the industry and his stores as a test bed. The technology company assigned product developers to create the solutions. The initiative was successful as far as it went: The grocery chain put a few customer-pleasing innovations in place, and the technology company got a start on some new products it could potentially sell to others. The CIO left the grocery company shortly afterward, and all progress stopped.

If these two companies had adopted fluid sourcing, however, things might have been different. Driven by a provocative joint-business model, they would have established a deep partnership. The grocery company CIO would have led the technology development initiative in a virtual joint venture that called on the resources and expertise of both organizations. In addition to improving the retailer's business with innovative technologies, the venture could have explored growth opportunities on both sides of the relationship. The CIO, for one, envisioned a profitable solutions business in providing these technologies to other retailers.

Whether this particular venture would have panned out or not isn't really important. The point is that fluid sourcing is a way of exploring new avenues to growth that seem to be eluding the players in this and many other industries.

How will companies manage their people in an environment of fluid sourcing? Leading companies will recognize their key employees as flexible resources rather than branding them with their current organizational identity. They will acknowledge that business models reside in people, not the other way around. Just as they learn to establish deep, committed relationships with other companies, they will grant employees dual citizenship that enables them to move across porous organizational boundaries easily.

These companies will also rid themselves of the creaky organizational machinery that stands in the way of fluid change. They will establish broad roles, goals, and incentive systems that span multiple models and reach into partnered companies. Fidelity Investments, a U.S.–based financial services firm, for example, currently gives its office staff the latitude to handle customer-service calls when the stock market melts down or the call volume peaks. These people are instantly added to the service center without any disruptive organizational change, simply by routing calls to them in nearby conference rooms commandeered for the emergency.

In the future, fluid companies will extend this latitude across their boundaries and into partner organizations. When Zing wants to try its hand at digital music distribution, it will call on a sister company to contribute technology expertise. Companies will use cross-partner employee stock ownership to encourage employees to consider the goals of their extended organization first and change roles as needed.

At a broader, corporate level, companies will need new, more flexible legal entities that more closely match the spirit and timing of fluid sourcing. For example, companies could use virtual joint ventures, as in the grocery chain, to house cross-company initiatives. It would provide focus and identity, expert management, and motivating risk/reward structures without forcing individuals to leave one company and join another to contribute. Unlike some partnerships, however, it would have clear leadership based on where the know-how resides.

For companies to use this kind of fluid sourcing, they will have to dramatically improve organizational navigation. Individuals on both sides of every partnership will need ways to find the right organizational touch points quickly to call cross-boundary plays. For example, how would the fluid-sourcing partner responsible for market research in a newly deregulated utility identify the individuals who should be involved in a big, time-sensitive decision? The right group would be pulled from the utility's senior staff, the partner's cadre of experts, and perhaps even the organization from which the intellectual property was sourced. Today we are at sea without a compass when it comes to navigating across organizational boundaries.

* * *

Despite its importance, transformational outsourcing is certainly not the right answer to every strategic change management question. It is one alternative. Effective executives will master the ability to use it and will know when it applies. They will start up new companies, drive growth, consolidate mature industries, and execute stunning strategic turnarounds. In addition, executives who learn to use fluid sourcing to manage mindsets will gain competitive resilience and a remarkable ability to adapt in an uncertain environment.

Notes

1. Unpublished Accenture survey of 325 U.S. executives, January 2003.

2. Unpublished survey conducted by The Economist Intelligence Unit, and sponsored by Accenture.

3. Unpublished survey sponsored by Accenture.

4. Colin C. Haley, "EMC, Accenture form Storage Consulting Unit," *Aspnews.com*, July 10, 2002. See http://www.aspnews.com/news/article/0,,4191_1383011,00.html.

5. See http://www.emc.com/partnersalliances/partner_pages/accenture.jsp.

6. Personal interview, October 2002.

7. See www.hoovers.com.

8. See www.nortelnetworks.com/corporate/news/newsreleases/2000c/10_02_0000632_square.html.

9. Jane Linder and Susan Cantrell, "It's All in the Mind (Set)," *Across the Board*, May/June 2002, pp. 38–42.

Index